The

ANCIENT
MYSTERIES
OF THE
ESSENES

The Ken Johnson Collection

THREE BOOKS IN ONE

The ANCIENT MYSTERIES OF THE ESSENES

The Ken Johnson Collection

DEFENDER
CRANE, MO

Ancient Mysteries of the Essenes: The Ken Johnson Collection
by Ken Johnson, Th.D.

Unless otherwise indicated, Bible quotations are taken from the King James
Version.

Quotations from the Testaments in Part 1 are from *Ancient Testaments of the
Patriarchs* by Ken Johnson, Th.D.

Cover design by Jeffrey Mardis

ISBN: 978-1-948014-50-2

CONTENTS

PART 1
THE ANCIENT DEAD SEA SCROLL CALENDAR
AND THE PROPHECIES IT REVEALS

PART 2
ANCIENT TESTAMENTS OF THE PATRIARCHS:
AUTOBIOGRAPHIES FROM THE DEAD SEA SCROLLS

PART 3
ANCIENT ORDER OF MELCHIZEDEK

FOREWORD
by Josh Peck

The three most important rules of Bible study:
context, context, and context.

I have no idea who was the first to say that. We who are involved in full-time ministry and continuous Bible study hear that quote so often, it has almost become a cliché. The reason it has become popular enough to become cliché is because it is absolutely true. Having a proper understanding of the context is the most important thing in understanding any work of ancient writing, especially the Bible. I say "especially," because, as a born-again Christian, I recognize the Bible as something special and set apart. It is not just an ancient library of ancient texts spanning thousands of years. It is the inspired Word of God, written through His chosen ones. It is our job, if we want to fully understand it, to study the context of each piece of writing. Why was it written? Who wrote it? Who was it written to? Was it written in response to something? What was the culture of the originally intended audience? Did they have idioms that may have made their way into the text that we are unfamiliar with today? What was God's original purpose for this text, and how can we most responsibly benefit from it today? These, and many more, are all questions of context.

The book you currently hold in your hands comprises three pieces of the ultimate context puzzle of the Bible. There are many more out there, of course, but this will give you an excellent foundation to clearly understand what's being addressed throughout the Holy Scriptures. First, in part 1, you will learn about the ancient calendar that Jewish people throughout time have used. This calendar shows up in the Bible quite frequently. According to ancient sources, this is the calendar that God gave directly to Adam and commanded the Jewish people to maintain. However, as you will learn, some decided to abandon God's original calendar for a lunar system popular with pagans of the time. In doing so, the original feasts and festivals of the Jewish people became confused and were celebrated on the wrong days. The original calendar has been pieced back together from the Dead Sea Scrolls and can help explain biblical mysteries. Why does it seem like the timeline in the Gospel of John differs from those in the other Gospels? How do the day counts of Noah's Flood, Moses' Exodus, and the ascension from Mount Sinai, or prophecies of Daniel and Revelation actually work? Without the context of the original calendar, these mysteries would be practically impossible to solve. However, now, thanks to the amazing work of Dr. Ken Johnson, the information is available to us today.

In part 2, you will learn about ancient writings from the people of God that predate the Bible itself. According to tradition, before the Old Testament was written, biblical patriarchs would write their own testaments to their descendants. Surprisingly, a few of those testaments still exist today. Dr. Ken Johnson has gone through painstaking work to track down, translate, and provide commentary for these testaments. Knowing what led up to the Old Testament can help us understand it more, just like learning context from the Old Testament can help us understand the New Testament. The testaments are full of wise advice, history, and even prophecy. While they are not considered canonical and are not meant to be lifted up to the same level as the inspired Scripture of the Bible, we can learn a great deal of context from the testaments that can open the Bible up to us in new and exciting ways.

Finally, in part 3, you will be given some new insights into the New Testament. This comes in the form of explaining the book of Hebrews (easily one of the most misunderstood books of the New Testament) from the context of the original author and culture. Without knowledge of the Dead Sea Scrolls, Testaments of the Patriarchs, and the original solar calendar system, it can be incredibly difficult to know what is being discussed in the book of Hebrews. This lack of information is what has led to strange interpretations and misunderstandings of the text in our modern day. No longer do we have to wonder about or even fear some of the more extreme-sounding passages concerning salvation in Jesus Christ. Dr. Ken Johnson explains the Melchizedekian context of the book of Hebrews in a way anyone can understand and benefit from.

It is my absolute honor to be providing the foreword for this phenomenal book. I truly believe this will become a staple in every serious, and even casual, Bible researcher's collection. Personally, I have been a follower of Dr. Ken Johnson's work for several years now, and it has greatly helped me in my understanding of the Bible. His research on the Dead Sea Scrolls is second to none. If you haven't yet had the pleasure of reading Dr. Johnson's materials, this is a great place to start. If you already are familiar with some of the things in this book that Dr. Johnson has thought about throughout the years, then you know as well as I do that this will all deserve a second, third, and even fourth readthrough. Dr. Johnson's writing is very easy to read and understand, yet it is so packed with information, it's easy to miss some of the details the first time around. It is my belief that once you finish reading this book, even if it is not your first time, you will want to turn back to page 1 and start it over again. I know I will.

Enjoy the journey!

Josh Peck

www.SkyWatchTV.com

PART 1

THE ANCIENT
DEAD SEA SCROLL CALENDAR
AND THE
PROPHECIES IT REVEALS

INTRODUCTION

Most of us who study ancient history and church history in general, know about the modern Jewish Calendar. It is a lunar calendar consisting of a 354-day year. Its months start on a new moon and every three to five years there is a leap month to keep it somewhat in sync with the four seasons.

The calendar most of us are familiar with, and use on a daily basis, is called the Gregorian Calendar. It is a solar calendar consisting of a 365-day year. There is a leap day once every four years.

Some holidays are set on the solar calendar. The American Independence Day always occurs on the fourth of July. Other holidays are set on the lunar calendar. This is why Easter is always on a different Sunday each year. Easter is calculated to occur on the first Sunday after the first full moon occurring on or after the spring equinox.

What we were never told is that there was another calendar; a solar one, used by the Essenes. This is their story.

The Essenes taught that God gave us the perfect calendar. The base unit for the calendar was a twenty-four-hour day that was put in sets of seven, called weeks. Their calendar year was 364 days long, which was evenly divided into fifty-two weeks. This made all holidays fall on the same day of the week every year. Our Gregorian calendar shifts week-days one or two days every year. This makes the seven-day cycle and the holidays off from year to year.

The Essenes said this calendar was observed unbroken from the time of Adam to Moses and down to the time of David. David wrote songs for each of the fifty-two Sabbaths of the year. We actually have some of those in the Dead Sea Scrolls! It remained the only calendar used by the Jews until the Greeks tried to force them to use the Seleucid Greek calendar. Unlike the 364-day solar calendar, this was a 354-day lunar calendar. It changed New Year's Day from the spring to the fall. It cal-culated the months, not by the solstices and equinoxes, but by the lunar new moon. To do this they had a leap month added to the calendar every three years. The Maccabees rose up and drove out the Greeks. Antiochus Epiphanes died, and the new ruler was more interested in taxes than religion. Antiochus V Eupator made a deal with the Mac-cabees. The Jews could keep their religion, but they had to pay tribute and use the Seleucid Empire's calendar. The Maccabees accepted the offer seeing no problem with using a different calendar. If we believe the Dead Sea Scrolls, this is the true origin of the modern Jewish Calendar. The Zadok priests said that giving up the original solar calendar alone would be a grievous sin. Eventually the Zadok priests were driven out and settled in Qumran. They took with them copies of everything in the temple library.

Now for the first time in almost two thousand years, we can recreate their calendar and see what secrets it may hold.

1

Calendar History

Gregorian Calendar

We should start by studying the common calendar in use today in most of the modern world. It is called the Gregorian calendar. This calendar was put in the form we have today by Julius Caesar in 46 BC. In the Middle Ages the Julian calendar became off more than a week because of the way the leap years were calculated. Pope Gregory ordered a reformation of the Julian calendar in October of AD 1582. This just changed the way the leap years were calculated. It did not change any other aspect of the Julian calendar. Unless we are discussing the leap year calculation the Julian and Gregorian calendars are identical.

Calendar Months

Julius Caesar started his year in the winter season.

The first month of the year is January, which has 31 days.

The second month is February with 28 days, except for leap years, when it has 29 days.

The third month is March having 31 days.

The fourth month is April having 30 days.

The fifth month is May having 31 days.

The sixth month is June having 30 days.

The seventh month is July having 31 days.

The eighth month is August having 31 days.

The ninth month is September having 30 days.

The tenth month is October having 31 days.

The eleventh month is November having 30 days.

The twelfth and final month is December which has 31 days.

According to the Dead Sea Scroll calendar, the year originally started at the spring equinox and the months did not have names; they were simply numbered one through twelve.

Can we see any evidence of this in the Gregorian calendar itself?

Start of the Year

The first month would have just been numbered month one. Roman historians Titus Livius (Livy) and Plutarch record the second king of Rome, Numa Pompilius, ordered the first month to be named after the first Italian king of the empire.

The Ancient Book of Jasher records that the name of the first Italian king was Janeas. That is where we get the name "January."

> And in those days died Janeas king of the children of Chittim [Rome], and they buried him in his temple which he had built for himself in the plain of Canopia for a residence, and Latinus reigned in his stead. Ancient Book of Jasher 74:6

July is named after Julius Caesar and August is named after Augustus Caesar. When we get to the last four months of the Gregorian calendar, we see something very interesting.

The names of the last four months of the year are September, October, November and December. If we look closer at their names, we notice the prefixes. "Sept" means seven, "oct" means eight, "nov" means nine, and "dec" means ten. So, the ninth through the twelfth months are actually the seventh through the tenth months. This makes January the eleventh month and February the twelfth month on the old calendar.

Also, when we have a leap year, where should we put the extra day or days? They should be placed at the end of the year. If March is the first month, then the extra day should be placed at the end of February, which is what we do. It is not placed at the end of December.

Starting of the Months

The spring equinox does occur in the month of March, so, March should be the first month of the year. Why then does the equinox occur on March 20th and not on March 1st? At first glance it may seem that the beginnings of the months are not related to the equinox at all. Each season is ninety-one days long. If we divide the season in two, we find the approximate time of the mid-season. Depending on how you divide each season the date of the mid-season can vary a few days.

Between the start of winter (December 21st) and the start of spring (March 20th) is February 2nd, also called Groundhog Day. Between the start of spring (March 20th) and the start of summer (June 20th) is May 1st, which is called May Day. Between the start of summer (June 20th) and the start of fall (September 20th) is July 31st, which is Mid-summer. Between the start of fall (September 20th) and the start of winter (December 21st) is November 1st, which is All Saints Day on the Roman Catholic calendar and the day after Halloween. This clearly shows that the Romans used the mid-season days as the start of their months.

Conclusion

After looking closely at the Gregorian calendar, we can see that before Julius Caesar reformed the old Roman calendar, the original new year was the spring equinox, just as the Dead Sea Scrolls state. Julius changed the start of the months to align with the mid-seasonal points instead of the turn of the seasons.

Modern Jewish Calendar

Now we need to compare the Dead Sea Scroll calendar with the modern Jewish calendar.

The modern Jewish calendar is a luni-solar calendar. It is based on the solar year but incorporates the moon phases for its months. This means the calendar year consists of 354 days, with a leap month, called Adar II, about every three years. This makes the modern Jewish calendar ten days shorter than the Dead Sea Scroll calendar and eleven days shorter than the modern Gregorian calendar. The modern Jewish calendar's new year starts in the fall.

The calendar used by the Pharisees in the first century was said to be based on observation. When a committee of priests would spot the crescent moon, they would declare a new month. When the Jerusalem temple was destroyed, and the nation of Israel was dispersed, various Jewish groups began to have problems keeping the calendar in sync with other Jewish groups. The modern calendar came into being in the fourth century AD, when rabbi Hillel III created the rules governing the current Jewish calendar. These changes to the calendar system move holy days so they would not fall on Sabbaths and other similar things.

Calendar Months

For the last seventeen-hundred years, the days for each month are as follows:

The first month of the year is Tishrei, which has 30 days.

The second month is Heshvan which has 29 or 30 days.

The third month is Kislev which has 29 or 30 days.

The fourth month is Tevet which has 29 days.

The fifth month is Shevat which has 30 days.

The sixth month is Adar which has 29 days.

The seventh month is Nisan which has 30 days.

The eighth month is Iyar which has 29 days.

The ninth month is Sivan which has 30 days.

The tenth month is Tammuz which has 29 days.

The eleventh month is Av which has 30 days.

The twelfth and final month is Elul which has 29 days.

Start of the Year

The modern Jewish calendar starts in the fall, but the calculations for starting the new year are done by calculating the new moon closest to the spring equinox. These calculations are very similar to how we calculate the date of Easter. This shows an ancient memory that the original new year was in the spring.

There is a rare Jewish ceremony done by the rabbis every twenty-eight years called the Birkat Hachama. Talmudic tradition teaches that the sun was created in its spring equinox position at the beginning of the Jewish month of Nissan (Bavli Rosh Hashanah 10b). The Birkat Hachama involves saying a blessing for the sun and the calendar.

> Blessed are You, LORD, our God, King of the Universe, Maker of the works of creation.

According to the Talmud, Bavli Berachot 56-59, every twenty-eight years the sun returns to its original place when the world was created. This would be Tuesday evening and Wednesday to sunset that occurs on the spring equinox, March 20. This twenty-eight-year cycle is called the "machzor gadol," meaning "the great cycle."

The Birkat Hachama is a second witness to the fact that the original calendar started at the spring equinox.

Start of the Months

The first century Pharisees declared the start of a new month at the first sign of a crescent moon. The new year was calculated by observing the first new moon (sign of the crescent) closest to the spring equinox. The modern Jewish months are based on these same lunar months, but are changed according to Hillel's formulas.

Conclusion

The modern Jewish Calendar is close to the original Pharisee calendar used in the first century AD, but it is a modified version. That means it is not entirely accurate, even by Pharisee standards. Even though the Pharisees taught the new year began in the fall, there is evidence that shows this was a change the Pharisees made further back in time. Pharisee records show the new year originally started in the spring.

Essene History

When we look at the history of the Gregorian calendar and the modern Jewish calendar, we see both originally started in the spring and relied heavily on the equinoxes and solstices for their calendar year. Let's turn our attention to what the Essenes of Qumran have to say about the history of the calendar.

The basic history of the calendar is seen in the Community Rule, Damascus Documents, the calendar fragments (4Q319 to 4Q394), the songs and psalms of David, and other works found in the Dead Sea Scrolls. There are also accounts of some of this material from the ancient church fathers and the Talmud. Pulling all these together they paint a fairly complete picture of what happened in what we call the "four hundred silent years."

Calendar History

The Essenes taught that the calendar was a completely solar calendar that started with the spring equinox. This was handed down from the beginning of time and used to calculate all the Jewish festivals in the tabernacle and temple. When the Exodus from Egypt occurred, which is the first month of spring, God told Moses:

> This month shall be unto you the beginning of months: it shall be the first month of the year to you. (Exodus 12:2)

The Essenes taught that the original calendar was still in use when King David reigned; and that he wrote fifty-two songs, one for each Sabbath. The Sabbath songs have the dates in them showing which Sabbath it was and what the solar date was for each of the Sabbaths.

Ezra and Nehemiah

Some Levitical priests began mixing pagan practices into temple worship. This made God angry. God exiled the nation of Israel into Babylon. After seventy years of exile the Persians conquered the Babylonians. The Persian king, Cyrus, then freed the Jews in 536 BC. Under the guidance of Ezra and Nehemiah the nation of Israel was reborn. Ezra taught all the people the laws of God for the nation of Israel. The newly born nation re-entered the covenant of God. They put away all the idolatry, rebuilt the Jerusalem temple, and restored the worship of God in the original way God had commanded.

The high priests from the time Cyrus freed the Jews to the beginning of the Grecian era were:

Joshua, son of Jehozadak (536 BC)
Joiakim, son of Joshua
Eliashib, son of Joiakim (~ 444 BC)

Joiada, son of Eliashib
Johanan, son of Joiada (~ 410 BC)
Jaddua, son of Johanan

The Grecian Era

The Persian Empire fell to the Greeks in 323 BC. The Greek empire then split into four smaller empires. Two of these four empires claimed the territory of Israel as their own. One of these was the Seleucid Empire, which ruled from the area of modern Syria. The other one was the Ptolemaic Empire, which ruled from Egypt to the South. From the time of the split of the Grecian Empire to when the Maccabees arose is known as the Grecian Era. This era extended from 323-164 BC.

During this time period the Seleucid Empire and the Ptolemaic Empire had many battles. The nation of Israel was always caught in the middle of these wars. One solution to the constant battles was to replace all the various customs of each nation under their control and require them all to embrace the Greek way of life. For the nation of Israel this meant to abandon their practices of things like the Jewish sacrifices, circumcision, and Torah reading. On what would appear to be the secular side of things, everyone was required to use Greek money and pay taxes on the proper due dates of the Grecian calendar.

The Grecian Calendar

The Grecian calendar used by the Seleucid Empire was a lunar calendar totaling 354 days per calendar year. The new year began when the crescent of the new moon of October was seen. The year consisted of twelve lunar months. A leap month was added six times in nineteen years between March and April (around the spring equinox). There was also a leap month added once sometime in the nineteen-year cycle between September and October (around the fall equinox).

The first month was Dios, (the new moon of October).

The second month was Apellaiios, (November).

The third month was Audunaios or Audnaios, (December).

The fourth was Peritios, (January).

The fifth month was Dystros, (February).

The sixth month was Xandikos or Xanthikos, (March)

The first leap month was Xandikos Embolimos.

The seventh month was Artemisios or Artamitios, (April).

The eighth month was Daisios, (May).

The ninth month was Panēmos or Panamos, (June).

The tenth month was Lōios, (July).

The eleventh month was Gorpiaios, (August).

The twelfth month was Hyperberetaios, (September).

The second leap month was Hyperberetaios Embolimos.

High Priest Rituals

All of this was unacceptable. The temple rituals had to continue, and they had to be done in the proper manner. When Nadab and Abihu offered strange fire, they changed the ritual and God killed them (see Leviticus 10). The robe of the high priest had bells on the hem of the garment. This would let everyone know the priest was walking around and doing his rituals on the Day of Atonement. There was always a rope tied around his leg in case he did the ritual incorrectly and died by being in the presence of God improperly. If the bells stopped making sounds, those outside of the Holy of Holies could pull the high priest out without endangering themselves.

The Talmud, in Yoma 9a, has a record of high priests up to the destruction of the Jerusalem temple. The interesting thing about that list is that it shows that there were eighteen high priests during the four hundred years that the Temple of Solomon stood. But during the 420-year period of the Second Temple, there were over three hundred high priests! The first few righteous high priests served many years. After them the Talmud says:

...after the righteous priests the last three hundred did not live past one year (passing beyond the veil died). Talmud, Yoma 9a

This seems to be saying that any high priest who tried to perform the ritual of Yom Kippur on the wrong day or in some other wrong way, died when they tried to do it. There may have been high priests who refused to perform the ritual. Part of doing the ritual in the proper manner was to do them on the proper dates. This could not be done if everyone was forced to use the Greek calendar system.

From the beginning of the Grecian era to the rise of the Maccabees, the high priests were:

Onias I (~ 309-265 BC)
Simeon I (Simeon the Just)
Eleazar (?–246 BC)
Manasseh
Onias II (~ 246-221 BC)
Simeon II (~ 221-204 BC)
Onias III (?–175 BC, murdered in 170 BC)
Onias IV
Jason (175–172 BC)
Menelaus (172–165 BC)
Judas Maccabeus (165–162 BC)
Alcimus (162–159 BC)

The push to stop being Jewish and start being Greek came in waves starting in the time of Onais I, around 300 BC. It got so bad that most Jews stopped practicing circumcision, reading Torah, and took Greek names. We can see in the list Jason's name was Greek and not a normal Hebrew name. His Hebrew name before he took the Greek name of Jason, was Yeshua. Jason was the last of the Zadok priests to be a high priest of the Jerusalem temple. But since he betrayed the order and was betrayed by Menelaus, he had to flee Jerusalem and live the rest of his life in exile. Some of the remaining Zadok priests were led by the Holy Spirit to avoid the apostasy by taking copies of the temple library to Qumran for safe keeping. They stayed there awaiting the first coming of the Messiah.

Onias IV read this prophecy of Isaiah:

In that day shall there be an altar to the LORD in the midst of the land of Egypt, and a pillar at the border thereof to the LORD. (Isaiah 19:19)

He then felt that this prophecy was referring to his time and fled to Egypt for safety and asked permission to build a second Jewish temple. His petition was granted, and a Jewish temple was built in Leontopolis, Egypt. It functioned as a complete sacrificial Jewish Temple until it was closed by Titus in AD 73, just three years after Titus destroyed the Jerusalem temple.

The Maccabean Era

The Essenes record that the Maccabees rose up and drove out the Greek forces. They rededicated the Jerusalem temple and reinstated Mosaic law; but for some reason the Maccabees never reinstated the original solar calendar.

High priests in the Maccabean era were:

Johnathan Apphus (153–143 BC)
Simon Thassi (142–134 BC)
John Hyrcanus I (134–104 BC)
Aristobulus I (104–103 BC)
Alexander Jannaeus (103–76 BC)
John Hyrcanus II (76–66 BC)
Aristobulus II (66–63 BC)
John Hyrcanus II (restored to power, 63–40 BC)
Antigonus (40–37 BC)

History records that about 110 BC the Roman and Seleucid Empires recognized Israel as an independent state. At that time John Hyrcanus I started a campaign of conquest to capture neighboring nations and city states and force them to convert to Judaism. Forced Gentile conversion is forbidden. He also took the title of high priest and king which was also forbidden. The Jews who felt they should follow the high priest, no matter what he says, became known as Sadducees. Even though none of them were Zadok priests, they took their name from the Zadok priestly line. The remaining Zadok priests were in Qumran at this time. Those Jews who felt the need to follow the Mosaic law, refused to support this high priest. They became known as Pharisees, or dissenters. This calmed down when Aristobulus became ruler but flared up again when Alexander Jannaeus became the next ruler. Alexander Jannaeus continued the practice of forcing non-Jews to become Jewish but went further in requiring all Jews and non-Jews under his control to start practicing some of the Levitical priestly regulations. This led to an all-out war between the Sadducees and Pharisees that lasted over eight years, 96-88 BC. Even after the war there were flair ups and sub-factions developed. Everyone claimed to be the rightful rulers and kept trying to assassinate the leaders of the other parties. The Dead Sea Scrolls say at this time "all of Israel was walking in madness."

The Roman Era

The Roman Era extended from 64 BC to when the nation of Israel was dissolved in AD 135. This constant infighting led to the leaders of both the Pharisees and Sadducees, Aristobulus II and John Hyrcanus II, to petition Rome to step in to restore order. Rome took control and deposed all leaders of all parties. After a time, they placed John Hyrcanus II back into power in 63 BC. After John Hyrcanus II reigned from 63-40 BC, the last Maccabean ruler, Antigonus reigned from 40 BC to 37 BC. Complete civil order was never restored, so in 37 BC the Romans appointed Herod, an Idumean, as king of the nation of Israel in hopes that it would end the conflict. But as we see from the Gospels, it did not. The factions kept rising up and the nation of Israel ceased to exist in AD 135.

Prophecy of Calendar Corruption

The Ancient Book of Jubilees gives a prophecy that at some point the Jews would make the grave error of replacing their solar calendar with a lunar one. Here is part of that prophecy:

> For there will be those who will assuredly make observations of the moon – how it disturbeth the seasons and cometh in from year to year ten days too soon. For this reason the years will come upon them when they will disturb the order, and make an abominable day the day of testimony, and an unclean day a feast day, and they will confound all the days, the holy with the unclean, and the unclean day with the holy; for they will go wrong as to the months and sabbaths and feasts and jubilees. For this reason I command and testify to thee that thou mayest testify to them; for after thy death thy children will disturb them, so that they will not make the year 364 days only, and for this reason they will go wrong as to the new moons and seasons and sabbaths and festivals. (Ancient Book of Jubilees 6:36–38)

Conclusion

The Dead Sea Scrolls describe how God created one calendar and that the Jews kept it pure by down through the ages until the time when the Greek Seleucid Empire forced the nation of Israel to adopt their pagan lunar calendar. They also record a prophecy that this would occur. The Maccabees rose to power and restored Israel's independence but never restored the original solar calendar.

If this Essene history is correct, Israel has been using a forbidden pagan version of the calendar for well over two thousand years. We can understand why the Essenes referred to the Pharisees as "sons of darkness" and their dark lunar calendar as a corruption. They referred to themselves as the "sons of light" because they used God's original solar calendar.

The Calendar Remains Intact

Some people will say, "Ok, even if we can recalculate what day and year it is on the Essene calendar, how do we know that nothing has changed in almost six thousand years?"

That is a very important point to consider. Did the Flood of Noah change the orbit of the earth as to throw off the calendar? Were there 360 days in a year before the Flood and 365 days in the years after the Flood? Or did the number of days in a year change at another time? If so, how could we accurately calculate what time is now? How did Joshua's long day affect the calendar? What about Elijah turning back time on Hezekiah's sundial? How can we really be sure about any of these issues?

The Essenes recorded these events and took them literally. The numerous calendar records in the Dead Sea Scrolls, along with the Enoch calendar and Jubilees calendar documents, show that the Essenes believed that the calendar was to consist of only 364 days. No calendar system can be more than the total number of days in the real tropical year. A tropical year is the number of days between spring equinoxes. A tropical year has always been 365.2422 days long. The Essenes understood the pre-flood Enoch calendar year to be 364 days long and the tropical year to be more than 364 days long.

> On that day the night decreases to nine parts day and nine parts night, and the night is equal to the day and the year is exactly 364 days long. (Ancient Book of Enoch 72:32)

The Essenes also believed that Noah used that same 364-day calendar both before and after the Flood.

> And command thou the children of Israel that they observe the years according to this reckoning—364 days, and these will constitute a complete year, and they will not disturb its time from its days and from its feasts. (Ancient Book of Jubilees 6:32)

If this is true, then there has been no change in the number of days in the tropical year from Creation to the time of the Essenes.

The Essenes taught the lunar Pharisee calendar was corrupt, but never said the same of the Julian calendar that had been in use in Rome since 46 BC. The only thing recorded about the Julian calendar was that it has the same seven-day pattern that the Essenes used (see the chapter entitled the Seven Day Week for details). This means that if we can place the Essenes calendar alongside the Julian/Gregorian calendar we use today; we can recreate the original calendar.

What about Joshua's long day and Elijah turning the sundial back? If the earth stopped rotating or went backward for this to happen, it would have destroyed most—if not all—life on this planet. Rather, there must have been something in the atmosphere that reflected the sunlight in such a way to cause these two phenomena to occur. This would have changed the daylight hours on these two days, but would not have affected the calendar in any way.

Sun and Moon Signs

Mark 13:24; Revelation 8:12–13 and 16:8–11 refer to the sun's heat and darkness over a third part of the earth and the moon either being so dark it is not seen or is blood red. These could be caused by a phenomenon that blocks light in varying degrees during the Tribulation period. Scripture never says that afterwards the sun and moon will not have the same courses as they did before. Revelation 21:1 reveals a new heaven and new earth; but until then, the old ones with their same patterns remain.

There are also lying signs and wonders produced by the Antichrist that may make it appear that the sun and moon are coming up in different courses but apparently they are merely the Antichrist's deception.

The prophets record that these cycles will continue undisturbed. The prophet Isaiah records that in the millennial kingdom people will still be observing the same seven-day Sabbath cycle and the same Rosh Chodesh, or cycle of months. This would include the observance of the equinoxes and solstices.

> And it shall come to pass, that from one new moon to another, and from one sabbath to another, shall all flesh come to worship before Me, saith the LORD. (Isaiah 66:23)

The prophet Ezekiel predicted these cycles would be observed again in the millennial temple.

> Thus saith the Lord GOD; The gate of the inner court that looketh toward the east shall be shut the six working days; but on the sabbath it shall be opened, and in the day of the new moon it shall be opened. (Ezekiel 46:1)

Conclusion

Many nations invented their own calendar systems; but the courses of the sun, moon, and stars did not change. Enoch's prophecy states they do not change until the new heaven and the new earth. This means we can put the original calendar back together!

> He showed me exactly how the astrological laws work in regard to all the years of the world, till the new creation is made which endures for all eternity. (Ancient Book of Enoch 72:1b)

The Calendar Year

The Seven-Day Week

The heart of the calendar is the seven-day week. Moses recorded in Genesis that God created the cycle of seven days at creation. Genesis chapter one lists what God created on each of the first six days.

First Day — Light
Second Day — Atmosphere
Third Day — Dry Land and Plants
Fourth Day — Sun, Moon, and Stars
Fifth Day — Fish and Fowls
Sixth Day — Land Animals and Man

God rested on the seventh day. Modern Jews refer to this as a Sabbath, or Sabbos. God also sanctified the Sabbath. This means it is set apart for a special purpose.

And on the seventh day God ended His work which He had made; and He rested on the seventh day from all His work which He had made. And God blessed the seventh day, and sanctified it: because that in it He had rested from all His work which God created and made. (Genesis 2:2–3)

If they observe a Sabbath every seven days, then that is the basis of the calendar system. We are told that the ancient Jews did not name their days except for the day of rest, which they called the Sabbath. They numbered the days one through six and then had the Sabbath.

And God said, Let there be lights in the firmament of the heaven to divide the day from the night; and let them be for signs, and for seasons, and for days, and years: And let them be for lights in the firmament of the heaven to give light upon the earth: and it was so. And God made two great lights; the greater light to rule the day, and the lesser light to rule the night: He made the stars also. And God set them in the firmament of the heaven to give light upon the earth, And to rule over the day and over the night, and to divide the light from the darkness: and God saw that it was good. And the evening and the morning were the fourth day. (Genesis 1:14–19)

This special purpose was to rest one day out of the week, but it also was to be the basis for the world calendar. Josephus wrote in his history that there was a time when all nations observed a seven-day cycle in their calendar, but they never observed the Jewish rituals. This tells us that the original God-given calendar consisted of a seven-day week. The Romans changed this to an eight-day cycle but then it was changed back into a seven-day cycle by Julius Caesar in 46 BC.

There is not any city of the Grecians, nor any of the barbarians, nor any nation whatsoever, whither our custom of resting on the seventh day hath not come, but our fasts and lighting up lamps, and many of our prohibitions as to our food, are not observed. (Josephus, Against Apion 2.40)

CREATION WEEK						
Sun	Mon	Tues	Wed	Thur	Fri	Sat
			sun, moon, & stars			

The Essenes and Pharisees both taught that the seven days of Creation were the very first week. If they are correct, then the day we call Sunday would be the first day of creation, which is when God created the light. Monday would have been the creation of the atmosphere. Tuesday would have been the creation of the dry land. The sun, moon, and stars would have been created on Wednesday. With this in mind, we can see why the Essenes start their year on a Wednesday. The fourth day of the week would have been the first day a solar calendar could start.

Have the Days of the Week Been Changed?

Before we go any further, we need to find out if it can be proven that the fourth day of the week that the ancients observed on their calendar is the same fourth day of the week that we observe today. If it is, then our Saturday Sabbath is still Saturday. If not, then the real Saturday Sabbath might be on a Tuesday or Friday, for instance. We do not need to go all the way back to Creation to find out. Since the Essenes held their calendar so sacred and believed that the Pharisees corrupted the calendar by going on moon phases, they made numerous comments about all the things the Pharisees did wrong on their calendar, repeatedly calling them the sons of darkness for following a lunar calendar. That being the case we can assume that the Essenes and Pharisees in Jesus' day kept the same seven-day pattern for their week. They had the same weekly Sabbaths or that would have been listed as yet another Pharisee error.

The Dead Sea Scrolls record that Noah commanded all of his children to observe the solstices and equinoxes as days of remembrance of the Flood, the coming judgment, and to walk in holiness toward the Lord. See the next chapter for details.

The Romans had turned the ancient winter solstice observance into a pagan festival called Saturnalia. The word comes from the word Saturn. Today that word is used as a name of one of the planets in our solar system, but anciently it simply meant "rest." This was the festival of rest held at the end of the Roman year. Romans were to refrain from working during the seven-day holiday. In ancient Roman records the Jews were made fun of because they kept the seventh day of their cycle as a day of rest. The Romans referred to the Jews as keeping their own Saturnalia, or rest, on the seventh day of each week. See Tacitus Histories. 5.4 and Justin, History and Origins of the Entire World and All of its Lands 36.2 for details.

The Roman calendar was originally a seven-day cycle that was changed into an eight-day cycle for a time. Julius Caesar created the Julian calendar in 46 BC. This is identical to the weekday structure used in the modern Gregorian calendar.

If the Essenes and Pharisees observed the same Sabbath and the Romans recorded their day of rest was the weekly Saturday, then we can be assured that the Sabbath has not changed from Creation up to the first century AD.

But has it changed since 46 BC? The only time it might have changed was when the world switched from the Julian calendar to the Gregorian calendar. The Julian calendar used a leap day every four years. Doing it this way, the spring equinox drifted away from the beginning of spring by eleven days by the Middle Ages. Pope Gregory authorized the Gregorian calendar in AD 1582, which is identical in every way to the Julian calendar except the calculation of leap years. On the Gregorian calendar one day is added every four years except at the end of a century. If the century is divisible by four a leap day is added, but if the century is not divisible by four evenly, no extra day is added. As each country accepted the Gregorian calendar, they were all careful to keep the seven-day cycle unchanged. For instance, when the change occurred in America, Wednesday September 2, 1752, was followed by Thursday September 14, 1752.

Conclusion

After looking at the evidence we can determine that the Essenes kept what they considered to be the original seven-day cycle from Creation. We can also be reasonably certain that it is the same seven-day cycle we keep today. This means that the weekday system we use today is unchanged.

This is important since we must use the correct seven-day cycle to calculate the leap years correctly.

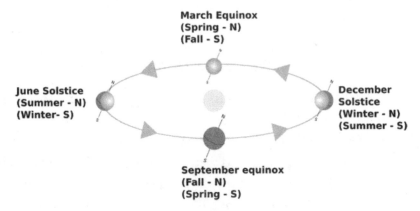

The most important function of any calendar is to mark the beginning of spring. Without this we would plant our crops at the wrong time and hunt our food at the wrong time. Eventually everyone would starve or freeze to death.

The summer solstice is the day when summer begins. It is the season of three months that are the hottest because the strongest rays from the sun are shining straight down on the northern hemisphere. The winter season is the opposite when the strongest rays of the sun are focused on the southern hemisphere making the northern hemisphere its coldest for the year. In the southern hemisphere, summer occurs when the northern hemisphere has its winter. Because of the tilt of the earth's axis, the days are longer in the summer and shorter in the winter. This adds to the cold and heat. At the winter solstice there is approximately eight hours of day and sixteen hours of night in one twenty-four-hour period. At the summer solstice it is the opposite, about sixteen hours of light and eight hours of darkness.

Ancient historical records are written from the view of the northern hemisphere, so we will concentrate on that. When the day and night is equal (twelve hours of each) that is called an equinox. On the American calendar, the spring equinox that heralds the beginning of planting time occurs around March 20 each year.

The Hebrew word Tekufah is used to describe the divisions of the four seasons, so Tekufah refers to both the summer and winter solstices and spring and fall equinoxes. There are four Tekufahs in all.

The Four Seasons

According to the Dead Sea Scrolls, Noah gave the Noahide laws to his sons to pass down to all mankind. These were to establish courts of justice and enforce moral law. The Mosaic law would come 792 years later. At the Exodus, God commanded that they stop using the Egyptian calendar they were used to when they were slaves in Egypt, and return to His original calendar, which begins at the spring equinox.

> You are to begin your calendar with this month; it will be the first month of the year for you. (Exodus 12:2 CJB)

The Egyptian calendar used during that time consisted of three seasons, which were one hundred and twenty days long. Each season had four thirty-day months. After the three seasons there was an intercalary month of five epagomenal days treated as outside of the calendar year.

The original calendar consists of twelve months. Each month is divided into thirty days. This totals 360 days. The four tekufahs are outside of the months. So, we have:

The spring equinox (1 day)
The three spring months (90 days)
The summer solstice (1 day)
The three summer months (90 days)
The fall equinox (1 day)
The three fall months (90 days)
The winter solstice (1 day)
And the three winter months (90 days)

The 360 days inside the months and the four tekufahs outside of the months total a 364-day calendar year.

Days of Remembrance

In the Book of Jubilees, Noah commands that the first day of each season is to be set aside as a "day of remembrance."

For I have written in the book of the first law, in that which I have written for thee, that thou shouldst celebrate it in its season, one day in the year, and I explained to thee its sacrifices that the children of Israel should remember and should celebrate it throughout their generations in this month, one day in every year. And on the new moon of the first month, and on the new moon of the fourth month, and on the new moon of the seventh month, and on the new moon of the tenth month are the days of remembrance, and the days of the seasons in the four divisions of the year. These are written and ordained as a testimony forever. (Ancient Book of Jubilees 6:22–23)

These days are set aside as holidays where the family leaves their work and comes together for a feast. They remember the Flood and practice repentance. They also study the writings of the prophets.

Three Calendar Types

All the ancient nations knew that the tropical year was about 365.25 days long, but you cannot create a calendar with a partial day.

The Gregorian calendar has a 365-day calendar and adds a leap day every four years. This is the most accurate way to calculate the seasons, but it causes the seven-day Sabbath cycle, to start on a different day each year. It also causes the moon phases to occur on different days throughout each year. We do this because the seasons are the most important part of the calendar to us. The Sabbath and moon cycles are not needed for the Gregorian system.

The Dead Sea Scroll calendar has a 364-day year, because the seasons and the seven-day Sabbath cycle were equally important to the Essenes. They did not care about the moon phases.

The Pharisee calendar was a 354-day luni-solar one. They needed to keep track of the seven-day Sabbath cycle and the seasons; but the moon phases were of utmost importance. They began each month on the new moon. To do this they had to start their first month of the year on the new moon closest to the equinox and about every three years they would have to add a leap month.

Gilgals

Gilgal is a Hebrew word meaning circle of standing stones. There were several of them. If it was cloudy on the day of the spring equinox and the date could not be verified from the tabernacle or temple, it could always be verified from a gilgal. A gilgal is similar to Stonehenge. If the circle of standing stones was large enough, it could be used to pinpoint the exact day of the year. There still exists a gilgal called Gilgal Rephaim in the Golan heights area of northern Israel. Gilgal Rephaim still works well. On the summer solstice light shines down into the center chamber of the gilgal. This only happens on that one day of the year.

Gilgal Rephaim by Abraham Graicer, 2010; courtesy Wikipedia

The kings of Israel would always meet the prophets at a gilgal on the high Sabbaths (festival days) and on the heads of the months.

> Send me, I pray thee, one of the young men, and one of the asses, that I may run to the man of God, and come again. And he said, Wherefore wilt thou go to him today? it is neither new moon [Rosh Chodesh or head of the months], nor sabbath. (2 Kings 4:22–23)

Remember that the apostle Paul stated that the Gentiles are not obligated to observe these customs, but we are free to learn about them.

Let no man therefore judge you in meat, or in drink, or in respect of an holyday, or of the new moon, or of the sabbath days: Which are a shadow of things to come; but the body is of Christ. (Colossians 2:16–17)

Dead Sea Scroll sundial

Sundials were found in Qumran. When examined carefully, we can see how they used these sundials to mark the eact day of the summer and winter solstices and the spring and fall equinoxes. The sundials are round and have a gnomon in the center to cast a shadow. There are seven circles embossed on the sundial. The circles mark equinoxes, solstices, and months. When the sundial is set at the proper angle and the end of the shadow sets exactly on the specific circle, it indicates that the equinox or solstice as arrived.

Shadow on the
summer solstice

Shadow on
the fall equinox

Shadow on the
winter solstice

Shadow on
the spring equinox

The Essene Year

The Seasonal Pattern

The divisions of the year are grouped into four seasons, starting with spring, then summer, fall, and finishing with winter. The spring season would be marked with the spring equinox. The equinoxes and solstices are named after the months that start the seasons. The spring equinox is called Tekufah Nisan. The day after the spring equinox is the first day of spring and New Year's Day. This would be the first of Nisan, or the first day of the first month. Each month would consist of thirty days each. After the three spring months, the ninety-first day of the year, would mark the summer solstice called Tekufah Tammuz. The following day is the first day of Summer. This is the first of Tammuz, or the first day of the fourth month. After the three summer months which would be another ninety days, the fall equinox would occur on the 182 day of the year. The fall equinox is called Tekufah Tishrei. The next day would be the first day of Tishrei or the first day of the seventh month. After the ninety days of fall, on the 273 day of the year the winter solstice would occur. The winter solstice is called Tekufah Tevet. The next day would be the first of Tevet, or the first day of the tenth month. After the ninety days of winter on the 364th day of the year would be the spring equinox called Tekufah Nisan. The next day would be the start of the following year.

The Twelve Months

Nisan is the first month of the year.
Iyar is the second month.
Sivan is the third month.
Tammuz is the fourth month.
Av is the fifth month.
Elul is the sixth month.
Tishrei is the seventh month.
Heshvan is the eighth month.
Kislev is the ninth month.
Tevet is the tenth month.
Shevat is the eleventh month.
Adar is the twelfth month.

Fifty-two Weeks

A 364-day calendar year divides into fifty-two weeks exactly. That means every year starts on the same day of the week; a Wednesday. Every holy day is on the same day of the week in the same month. Passover is always Tuesday, Nisan 14.

Calculated vs. Actual Equinox

The Essene calendar scrolls show the spring equinox on a Tuesday. The very next day is Wednesday the first of Nisan. This Wednesday is New Year's Day. The following year, 364 days later, the spring equinox would be one day off. With each successive year the actual spring equinox would drift further away from the Tuesday it is observed on the calendar. This would keep occurring until a leap year which would correct it. Before figuring out the Leap year system the Essenes used, we should map out the entire calculated calendar year.

The Yearly Pattern

The spring equinox occurs on a Tuesday, the last day of the previous year. New Year's falls on Wednesday, the first Sabbath of the new year always falls on the fourth day of the month of Nisan. Anciently Nisan was called Abib. The week of unleavened bread occurs from Wednesday Nisan 15 to Tuesday Nisan 21. The festival of the first fruits of the barley harvest is on Sunday Nisan 26. The next day begins the "counting of the Omer."

Nisan						
S	M	T	W	T	F	S
		Spring equinox	1	2	3	4
5	6	7	8	9	10	11
12	13	14 Passover	15	16	17	18
19	20	21	22	23	24	25
26 FF-B	27	28	39	30		

FF-B, First Fruits of the Barley Harvest

Iyar						
S	M	T	W	T	F	S
					1	2 07
3	4	5	6	7	8	9 014
10	11	12	13	14	15	16 021
17	18	19	20	21	22	23 028
24	25	26	27	28	29	30 035

01-49, the counting of the Omer

The counting of the Omer is a daily count for fifty days. They fiftieth day is Pentecost Sunday, which occurs on Sunday, Sivan 15. This begins the fifty-day count to the Festival of New Wine. For the prophetic significance of the festivals see Chapter 4 of this book, *Festivals in Prophecy*.

Sivan						
S	M	T	W	T	F	S
1	2	3	4	5	6	7 042
8	9	10	11	12	13	14 049
15 Pent.	16	17	18	19	20	21 W7
22	23	24	25	26	27	28 W14
29	30					

Pent., Pentecost; W1-49, the daily count to the Festival of New Wine

Tammuz						
S	M	T	W	T	F	S
		Summer solstice	1	2	3	4 W21
5	6	7	8	9	10	11 W28
12	13	14	15	16	17	18 W35
19	20	21	22	23	24	25 W42
26	27	28	39	30		

The summer solstice occurs the day after Sivan 30 which is also the day before Tammuz 1.

The festivals of new wine, oil, and wood are celebrations that have been forgotten by modern Judaism. Since Passover and Pentecost were prophetic, these other festivals must be studied to see if they teach prophecy.

Av						
S	M	T	W	T	F	S
					1	2 W49
3 FF-NW	4	5	6	7	8	9 NO7
10	11	12	13	14	15	16 NO14
17	18	19	20	21	22	23 NO21
24	25	26	27	28	29	30 NO28

FF-NW, First Fruits of New Wine; NO1-49, the daily count to the Festival of New Oil

Elul						
S	M	T	W	T	F	S
1	2	3	4	5	6	7 NO35
8	9	10	11	12	13	14 NO42
15	16	17	18	19	20	21 NO49
22 FF-NO	23 WO	24 WO	25 WO	26 WO	27 WO	28 WO
29	30					

FF-NO, First Fruits of New Oil; WO, Wood Offering

The Festival of New Wine falls on Sunday, Av 3. Then the count to the festival of New Oil begins. The festival of New Oil occurs on Sunday, Elul 22. Notice that the festivals of the first fruits of the barley harvest, Pentecost, new wine, and new oil all occur on a Sunday. Elul 23-28 are the wood offerings for the twelve tribes.

Tishrei						
S	M	T	W	T	F	S
		Fall equinox	1 Trump.	2	3	4
5	6	7	8	9	10 Atone.	11
12	13	14	15 T1	16 T2	17 T3	18 T4
19 T5	20 T6	21 T7	22 GD	23	24	25
26	27	28	39	30		

Trump., Festival of Trumpets; Atone., Day of Atonement; T1-7, the seven days of Tabernacles

Heshvan						
S	M	T	W	T	F	S
					1	2
3	4	5	6	7	8	9
10	11	12	13	14	15	16
17	18	19	20	21	22	23
24	25	26	27	28	29	30

The day after Elul 30 is the calculated fall equinox. The following day is Wednesday, Tishrei 1. This is the Festival of Trumpets. On Friday, Tishrei 10 is the Day of Atonement. Wednesday, Tishrei 15 through Tuesday, Tishrei 21 is the Festival of Tabernacles. Wednesday, Tishrei 22 is the Festival of the Great Day.

Kislev						
S	M	T	W	T	F	S
1	2	3	4	5	6	7
8	9	10	11	12	13	14
15	16	17	18	19	20	21
22	23	24	25 H1	26 H2	27 H3	28 H4
29 H5	30 H6					

H1-8, the eight days of Hanukkah

Tevet						
S	M	T	W	T	F	S
		Winter Solstice H7	1 H8	2	3	4
5	6	7	8	9	10	11
12	13	14	15	16	17	18
19	20	21	22	23	24	25
26	27	28	39	30		

Wednesday, Kislev 25 through Wednesday, Tevet 1 is the festival of Hanukkah. Notice this includes the winter solstice, the day between Monday, Kislev 30 and Wednesday, Tevet 1.

Shevat						
S	M	T	W	T	F	S
					1	2
3	4	5	6	7	8	9
10	11	12	13	14	15	16
17	18	19	20	21	22	23
24	25	26	27	28	29	30

Adar						
S	M	T	W	T	F	S
1	2	3	4	5	6	7
8	9	10	11	12	13	14
15	16	17	18	19	20	21
22	23	24	25	26	27	28
29	30	Spring Equinox				

The last month of the year is Adar. The last day of the month is Monday, Adar 30. The next day is Tuesday, Tekufah Nisan, or the spring equinox. The following day is Wednesday, Nisan 1, or New Year's Day.

Leap Years

What is not stated clearly is how to calculate leap years. We need this to finish the calendar calculations. First, we will look at all possible theories and eliminate the ones that do not fit the evidence and see what is left.

Theory 1: No Leap Year

The first theory is that there was no leap year, leap month, leap week, or leap day at all. The Muslim calendar is like this. It follows the moon phases and never corrects itself. If the Dead Sea Scroll Calendar did this, we would eventually have summer in winter and Passover would be in the fall. Scripture states the year always begins in the spring month of Nisan, also called Abib.

You are to begin your calendar with this month; it will be the first month of the year for you. (Exodus 12:2, CJB)

Enoch states the year always begins with the spring equinox when the daylight hours and hours of darkness are equal and that the base calendar is 364 days long.

On that day the night decreases to nine parts day and nine parts night, and the night is equal to the day and the year is exactly 364 days long. (Ancient Book of Enoch 72:32)

Looking at these two sources and considering the fact that the Dead Sea Scroll calendar has the solstices and equinoxes built into it proves there has to be some kind of correction to keep the seasons correctly.

Theory 2: A Leap Month

This theory would have us add a whole month to the calendar every so many years. This is how the modern Jewish calendar does it. It works for the modern Jewish calendar because it is a lunar/solar calendar. This method does not work with the solar year given in the Dead Sea Scrolls. It would be twenty-two years or more before we would add a leap month to this calendar the way the Essenes did their calculations. That would make the seasons off by fifteen to thirty days before a correction. We have two witnesses against the idea of using the lunar leap month.

Before the discovery of the Book of Enoch in the Dead Sea Scrolls, the only full version we had was from the Ethiopic. The Ethiopic version mentions both the sun and the moon in the section for calendar calculations. This has led some to assume there is some lunar calculation required for the calendar. The version found in the Dead Sea Scrolls has "sun and stars" in place of the Ethiopic "sun and moon." This would indicate that we are to use only the sun and stars to properly calculate the calendar. The moon is only to be used to check the calculations, to ensure their accuracy.

> The sun and the stars bring in all the years exactly, so that they do not advance or delay their position by a single day unto eternity. (Ancient Book of Enoch 74:12)

The Book of Jubilees predicted that the Jews would abandon the God-given solar year and adopt lunar calculations. This would corrupt the calendar.

> For there will be those who will assuredly make observations of the moon—now it disturbeth the seasons and cometh in from year to year ten days too soon. For this reason the years will come upon them when they will disturb the order, and make an abominable day the day of testimony, and an unclean day a feast day, and they will confound all the days, the holy with the unclean, and the unclean day with the holy; for they will go wrong as to the months and sabbaths and feasts and jubilees. For this reason I command and testify to thee that thou mayest testify to them; for after thy death thy children will disturb them, so that they will not make the year 364 days only, and for this reason they will go wrong as to the new moons and seasons and sabbaths and festivals. (Ancient Book of Jubilees 6:36–38)

With all of this evidence I think we can safely conclude there should be no leap month.

Theory 3: A Leap Day

The third theory is to add a day or two at the end of the year to make the first of the year come out evenly with the spring equinox. This sounds like the most accurate way of doing it, but it would break the seven-day cycle. We can see in the calendar scrolls (4Q230–231a) the moon phases were added to the base calendar. The moon phases show there was no leap day each year to compensate for the drift.

Sun	Mon	Tue	Wed	Thu	Fri	Sat
			1 ○	2	3	4
5	6	7	8	9	10	11
12	13	14	15	16	17 ☽	18
19	20	21	22	23	24	25
26	27	28	29	30 ⊜	1	2
3	4	5	6	7	8	9
10	11	12	13	14	15	16
17 ☽	18	19	20	21	22	23
24	25	26	27	28	29	30 ○
1	2	3	4	5	6	7
8	9	10	11	12	13	14
15	16 ☽	17	18	19	20	21
22	23	24	25	26	27	28
29 ○	30					

The priestly calendar scrolls (4Q230-231a) have a repeating six-year cycle. In year one of that cycle the first of Nisan is a Wednesday. It is also a full moon. The new moon appears on Friday, Nisan 17 and the second full moon, called a blue moon, appears on Thursday Nisan 30.

The moon phases are recorded every month for six years. A close look at these calendar scrolls demonstrate no leap days in the first six years. If we added a leap day anywhere in the six-year period, the moon phases would be off.

It has been noted that 4Q230-31 do not take into account that the moon adds a day every two years and ten months, which calls into question if it can be trusted for accuracy. Dead Sea Scroll 4Q317 shows the calendar calculations with the same moon phases but it has scribal notes correcting the moon phases of 4Q319-320. All together these scrolls show that the Essenes were just using the moon as a second witness to mark time.

The addition of moon phases to the base calendar prove they did not use a leap day every year. These moon phases also help to pinpoint the year the Essenes were using for the calculations. The full moon would only show up on the same day in the same week every nineteen years. Coupling that with the spring equinox occurring on the Tuesday of that same week makes it much rarer: only once in over five hundred years.

Theory 4: A Leap Week

The fourth theory is to intercalate a leap week every so many years. This is the only theory left so it must be the correct one. This would keep the seven-day cycle uninterrupted and keep the seasons in check. But how do we find out exactly when to add the leap week to the end of the year? There have been several theories proposed to answer this question.

Leap Week Theory 1: Shemittahs and Jubilees. In this theory we would add a leap week at the end of every Shemittah (seven-year period) and add an extra leap week every Jubilee year (every fiftieth year). At first, this sounds logical because Shemittahs and Jubilees are a major part of the calendar system. The problem with this design is that there would be a maximum of thirteen days away from the equinox before the Jubilee year, and it would still have 6.11 days after the first Jubilee year. There would have to be extra leap weeks added somewhere, so the theory is incomplete and makes the year off too many days.

Leap Week Theory 2: Shemittahs and Sun Cycles. Another way of using Shemittah years for leap years is to replace the extra leap week on the Jubilee with one on every twenty-eight-year sun cycle. A ritual is performed every twenty-eight years thanking God for the creation of the sun and the calendar (see the Birkat Hachama in the chapter on the Modern Jewish Calendar). Adding a leap week at the end of each Shemittah and each twenty-eight-year-sun-cycle is more accurate than the Shemittah/Jubilee theory, but it still has 5.46 days left over at the end of seven hundred years.

The calendar fragments show years one through six and then year one repeats. This may not be the case every year, but since it is the case in some years the leap weeks cannot be every Shemittah year.

There are other variants of the Shemittah theory, but I believe all of them allow the start of the year to drift too far away from the equinox. In my opinion, theories three to five are the only viable ones.

Leap Week Theory 3: Wednesday after the Equinox. This theory places New Year's Day, Nisan 1, on the first Wednesday that occurs after the spring equinox. The idea that the spring equinox cannot be the first day of the new year is based on these passages from Enoch.

> In this way he rises in the first month [Nisan] in the great constellation, which is the fourth of those six constellations in the east... 8When the sun rises in the heaven, he comes out of that fourth constellation thirty mornings in succession, and sets accurately in the constellation in the west of the heaven... 32On that day the night decreases to nine parts day and nine parts night, and the night is equal to the day and the year is exactly 364 days long. (Ancient Book of Enoch 72:6, 8, 32)

So, it is true that the new year, the first of Nisan, occurs after the sun has entered the fourth portal, or constellation, which is after the equinox. But it is also true that the sun enters the other portals after the solstices and equinoxes.

The solstices and equinoxes are set to occur at a predetermined time on the calendar and are off a day or two from the actual time they would be observed. The function of the leap week is to keep the start of the year as close to the spring equinox without disrupting the seven-day week cycle.

This leap-week theory would keep New Year's Day closer to the equinox than the other methods while keeping the seven-year cycle uninterrupted. If the spring equinox fell on a Wednesday, the first of the year would be seven days later, on the next Wednesday. This would allow the first of the year to drift up to a maximum of seven days away from the spring equinox.

S	M	T	W	T	F	S
			VE	1	2	3
4	5	6	7			

Leap Week Theory 4: Wednesday on or after the Equinox. This theory is the same as theory 3 except that it is thought that if the vernal equinox falls on a Wednesday, it would also be the first day of the new year. This would allow the first day of the new year to occur up to a maximum of six days away from the equinox. This seems more accurate but there is an even more accurate method.

S	M	T	W	T	F	S
			1(VE)	2	3	4
5	6	7				

Leap Week Theory 5: Wednesday closest to the equinox. In my opinion, the best theory seems to be to place New Year's Day on the Wednesday closest to the spring equinox. This self-correcting method would keep the seven-year cycle intact and allow a drift of only up to a maximum of three days before or up to a maximum of three days after the spring equinox. This is by far the most accurate method.

S	M	T	W	T	F	S
-3	-2	-1	VE	1	2	3

In the next section the Jewish historian Josephus will give us a clue that this method is the correct one.

Enoch's Five, Six, and Eight Year Periods

Enoch 72:32 says that the calendar year is exactly 364 days. Enoch 74 discusses the difference in the calendar months of his system and the lunar months. Enoch says that the moon has 354 days in one lunar year. This makes 1,062 days in three lunar years, 1,770 days in five lunar years, and 2,832 days in eight lunar years. The number of his calendar days total 364 days in one solar year, 1,092 days in three solar years, 1,820 days in five solar years, and 2,912 days in eight solar years.

This has made some think years three, five, and eight are special and that they must be used in the calculation of the leap years in some way.

There are almost ten days' difference in one year. The basic principle is that in Enoch's septenary system, there are thirty-six lunar cycles every three years, sixty-one lunar cycles every five years, and ninety-nine lunar cycles every eight years. On the solar calendar you would have thirty-six months in three years, but sixty months in five years, and ninety six months in eight years. So in three years they appear to be equal, but there is one extra month by the time you get to year six and three extra months by the time you get to year eight. This is without taking into account any leap system so as not to confuse readers. In other words, you would think you would see the extra month in year six but it appears in year five instead and you might think to see three extra months by year nine but they show up in year eight instead.

Enoch is simply showing how off the calendar would be if it used the moon for any calculation. That's all. It has nothing to do with leap years.

Evidence for the Correct Method

If we recap the facts from this chapter, we can see that there must be a leap year sometime, and it has to be a leap week to fit all the criteria. Out of the three possible leap week theories using the Wednesday closest to the spring equinox is the most logical.

The spring equinox is the pointer for the start of the year.

The year always starts on a Wednesday.

There are no leap days that occur every single year.

The solstices and equinoxes are calculated, not observed.

The Wednesday closest to the equinox is a self-correcting method.

The priestly courses do not show any leap weeks. Therefore, the leap weeks are not counted as part of the year, in the same way that the teku-fahs are not counted as part of the days inside of the months.

Conclusion

In my opinion, the correct leap week method is keeping the start of the calendar as close to the spring equinox as possible. This is best done by placing the first of the new year on the Wednesday closest to the spring equinox. This will keep the seven-day cycle intact.

Menorah as a Timepiece

The tabernacle of Moses always faced east. This would allow a priest in the tabernacle to record the day that the spring equinox occurred by observing the sunrise that morning.

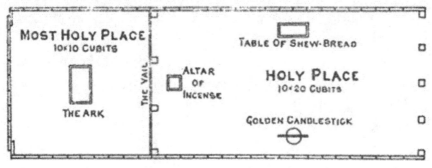

Plan of the Tabernacle

Josephus says this about the Menorah:

Over against this table, near the southern wall, was set a candlestick of cast gold, hollow within, and being of the weight of one hundred pound: which the Hebrews call cinchares: which, if it be turned into the Greek language, it denotes a talent. It was made with its knops, and lilies, and pomegranates, and bowls: which ornaments amounted to seventy in all. By which means the shaft elevated itself on high from a single base, and spread itself into as many branches as there are planets: including the sun among them. It terminated in seven heads, in one row, all standing parallel to one another; and these branches carried seven lamps, one by one, in imitation of the number of the planets: these lamps looked to the east and to the south, the candlestick being situate obliquely." Josephus' Antiquities 3.6.7

According to Josephus the lamps on the Menorah "imitated the number" of the planets. That might mean that they were named after the planets. Originally the days of the week were numbered one through seven, or one through six and "the Sabbath." Later, the days of the week were named after the planets. Saturday, Sunday, and Monday are obvious in English as Saturn, the sun and the moon. Tuesday, Wednesday, Thursday, and Friday are easier seen in the French language than the English language. Tuesday is *mardi* (Mars). Wednesday is *mercredi* (Mercury). Thursday is *jeudi* (Jupiter). Friday is *vendredi* (Venus).

Pagans later named their gods after the planets. So, by saying that the lamps on the Menorah were named after the planets, he could very easily be saying they represented the days of the week. The lamps could be "slanted" or turned to face either east or south. I believe Josephus has given us the Zadok priest's method of recording the day of the week that the spring equinox occurred, and thereby showing when to add the leap week into the calendar.

It would start with the lamps all pointing the same way accept the marker lamp pointing the other way. The Essenes used Wednesday to start their calendar because Genesis 1:14–19 records that the sun, moon, and stars were created on the fourth day of the week. Wednesday would be the middle or fourth lamp in the row. The next spring equinox would occur 365 days later, one day more than the 364-day calendar that they used. This would place the spring equinox on Thursday instead of Wednesday. So, the priest would turn the fourth lamp back in line with the others and turn the fifth lamp to mark that the equinox occurred on Thursday that year.

Continuing this pattern, the second year's equinox would fall on a Friday and the third year's equinox would fall on a Saturday.

In the fourth year something interesting would happen. The marker would naturally be moved from Saturday to Sunday, back to the first lamp on the Menorah. This would signal that the year was a leap year adding a "leap week." However, since this would be the fourth year in the cycle, it would also have an extra day (the 366th day on the Gregorian calendar). By adding this extra day, the marker would move from Saturday to Monday, instead of Saturday to Sunday.

The fifth year the marker would move to Tuesday, then in the sixth year it would move to Wednesday, and then in the seventh year it would move to Thursday. In the eighth year it should move to Friday but every four years we need to add that extra day (the 366th day on the Gregorian Calendar), so it would actually move from Thursday to Saturday.

The ninth year would be a normal year, it would only move from Saturday to Sunday (only one day). The marker would move off of Saturday, the seventh lamp, and return to the left side of the Menorah landing on Sunday. That means we would add a seven-day leap week. After eleven cycles the pattern repeats.

Sun	Mon	Tue	Wed	Thu	Fri	Sat
			X	1yr	2yr	3yr
→	4yr	5yr	6yr	7yr	→	8yr
9yr	10yr	11yr	→	12yr	13yr	14yr
15yr	→	16yr	17yr	18yr	19yr	→
20yr	21yr	22yr	23yr	→	24yr	25yr
26yr	27yr	→	28yr	29yr	30yr	31yr
→	32yr	33yr	34yr	35yr	→	36yr
37yr	38yr	39yr	→	40yr	41yr	42yr
43yr	→	44yr	45yr	46yr	47yr	→
48yr	49yr	50yr	51yr	→	52yr	53yr
54yr	55yr	→	X			

This would keep the calendar correct for approximately 20,806 years, until another "extra day" would add up. But, when it does, the priests could simply add an extra skip day on the Menorah and start all over. In other words, it is a self-correcting calendar. It would never get off.

This method keeps both the seven-day sequence uninterrupted and keeps the start of the new year within three days of the equinox. If you count the number of years between leap years using this method, it is either five or six years long. I believe this is more evidence that we are using the correct method.

After the Equinox Debate

The method taught in this chapter only allows the spring equinox to occur a maximum of three days away from the first of the new year, three days before to three days after.

There are those who believe that the sign of the spring equinox must always be before the Wednesday which is the new year. With their method, the counting and marking of the Menorah would be the same as this one, but they would place the leap week when the marker moves from Tuesday to Wednesday instead of moving from Saturday to Sunday. Their method would allow the spring equinox to vary a total of seven days away from the first day of the new year. This is the major reason I believe the "after the equinox" method is incorrect. The seasons would get too far out of alignment. It seems more natural to have the leap week when the Menorah lamp counter goes back a week.

3

THE AGES OF TIME

Ancient Chronology

We can begin to calculate the years by studying the chronology in Genesis 5. Adam was created. When he was in his 130th year, he fathered a child whom he named Seth. When Seth was 105 years old, he fathered a son whom he named Enos. It does not matter how long Adam was in the Garden of Eden. We know from his creation to the birth of Seth was one hundred and thirty years. By adding the 130 to the 105 we come to 235 years after Creation. The Jews call this dating system Anno Mundi and abbreviate it as AM. Anno Mundi means "the year of the world." If we compare this to Anno Domini meaning "the year of our Lord" we can see the similarity. The year AD 2020 means two thousand and twenty years after Jesus was born. This is if the AD calendar is accurate. So, when we add up the years to the Flood and find they were 1,656 years after creation, we would call that the year 1656 AM. That would be accurate if the AM calendar has not been tampered with.

We will begin building our chronology by using the books of Genesis, Exodus, Jasher, and the Seder Olam. We should all know what the biblical books of Genesis and Exodus are. The Ancient Book of Jasher is a Jewish history book dating from about 1500 BC, which makes it approximately 3,500 years old. It covers time from the Creation to the death of Joshua, which is the first 2516 years of human history. The Ancient Seder Olam is a Jewish history book written about AD 169 by a Jew who wanted to be respectful of his elders, but record accurate history and what actually happened when the calendar was deliberately tampered with.

Adam to the Flood

Genesis 5:1–28, Jasher 1:1–3:13, and the Seder Olam 1 all record the same dates. Jasher and the Seder Olam give a total number of years from Creation to the Flood as 1,656 years. We have the following from all three sources:

> Adam was 130 when Seth was born (130 AM).
> Seth was 105 when Enos was born (235 AM).
> Enos was 90 when Cainan was born (325 AM).
> Cainan was 70 when Mahalaleel was born (395 AM).
> Mahalaleel was 65 when Jared was born (460 AM).
> Jared was 162 when Enoch was born (622 AM).
> Enoch was 65 when Methuselah was born (687 AM).
> Methuselah was 187 when Lamech was born (874 AM).
> Lamech was 182 when Noah was born (1056 AM).
> Genesis 7:11, Jasher 4:1, and the Seder Olam 4 record the Flood occurring when Noah was six hundred years old. This would be 1656 AM.

> In the six hundredth year of Noah's life, in the second month, the seventeenth day of the month, the same day were all the fountains of the great deep broken up, and the windows of heaven were opened. (Genesis 7:11)

Notice also that the date is recorded. It was Iyar 17, 1656 AM. We have three independent witnesses, the Bible, Jasher, and the Seder Olam, that state from Creation to the flood was 1656 years, one month and seventeen days.

The Septuagint Chronology

Just a quick note about the Greek versions of the Bible. The original Septuagint was reported to be an extremely accurate translation of the Hebrew Scriptures. Church father Origin recorded that after the Messiah's death there were at least three people who tampered with the text to remove references to the divinity and timing of the Messiah. These three began to be intermingled and soon there were numerous versions created that were missing many random parts of the text. Origin created a work called the Hexapla to show the differences between all the texts. Today we have a movement who wants to use the Septuagint instead of the Hebrew text for their chronology for various reasons. It should be pointed out that almost every copy of the Septuagint text we have in Greek differs in some way from all the other Greek manuscripts. Even Josephus gives a different chronology in his Antiquities of the Jews. All the Hebrew works agree in the chronology including the texts of Genesis found in the Dead Sea Scrolls. More than that, both the Septuagint and the Hebrew state that their chronology can be checked against the book of Jasher.

> And he said to teach the sons of Judah The Song of the Bow. Behold, it is written in the Book of Jashar. (2 Samuel 1:18, LITV [Hebrew])

> And he spoke to teach the sons of Judah. Behold, it is written upon the scroll of the upright. (2 Samuel 1:18, APB [Greek])

> Is not this written in the book of Jasher? (Joshua 10:13, KJV [Hebrew])

> Is this not written in the scroll of the upright? (Joshua 10:13, APB [Greek])

To my knowledge, the Book of Jasher was never translated into Greek. Today it exists in Hebrew, English, and a few other languages. If both the Greek and Hebrew versions tell us to compare the text to Jasher, and Jasher agrees with all of the Hebrew manuscripts but disagrees with the numbers of the Greek text, that is amazing proof as to which set of numbers we should be using for our studies.

This is overwhelming proof that we should be using the Hebrew Masoretic text and Dead Sea Scroll texts for our Old Testament chronology. We should not use the Greek texts.

The Flood to Abraham

One mistake people make in chronology is using Genesis 5:32 instead of Genesis 11:10 for the post-Flood genealogy. This can cause calculations to be off by two years.

> And Noah was five hundred years old: and Noah begat Shem, Ham, and Japheth. (Genesis 5:32)

Were Shem, Ham, and Japheth triplets; all born in the same year? Or was the first or last of the three born in that year? We know from the text that Noah had only one wife, Naamah. So, they were all born from the same mother and father. Genesis 11:10 records the answer we are looking for.

> These are the generations of Shem: Shem was an hundred years old, and begat Arphaxad two years after the flood. (Genesis 11:10)

Arphaxad was born in the year 1658 AM, just two years after the Flood. Genesis 11:10–24, Jasher 7:19–22, and the Seder Olam 1 give the same chronology up to Terah, Abraham's father.

Arphaxad was born in 1658 AM.

Selah was born in 1693 AM.

Eber was born in 1723 AM.

Peleg was born in 1757 AM.

Reu was born in 1787 AM.

Serug was born in 1819 AM.

Nahor was born in 1849 AM.

Terah was born in 1878 AM.

Then we have that same problem again:

And Terah lived seventy years, and begat Abram, Nahor, and Haran. (Genesis 11:26)

Were Abraham, Nahor, and Haran triplets? Jasher and the Seder Olam state Nahor and Haran were Abraham's older brothers.

Terah was seventy years old when he begat him, and Terah called the name of his son that was born to him Abram, because the king had raised him in those days, and dignified him above all his princes that were with him. (Jasher 7:51)

This means Abraham was born in the year 1948 AM. It is almost prophetic that the nation of Israel, the children of Abraham, would be reborn in AD 1948!

Abraham to the Exodus from Egypt

We can record this period in two different ways from the Scriptures, Jasher, and the Seder Olam.

The long way:

Isaac was born in 2048 AM (Gen. 11:26, Jasher 8:51)

Jacob was born in 2108 (Gen. 25:20, Jasher 21:1)

Joseph was born in 2199 AM (Gen. 30, Jasher 31:21)

Joseph was enslaved in 2216 AM (Gen. 37:2, Jasher 41:9)

Joseph started ruling in 2228 (Gen. 41:46, Jasher 49:38)

Seven-year famine started in 2237 (Gen. 41:54, Jasher 50:19)

Jacob migrated into Egypt in 2238 (Gen. 47:28, Jasher 55:26)

Jacob died in 2255 (Gen. 47:28, Jasher 56:1)

Joseph died in 2309 (Gen. 50:26, Jasher 59:25)

Moses was born in 2368 (Exo. 2:2, 10; Jasher 68:4)

The Exodus occurred when Moses was eighty years old. Or in the year 2448 AM.

The short way:

The apostle Paul stated that the time from when God gave Abraham the promise to the Exodus from Egypt was exactly 430 years.

> Now to Abraham and his seed were the promises made. He saith not, And to seeds, as of many; but as of one, And to thy seed, which is Christ. And this I say, that the covenant, that was confirmed before of God in Christ, the law, which was four hundred and thirty years after, cannot disannul, that it should make the promise of none effect. (Galatians 3:16–17)

God gave the promise to Abraham when he was seventy years old. Isaac, Abraham's seed was born thirty years later when Abraham was one hundred. Then the four hundred years of Abraham's seed sojourning in lands not their own began, resulting in slavery in Egypt.

Using either method, we arrive at the date of the Exodus which was after dusk on Passover (Nisan 15) in the year 2448 AM, or the fifteenth day of the first month.

The Exodus to the Dedication of Solomon's Temple

This one is an easy one. First Kings records 487 years from the Exodus to the dedication of King Solomon's Temple. This places the dedication at 2935 AM. The ancient date would be the eighth month of 2935 AM.

> And it came to pass in the four hundred and eightieth year after the children of Israel were come out of the land of Egypt, in the fourth year of Solomon's reign over Israel, in the month Zif, which is the second month, that he began to build the house of the LORD. (1 Kings 6:1)

> And in the eleventh year, in the month Bul, which is the eighth month, was the house finished throughout all the parts thereof, and according to all the fashion of it. So was he seven years in building it. (1 Kings 6:38)

The Era of Solomon's Temple

This one is a bit tricky. The Book of Jasher ends with the death of Joshua, so it is of no help to us this time. If we add together all the dates in Kings and Chronicles, we come up with the temple standing anywhere between four hundred and four hundred ten years. This is because the terms used in Kings and Chronicles can be confusing. The Seder Olam shows Solomon's Temple stood for exactly 403 years. This places the destruction of Solomon's Temple by Nebuchadnezzar at 3338 AM.

So far, we have:

Creation: 1 AM
Noah's Flood: 1656 AM
Birth of Abraham: 1948 AM
Exodus from Egypt: 2448 AM
Dedication of Solomon's Temple: 2935 AM
Destruction of Solomon's Temple: 3338 AM

AM to BC

All secular historians agree that Nebuchadnezzar destroyed the Jerusalem Temple in either 586 or 587 BC. When we take 3,338 plus 587 BC we arrive at the year of Creation. Creation would have been 3925 BC.

Prophecy of the Messiah's First Coming

So far, we have seen the date of the destruction of Solomon's Temple was 3338 AM, or 587 BC. Cyrus freed the Jews from the Babylonian captivity in the year 3388 AM or 537 BC.

Daniel 9 gives a prophecy detailing the exact time between a decree to rebuild the Temple of Jerusalem to the cutting off, or death, of the Messiah.

> Seventy weeks are determined upon thy people and upon thy holy city, to finish the transgression, and to make an end of sins, and to make reconciliation for iniquity, and to bring in everlasting righteousness, and to seal up the vision and prophecy, and to anoint the most Holy. Know therefore and understand, that from the going forth of the commandment to restore and to build Jerusalem unto the Messiah the Prince shall be seven weeks, and threescore and two weeks: the street shall be built again, and the wall, even in troublous times. And after threescore and two weeks shall Messiah be cut off, but not for Himself: and the people of the prince that shall come shall destroy the city and the sanctuary; and the end thereof shall be with a flood, and unto the end of the war desolations are determined. (Daniel 9:24–26)

The angel Gabriel predicted that from the decree to rebuild Jerusalem until the Messiah would be seven weeks plus another sixty-two weeks. During the first seven weeks (forty-nine years), the wall of the city of Jerusalem and the city itself would be rebuilt.

And it came to pass in the month Nisan, in the twentieth year of Artaxerxes the king, that wine was before him: and I took up the wine, and gave it unto the king. Now I had not been beforetime sad in his presence. Wherefore the king said unto me, Why is thy countenance sad, seeing thou art not sick? this is nothing else but sorrow of heart. Then I was very sore afraid, And said unto the king, Let the king live for ever: why should not my countenance be sad, when the city, the place of my fathers' sepulchres, lieth waste, and the gates thereof are consumed with fire? Then the king said unto me, For what dost thou make request? So I prayed to the God of heaven. And I said unto the king, If it please the king, and if thy servant have found favour in thy sight, that thou wouldest send me unto Judah, unto the city of my fathers' sepulchres, that I may build it. And the king said unto me, (the queen also sitting by him,) For how long shall thy journey be? and when wilt thou return? So it pleased the king to send me; and I set him a time. (Nehemiah 2:1–6 KJV)

Nehemiah 2:1 recorded that the decree to restore and rebuild Jerusalem occurred in the month of Nissan in the twentieth year of the reign of the Persian king, Artaxerxes. Encyclopedia Britannica gives the date Artaxerxes Longimanus took the Persian throne as July of 465 BC. Therefore, his twentieth year began in July of 445 BC. The month of Nissan following that would have been in March of 444 BC, which occurred before the twenty-first anniversary of Artaxerxes' reign. The seven weeks, or forty-nine years, ran from Artaxerxes' decree to the year Jerusalem's wall and moat were finished in the period of Ezra and Nehemiah. From that time another sixty-two weeks went by until the Messiah was "cut off," a term meaning "executed."

Messiah's Death ~ AD 32

In the early third century, ancient Church Father Julius Africanus wrote a book entitled *On the Weeks and This Prophecy*. Only fragments remain today; but in fragment 16, he tells us how to calculate the exact date by converting the years to days and changing them from the Jewish prophetical calendar to the Roman calendar used in his day. Julius says that the "seventy weeks" prophecy of Daniel 9 started when Artaxerxes gave the decree in his twentieth year. Years later, Sir Robert Anderson recreated the conversion process for our modern calendar as follows: first, the sixty-nine weeks of years ends with the Messiah's death. If we multiply 69 times 7 this gives us the 483 prophetic years between Artaxerxes' decree and the death of the Messiah.

We convert from the Jewish/prophetic calendar to the Gregorian/Roman calendar this way: We take the 483 years times 360 days per year (the sacred Jewish calendar) and that equals 173,880 days. The 173,880 days on the modern calendar comes out to be 476 years and 21 days (476 x 365.25 = 173,859 and 173,880-173,859 = 21). March 14, 444 BC plus 476 years comes out to be March 14, AD 31. We add one year because there was no "0" year between AD and BC. We then add the 21 days. The final date arrives at April 6, AD 32!

70 Weeks Prophecy

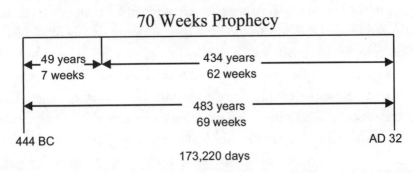

The ancient rabbis agreed Daniel accurately gave the date for the Messiah's coming. They simply say something was supposed to happen, but it did not occur.

Ancient Rabbis Agree on the Coming of Messiah

When witnessing to Jews, most will say Daniel's 70 weeks prophecy has nothing to do with the Messiah; but the ancient rabbinical writings, including the Talmud, state the prophecy does refer to King Messiah. Please point out to them that the Messiah, whoever he was, had to have come before the destruction of the Temple in AD 70. If the Messiah was not Jesus Christ, then who was he? Here is a small list of quotes from the ancient rabbis about this passage in Daniel:

> Daniel has elucidated to us the knowledge of the end times. However, since they are secret, the wise [rabbis] have barred the calculation of the days of Messiah's coming so that the untutored populace will not be led astray when they see that the End Times have already come but there is no sign of the Messiah. (Maimonides: Igeret Teiman, Chapter 3)

> The anointed King is destined to stand up and restore the Davidic Kingdom to its antiquity, to the first sovereignty. He will build the Temple in Jerusalem and gather the strayed ones of Israel together. All laws will return in his days as they were before: Sacrificial offerings are offered and the Sabbatical years and Jubilees are kept, according to all its precepts that are mentioned in the Torah. Whoever does not believe in him, or whoever does not wait for his coming, not only does he defy the other prophets, but also the Torah and Moses our teacher.... Bar Kokhba claimed that he was King Messiah. He and all the Sages of his generation deemed him King Messiah, until he was killed by sins; only since he was killed, they knew that Bar Kokhba was not the Messiah. (Maimonides: Mishneh Torah, Hilkhot Melakhim Umilchamoteihem, Chapter 11)

These times (Daniel's 70 Weeks) were over long ago. (Rabbi Judah: Babylonian Talmud, Sanhedrin)

I have examined and searched all the Holy Scriptures and have not found the time for the coming of Messiah clearly fixed, except in the words of Gabriel to the prophet Daniel, which are written in the 9th chapter of the prophecy of Daniel. (Rabbi Moses Abraham Levi)

Similarly, one should not try to calculate the appointed time [for the coming of Messiah]. Our Sages declared: [Sanhedrin 97b] 'May the spirits of those who attempt to calculate the final time [of Messiah's coming] expire!' Rather, one should await [his coming] and believe in the general conception of the matter, as we have explained. (Maimonides: Mishneh Torah, Hilkhot Melakhim Umilchamoteihem, Chapter 12)

...all we need is to do teshuva until Messiah comes, for all the predestined dates for the redemption have already passed. (Talmud: Sanhedrin 97b)

All the time limits for redemption (the coming of Messiah) have passed and the matter now depends only on repentance and good deeds. (Babylonian Talmud: Rabbi Rabh)

Notice the rabbis placed a curse on those who would read Daniel 9 and calculate the time of the Messiah's coming to earth. They did this because it clearly points to Jesus Christ.

The Daniel 9 prophecy pinpoints the dates of Artaxerxes' degree and the year of the death of Jesus Christ. When we add this information to our calendar calculations we arrive at these dates:

Solomon's Temple Destroyed, 3338 AM, or 587 BC.

Cyrus freed the Jews, 3388 AM or 537 BC.

Artaxerxes' degree, 3481 AM, or 444 BC,

Death of Messiah, Passover, 3957 AM, or AD 32

So why does the modern Jewish calendar have 5780 AM instead of 5944 AM for the AD year of 2020?

Tampering with the Timeline

We know the Essenes teach the Pharisees changed the calendar system but did any of them try to change the years? To answer that question, we turn to the Seder Olam.

The Seder Olam is a history book written by an unknown Jew about the year AD 169. The author tried to put together a timeline of events starting with Creation up to the Flood and going beyond that up to his time. What is interesting is that the Talmud says that the Seder Olam is accurate history and uses it to prove its timeline.

Chronology of the Persian Era

History records that Cyrus conquered Babylon and freed the Jews in 537 BC. After Cyrus there was Darius the Mede of whom Daniel predicted there would be four more Persian kings before the coming of the Grecian kingdom led by Alexander the Great:

> Also, I in the first year of Darius the Mede, even I, stood to confirm and to strengthen him. And now will I shew thee the truth. Behold, there shall stand up yet three kings in Persia; and the fourth shall be far richer than they all: and by his strength through his riches he shall stir up all against the realm of Grecia. And a mighty king shall stand up, that shall rule with great dominion, and do according to his will. (Daniel 11:1–3)

Darius the Mede ruled from 536–530 BC.

Cambyses ruled from 530–522 BC.

Pseudo-Smerdis tried to take the kingdom but was executed in 522 BC.

Darius I ruled from 522–486 BC. The Jerusalem temple was rebuilt under his reign.

Xerxes I ruled from 486–465 BC. He attacked Greece as prophesied.

Artaxerxes I ruled from 465–424 BC.

Alexander the Great reigned over the Persians for only three years before his death, from 326–323 BC. Babylon fell to Alexander in 327 BC, exactly 210 years after Babylon fell to Cyrus in 537 BC. This is what we read in the Seder Olam.

> The kings of Media/Persia ruled for 210 years total before the coming of Alexander the Great. (Seder Olam 30)

The Missing Years

The Seder Olam was written to preserve the true history in its day and bring to light the attempts of certain rabbis to change dates in history. The history in the Seder Olam agrees with the Bible, Jasher, and other works up to the time of the Persian rule over the Jews. Cyrus conquered the Persian empire in 3388 AM, or 537 BC.

In the previous chapter we learned that the standard interpretation of the Messiah's death recorded in Daniel 9 was that it pointed to when the Messiah should die, but it did not occur because God changed His mind due to the sins of the nation of Israel. This does not make sense because it would cause God to be a liar. One rabbi came up with a way to fix this problem.

The author of the Seder Olam describes a rabbi named Yose who came up with an idea that the prophecy given in Daniel 9 did not point to the death of the Messiah, as all other rabbis had taught, but that it pointed to the destruction of the second temple in AD 70. But this caused the chronology to be off by at least forty years.

To fix this, Rabbi Yose came up with the idea that Cyrus, Artaxerxes, and Darius were titles, not proper names. He said that they were all the same person.

The author of the Seder Olam recorded the calculations of the rabbi and then stated he changed his mind because the numbers did not match up well with other dates. Rabbi Yose's second theory turned out to be off even more. The author of the Seder Olam tried to be very respectful of his elders, but at the same time point out that they were trying to deliberately tamper with the timeline for the purpose of rejecting the Messiah.

The Seder Olam records Rabbi Yose came up with this interpretation:

Rabbi Yose said: The 70 weeks are figured from the destruction of the First Temple to the destruction of the Second Temple. The seven took place while they were still in Babylonian exile. Then the one week took place while they were moving back into the land. Finally, there were 62 weeks to the destruction of the Second Temple. Rabbi Yose also said: It was 70 years between the destruction of the First Temple to the dedication of the Second Temple. Add to that 410 [420] years and we come to the 490 years of the prophecy which ended at the destruction of the Second Temple. (Seder Olam 28)

By doing this he managed to get the time of the Persian rule over the Jews from around two hundred years down to about twenty-five years.

Rabbi Yose said: the Persian Empire continued to exist for twenty-four years after the new Temple was completed. The Grecian Empire ruled after Persia for 180 years. After the fall of the Grecian Empire, the Hasmonean Dynasty, starting under

Judas Maccabee, ruled Israel for 103 years. Then under Roman rule, the kingdom of Herod existed for 103 years before the Temple was destroyed. (Seder Olam 30)

Eventually Rabbi Yose's theories with a few other modifications, became the basis for the official Jewish year. See the Jewish Time Line Encyclopedia by Mattis Kantor for the Talmudic account of history.

Event	Yose	History
Temple built to the fall of Persia	24	192
Fall of Persia to the fall of Greece	180	161
Fall of Greece to the coming of Rome	103	100
Coming of Rome to the end of Temple	103	134
Total	410	587

Later, when the rabbis took rabbi Yose's theories and tweaked them yet again, the calendar year was set.

The difference between these rabbis' calculations and the dates set forth in the Seder Olam is the famous 164 missing years.

Conclusion

The author of the Seder Olam agrees with all other Jewish history books and keeps the correct number of years past the destruction of Solomon's Temple in 3338 AM, 587 BC. He then continues to give correct chronology and makes it clear who corrupted the calendar and when. This is one of the most well-known deliberate corruptions to the Jewish calendar by those who rejected the Messiah. We can skip all the corruption by switching to the AD / BC timeline at 587 BC.

Biblical Timeline Prophecies

There are two other prophecies we should look at that prove we have the correct dating system. We looked at the prophecy of Daniel 9 about the number of days between Artaxerxes' decree and the death of the Messiah. We learned that it was fulfilled to the day.

Two prophecies we need to look at give the exact number of days between events in the distant past and the rebirth of the modern state of Israel on May 14, AD 1948. Another prophecy records that the modern state of Israel would take back the temple mount on June 7, AD 1967. This gives a direct connection between Cyrus' decree in 537 BC and 1948 and 1967. Look back at the chapter on the Prophecy of Messiah's First Coming for details on that timeline prophecy. These will be calculated in the exact same way.

The Second Return—May 14, 1948

Both Daniel and Ezekiel foretold the exact date of the reestablishment of Israel.

> [4]Lie thou also upon thy left side, and lay the iniquity of the house of Israel upon it: according to the number of the days that thou shalt lie upon it thou shalt bear their iniquity. [5]For I have laid upon thee the years of their iniquity, according to the number of the days, three hundred and ninety days: so shalt thou bear the iniquity of the house of Israel. [6]And when thou hast accomplished them, lie again on thy right side, and thou shalt bear the iniquity of the house of Judah forty days: I have appointed thee each day for a year. (Ezekiel 4:4–6)

In this passage, the sin of Israel and Judah was three hundred ninety years and forty years. To symbolize this, Ezekiel had to lie on his left side

for 390 days, a day for each year of Israel's sin, and forty days on his right
side, a day for each year of Judah's sin. The total time then was 430 years
of sin. The Babylonian captivity took up seventy years of this punishment, leaving 360 years.

> [14]But if ye will not hearken unto Me, and will not do all these
> commandments; [15]And if ye shall despise My statutes, or if your
> soul abhor My judgments, so that ye will not do all My com-
> mandments, but that ye break My covenant... I will set My face
> against you, and ye shall be slain before your enemies: they that
> hate you shall reign over you; and ye shall flee when none pur-
> sueth you. [18]And if ye will not yet for all this hearken unto Me,
> then I will punish you seven times more for your sins. (Leviticus
> 26:14–18)

Here God declares that if Israel does not repent after the Babylonian
captivity, when Cyrus freed Israel, then the remaining time would be
multiplied sevenfold. If you multiply 360 years by seven, you get 2,520
prophetical years. The prophet Daniel predicted this same time period
in another way.

In Daniel 4, God punished King Nebuchadnezzar with insanity for
seven years, in order to humble him. God had Nebuchadnezzar act out
a prophecy, just as Ezekiel acted out his 430-day prophecy by lying on
his side. In Nebuchadnezzar's case, the restoration of his kingdom after
seven years is also a symbolic prophecy that illustrates that the children
of Israel would be restored a second time to their land after seven years
of days. Since the prophetic calendar uses a 360-day year, if you multiply
Nebuchadnezzar's seven years by the 360-day calendar, you get 2,520
years—just like Ezekiel's prophecy. From these two prophets we are told
the time of the second return of Israel. We will first convert the Jewish
years to Roman years the same way we did for the timeline prophecy of
the Messiah's death.

Cyrus issued his decree freeing the Jews and declaring the state of Israel to exist again on August 3, 537 BC. Multiply 2,520 Jewish years times 360 days per year to get 907,200 days. The 907,200 days on the modern calendar is 2,483 years and 285 days (2,483 years x 365.25 = 906,915; 907,200 − 906,915 = 285 days). August 3, 537 BC plus the 2,483 years comes to August 3, AD 1946. Add one year because there was no year "0" and the date becomes August 3, AD 1947. When we add the extra 285 days, we arrive at May 14, AD 1948!

This was the very day that the UN declared Israel to be a sovereign state!

Cyrus' Decree   **War of Independence**

August 3, 537 BC   **"907,200 Days"**   **May   14,   1948**

Control of the Temple Mount—June 7, 1967

Just as Daniel 4 predicted the reestablishment of the modern state of Israel, Daniel 5 also predicted Israel would take control of the Temple Mount in AD 1967.

In Daniel 5, we read of the account of the handwriting on the wall. This handwriting is an inscription prophecy with a double fulfillment. Daniel left out the first *mene* in this riddle and interpreted only the second *mene*, plus the *tekel*, and *pharsin* as Hebrew verbs which literally read "numbered," "weighed," and "divided." Daniel told Belshazzar that the words of the handwriting on that wall meant that he personally had been weighed and found to be godless. Therefore, the days of his kingdom had been numbered and had come to an end. His kingdom would be divided and given to the Medes and Persians.

And this is the writing that was written, MENE, MENE, TEKEL, UPHARSIN. (Daniel 5:24)

Mene	1,000	garahs
Mene	+1,000	garahs
Tekel	+ 20	garahs
Peres	+ 500	garahs
	2,520	garahs

The double fulfillment is for the latter days. First, notice that *mene* is stated twice. If we take these words as nouns instead of verbs, a different meaning becomes clear. If we decipher them as nouns, they turn out to be names for weights or money. A *mene* is 1,000 *garahs*. (A *garah* is a base unit of weight like our penny.) A *tekel* is 20 *garahs*, and a *peres* is half a *mena*. *Upharsin* is the Hebrew way of saying "and Peres." So the inscription reads 2,520 *garahs* or 2,520 periods of time. On this night the control of the temple vessels passed to the children of Israel. Real control of the Temple Mount would be given later by Darius. The actual building of the Temple would be much later still.

This prophecy tells us that from the decree Darius would give granting full control of the Temple Mount, plus 2,520 Jewish years, the children of Israel would again be granted control of the Temple Mount—but not granted the right to build the temple itself. The calculations for this timeline prophecy are exactly the same as the ones given for AD 32, and AD 1948. The 2,520 garahs or prophetic years times 360 days comes out to be 907,220 days. The 907,220 days on the modern calendar is 2,483 years and 285 days (2,483 years x 365.25 = 906,915; 907,200 – 906,915 = 285 days).

Darius's decree to grant the Jews control of the Temple Mount was August 25, 518 BC. This date plus 907,200 days (plus one year changing from BC to AD) brings us to June 7, 1967. On this exact date the Israelis again gained control of the Temple Mount during the Six Day War!

Darius Decree   Six Day War

├──┤

August 25, 518 BC   "907,200 Days"   **June 7, 1967 AD**

Conclusion

These timeline prophecies are fantastic for the purpose of keeping the Dead Sea Scroll calendar accurate.

So far, we have:

Creation: 1 AM
Noah's Flood: 1656 AM
Birth of Abraham: 1948 AM
Exodus from Egypt: 2448 AM
Dedication of Solomon's Temple: 2935 AM
Solomon's Temple destroyed, 3338 AM, or 587 BC.
Cyrus freed the Jews, 3388 AM or 537 BC.
Artaxerxes' decree 3481 AM, or 444 BC,
Death of Messiah, Passover, 3957 AM, or AD 32
Israel reborn, 5873 AM, AD 1948
Israel retaking the temple mount, 5892 AM, AD 1967

The School of Elijah

Elijah ran a school of the prophets. Josephus stated there was a prophetical work called the Epistle of Elijah that still existed in his day. As far as I know, it does not exist in its entirety today. The Ethiopian Orthodox church has an epistle called the Epistle of Elijah in its cannon. If it is the original text, it is missing a lot of information. It has nothing new to teach us. However, there is a commentary on the Epistle of Elijah called the Tannah Eliyahu.

For our purposes we want to know what it teaches about the calendar. It is obvious that it has been edited by rabbis over the centuries, but it still does contain commentary about the ages as taught by the School of Elijah. The epistle taught that human history would be divided into four "ages." The first age was called the Age of Chaos and was a period of two thousand years. It started with Creation and ended with the call of Abraham. According to Jasher, God called Abraham in the year 2000 AM. The second age was also to last two thousand years. It was called the Age of Torah and was supposed to exist from the call of Abraham to the first coming of the Messiah. When Messiah came it would start the third age which was called the Age of Grace. This Age of Grace was also called the temporary messianic period. We are not told why in the commentary, but the Essenes believed it was because the Messiah would die for our sins at his First Coming and rule as king at his Second Coming. The third age was to last for two thousand years. After the Age of Grace there would be a Messianic Kingdom which would last for one thousand years.

The concept of the four ages lasting for seven thousand years is repeated afterwards in several other rabbinical manuscripts even though it goes against what is commonly taught by them, namely that the Messiah did not come.

The Ancient Church Fathers

Many ancient Church Fathers believed in this concept of six thousand years of human history and a day of sabbath rest in the Messianic kingdom. This is what the weekly Sabbath ritual was to teach us. There were several Church Fathers who taught that the Second Coming would be in the year 6000 AM. This was because of the Old Testament chronology, the Essene beliefs, and the teaching from the School of the Prophets. Here are some quotes from the ancient church fathers about the Second Coming.

> Therefore, children, in six days, or in six thousand years, all the prophecies will be fulfilled. Then it says, He rested on the seventh day. This signifies at the Second Coming of our Lord Jesus, He

will destroy the Antichrist, judge the ungodly, and change the sun, moon, and stars. Then He will truly rest during the Millennial reign, which is the seventh day. (Epistle of Barnabas 15:7–9)

The day of the Lord is as a thousand years; and in six days created things were completed. It is evident, therefore, they will come to an end in the six thousandth year. (Irenaeus, Against Heresies 5.28)

The Sabbath is a type of the future kingdom.... For "a day with the Lord is as a thousand years." Since, then, in six days the Lord created all things, it follows that in six thousand years all will be fulfilled. (Hippolytus, Fragment 2; Commentary on Daniel 2.4)

We will be immortal when the six thousand years are completed. (Commodianus, Against the Gods of the Heathens 35)

Resurrection of the body will be when six thousand years are completed, and after the one thousand years [millennial reign], the world will come to an end. (Commodianus, Against the Gods of the Heathens 80)

Satan will be bound until the thousand years are finished. That is, after the sixth day. (Victorinus, Commentary on Revelation 20:1–3)

In the seventh millennium we will be immortal and truly celebrate the Feast of Tabernacles. (Methodius, Ten Virgins 9.1)

The sixth thousandth year is not yet complete. When this number is complete, the consummation must take place. (Lactantius, Divine Institutes 7.14)

Jubilee and Shemittah Years

Every seven years there is a Shemittah year. On this year all the debts of Jews would be forgiven. This seven-year cycle is repeated seven times. After the seventh Shemittah (forty-nine years) there is a Jubilee year. The Jubilee year is when all of the debts of the Gentile Noahides would be forgiven.

Today, it is most commonly taught that there are seven Shemittahs (forty-nine years) and then a jubilee year (the fiftieth year), so two jubilees would total one hundred years. Others have taught that a jubilee year is not separate from the Shemittah cycles. The jubilee year would be the first year of a new Shemittah cycle. This would mean two jubilees would total ninety-eight years instead of one century. Who is right?

The Tannah Eliyahu teaches that there are ten jubilees in a five hundred-year period called an "onah." It also teaches that there are four onahs in the ages of Chaos, Torah, and Grace, but only two onahs in the age of the Messianic Kingdom. This shows that the jubilee year is every fifty years and not every forty-nine years.

The Melchizedek Document

There is a Dead Sea Scroll called 11QMelchizedek. The Messiah is described as God incarnate. He was to be a Melchizedekian priest, not a Levitical one.

This scroll mentions that the Messiah (Melchizedek) would come to earth and die to pay for our sin nature, reconciling us to God the Father. It then goes further to tell us exactly when this would occur.

The captives Moses speaks of are those whom Isaiah says "To proclaim freedom to the captives [Isa. 61:1]." Its interpretation is that the LORD will assign those freed to the sons of heaven and the lot of Melchizedek. Even those, whose teachers had deliberately hidden and kept secret from them the truth about their inheritance through Melchizedek. The LORD will cast their lot amid the portions of Melchizedek, who will make them return [or repent] and will proclaim freedom to them, to free them from the debt of all their iniquities. This event will take place in the first week of the jubilee that occurs after the ninth jubilee. (11QMelchizedek Column 2)

The Essene calendar used the Ages as taught by Elijah. Each age was broken up into four onahs, or four parts of ten Jubilees each. If we use the biblical timeline we have shown in this book, Creation was 3925 BC. This would make the third age start in AD 75. Notice that the Dead Sea Scroll stated that the Messiah would die one Shemittah (seven-year period) after the end of the ninth Jubilee of their age. If we subtract a fifty-year Jubilee period, not a forty-nine-year period, from AD 75, we come to AD 25. If we then add that one Shemittah (seven year-period) to AD 25 we arrive at AD 32. So, according to this Dead Sea Scroll the Messiah came and died for our sins in AD 32. That is exactly what Jesus Christ did!

The Ten-Week Prophecy

There is another Dead Sea Scroll containing an outline of human history and various predictions that occur throughout the seven thousand years. It is called the Ten-week Prophecy. It divides time into ten weeks. Each day is one hundred years. One week is seven hundred years and over ten weeks of time, seven thousand years. With each day representing a century and two jubilee periods it fits nicely with the Essene calendar. The ten-week prophecy can be found in the Ancient Book of Enoch 93.

Conclusion

We have learned that several of the ancient Church Fathers believed in the original calendar, the Essene teachings, and taught that the Second Coming would be in the year 6000 AM. The school of the prophets divided time into three ages of two thousand years each; the Ages of Chaos, Torah, and Grace. After which there would be a one-thousand-year reign of the Messiah starting at His Second Coming. Other Dead Sea Scrolls divide time into ten weeks, where each day is one century. These documents use a fifty-year jubilee cycle. All of this helps to show the consistency of the calendar system taught by the Essene community.

4

~

FESTIVALS IN PROPHECY

Festival Outline

There are seven festivals given in Leviticus that were to be practiced by the Jews. The rituals performed on the festivals taught prophecy. Here is a list of the seven.

Passover
Unleavened Bread
First Fruits of the Barley Harvest
Pentecost
Trumpets
Day of Atonement
Tabernacles

The Essene calendar puts some of the festivals on a slightly different date than does the Pharisee calendar that we are used to. The Dead Sea Scroll calendar also adds eight more festivals that might be just as prophetic. These previously unknown holy days are:

New Year's Day
the Festival of New Wine
the Festival of New Oil
the wood offering
Noah's four Days of Remembrance

The spring Day of Remembrance falls on New Year's (Nisan 1) and the fall Day of Remembrance falls on the Festival of Trumpets (Tishrei 1) so those four holidays combine into two holy days. There is also a second Passover on Thursday, Iyar 14. It is observed by those who were unclean during the actual Passover, Tuesday, Nisan 14. We assume there is nothing new in the ritual done on the second Passover, so we do not list it here.

For all practical purposes that makes thirteen holy days to remember. In order these would be:

New Year's Day, the spring Day of Remembrance (Nisan 1)
Passover (Nisan 14)
Unleavened Bread (Nisan 15–21)
First Fruits of the Barley Harvest (Nisan 26)
Pentecost (Sivan 15)
Summer Day of Remembrance (Tammuz 1)
Festival of New Wine (Av 3)
Festival of New Oil (Elul 22)
Wood Offering (Elul 23-28)
Feast of Trumpets, Fall Day of Remembrance (Tishrei 1)
Day of Atonement (Tishrei 10)
Tabernacles (Tishrei 15–21)
Winter Day of Remembrance (Tevet 1)

We will start with the first one and go through the list showing the Essene theology each represented.

New Year's Day

New Year's Day always falls on Wednesday, Nisan 1. It was just a time to mark the turn of the year. It is listed as a holy day, but it is currently unknown if there were any rituals performed for a New Year's celebration.

Spring Day of Remembrance

Another name for New Year's Day is the spring Day of Remembrance. Noah commemorated four Days of Remembrance. All Gentile families were to gather together on these Days of Remembrance for a feast, fellowship, and focus on the written Testaments of the Patriarchs and memorize prophecy. According to Jubilees, the spring Day of Remembrance marks the time when God commanded Noah to start building the ark and when the Flood was over, and the earth became dry.

> And Noah ordained them for himself as feasts for the generations forever, so that they have become thereby a memorial unto him. And on the new moon of the first month [Nisan 1, the first day of spring] he was bidden to make for himself an ark, and on that day the earth became dry and he opened the ark and saw the earth. (Ancient Book of Jubilees 6:24–25)

Passover

The Festival of Passover occurs on Tuesday, Nisan 14, each year. The Passover lamb depicts the death of the Messiah for our sins. John the Baptist points this out in John 1:29.

> The next day John seeth Jesus coming unto him, and saith, Behold the Lamb of God, which taketh away the sin of the world. (John 1:29)

The Apostle Paul taught that we should remember the Messiah's sacrifice and focus on righteousness and repentance. The leaven represented sin and we should purge ourselves of sin.

> Purge out therefore the old leaven, that ye may be a new lump, as ye are unleavened. For even Christ our passover is sacrificed for us: Therefore let us keep the feast, not with old leaven, neither with the leaven of malice and wickedness; but with the unleavened bread of sincerity and truth. (1 Corinthians 5:7–8)

The Temple Ritual

In the time of Jesus, the high priest, on the 10th of Nisan, would go to Bethany to choose an unblemished lamb and bring it into the temple to be inspected for four days. As the lamb was brought to the Eastern Gate, pilgrims would line the sides of the road leading to the gate and wave the palm branches and say *Baruch Ha Shem Adonai*, which means "Blessed is he who comes in the name of the Lord," quoted from Psalm 118:26–27. At 9 AM on the fourteenth of Nisan, the lamb was tied to one of the horns of the altar. At 3 PM, the high priest would slay the lamb while saying the words, "it is finished."

How Jesus Fulfilled the Passover

The temple ritual teaches us about the Messiah's death. Jesus left the house of Lazarus in Bethany on Nissan 10 to teach in the temple. There the scribes asked their hardest questions of Jesus and walked away saying "never a man spoke as this man." So, Jesus was without blemish. Jesus was hung on the cross at 9 AM and died at 3:00 PM, or "between the evenings" on Nissan 14. He acted as both priest and sacrifice when He said, "It is finished," and then died.

Unleavened Bread

Unleavened Bread is a seven-day festival that occurs from Wednesday, Nisan 15 through Tuesday, Nisan 21. During this festival Jesus was buried and resurrected three days later.

Passover occurs on Tuesday, Nisan 14, every year. Jesus predicted that He would be in the grave for three days and three nights. On the Essene calendar Jesus would have celebrated the Last Supper with His disciples on Passover, Tuesday evening, Nisan 14. Later that night He would have been arrested, tried, and convicted of blasphemy. He would have been crucified the next day, which would have been Wednesday. Jesus would have been in the grave the three days and three nights; lasting from Wednesday night to Saturday night.

For as Jonas was three days and three nights in the whale's belly; so shall the Son of man be three days and three nights in the heart of the earth. (Matthew 12:40)

When the women went to the tomb on Sunday morning, Nisan 19, He was already risen.

So, the Festival of Unleavened Bread teaches us to put away sin. Jesus fulfilled His part of the prophecies by dying for our sins and resurrecting.

First Fruits of the Barley Harvest

On the Essene calendar the First Fruits of the Barley Harvest occurs on Sunday, Nisan 26, each year. I was taught that this festival was on the Sunday following Passover. The Essenes, by connecting the Festivals of Passover and Unleavened Bread, taught it was the Sunday following the week of Unleavened Bread. If Jesus resurrected on Resurrection Sunday, Nisan 19, what does the Festival of the First Fruits of the Barley Harvest prophetically teach?

But now is Christ risen from the dead, and become the firstfruits of them that slept. (1 Corinthians 15:20)

On Resurrection Sunday, Jesus told Mary not to touch Him, probably because the offering was not completed in some way.

Jesus said to her, Do not touch Me, for I have not yet ascended to My Father. But go to My brothers and say to them, I am ascending to My Father and your Father, and My God, and your God. (John 20:17 LITV)

Later, He appeared to His disciples and told them to touch Him and see His flesh was real.

Then He said to Thomas, Bring your finger here and see My hands, and bring your hand and thrust into My side, and be not unbelieving, but believing. (John 20:27 LITV)

So, it is thought that Jesus died on Passover, was buried on the first day of Unleavened Bread. He resurrected the Sunday during the seven-day Festival of Unleavened Bread and presented atonement before the Father on the Festival of First Fruits. Jesus would have then appeared to the disciples and stated for them to touch Him because the atonement was complete. I believe our salvation was finished at the cross when Jesus said, "It is finished." I believe atonement here means ritually completed as it does when the grape and olive harvests are done, and the grapes and olives are said to be "atoned for." The meaning of this was that the first fruits were tithed, and everyone could now partake of the crops. We can see this kind of atonement is to set apart people or things for holy service. See Exodus 29:33. The altar (Exodus 29:37) and the tabernacle with the sanctuary (Leviticus 16:33) were atoned for in this manner.

Pentecost

The Jews held the three pilgrimage Festivals of Passover, Pentecost, and Tabernacles to be the most important. Among these, the Essenes held Pentecost as the single most important festival. Pentecost is the fiftieth day after the First Fruits of the Barley Harvest. In Hebrew it is called Shavuot. The word *sheva* means seven, week, or an oath. When a word is feminine plural, the Hebrew language adds *ot* to the end. Shavuot is usually translated as the festival of "weeks." I always assumed that it should be thought of as the Festival of Weeks because of the fifty-day count, but according to the Essenes there were four first-fruit festivals each having a fifty-day count. They taught Shavuot should be thought of as the "Festival of the Oaths." This was the time when God entered into covenants with people.

Shavuot, or Pentecost, was always on Sunday, Sivan 15 each year. According to the Essene calendar, God entered, or will enter, into the following covenants on Pentecost:

Adamic Covenant, Pentecost ~ pre-Flood
Noahide Covenant, Pentecost 1657 AM
Abrahamic Covenant, Pentecost 2018 AM
Mosaic Covenant, Pentecost 2448 AM
Covenant of Grace, Pentecost 3957 AM
Millennial Covenant, Pentecost 6000 AM

The Ancient Book of Jubilees 6 gives details about the Festival of Oaths:

It is ordained…that they should celebrate the feast of weeks [oaths] in this month once a year, to renew the covenant every year. And this whole festival was celebrated in heaven from the day of creation till…the day of Noah's death his sons did away with it until the days of Abraham… But Abraham…Isaac and Jacob and his children observed it…in thy days the children of Israel forgot it until ye celebrated it anew on this mountain… For it is the feast of weeks and the feast of first-fruits: this feast is twofold. (Ancient Book of Jubilees 6:17–21)

Jubilees teaches that there was some covenant between God and Adam that existed and was celebrated on Pentecost in the pre-Flood world. God gave the Noahide Covenant as recorded in Genesis 9 and the Law of Kings 9 which included the seven Noahide laws, the 364-day solar calendar, and the four Days of Remembrance.

God entered a covenant with Abraham as recorded in Genesis 12 and God entered into the Sinai covenant with the children of Israel through Moses, both on Pentecost Sundays. The Holy Spirit was given for those in the New Covenant of Grace. If the Essenes are right, the new Millennial Covenant will be given on the first Pentecost after the Second Coming and the establishment of the Millennial Kingdom.

Daniel's Pentecost Comment

In Daniel 12, the prophet mentions two mysterious numbers, 1290 days and 1335 days. He states they are "moedim" calculations, which means that they represent the number of days between festivals, like the First Fruits of the Barley Harvest to Pentecost is fifty days.

And I heard the man clothed in linen, which was upon the waters of the river, when he held up his right hand and his left hand unto heaven, and sware by Him that liveth for ever that it shall be for a time, times, and an half; and when he shall have accomplished to scatter the power of the holy people, all these things shall be finished. (Daniel 12:7)

The word in this verse for time and times is *moed* and *moedim*, respectively. The normal word for "year" is *shannah*. So, Daniel is telling us the following numbers of days are between festivals. They are still three and one-half years long, but they should start and end on festivals. Many people have tried to make these two numbers fit and they just do not fit between any two festivals! That is, if you use the modern Jewish calendar. Notice how Daniel gives the reference. He makes it into an idiom.

> Blessed is he who waits and comes to the thousand, three hundred and thirty-five days. (Daniel 12:12 LITV)

The 1335 has a specific meaning we have never been taught. On the Dead Sea Scroll calendar there is only one place where one 1,335 days fit between two festivals. That works out only if you start on a Tabernacles and end on a Pentecost.

So, Pentecost is when we rededicate ourselves to God for the covenant of our age and "the 1335" is an idiom Daniel uses to refer to entering into a covenant at a Pentecost. In saying you are blessed if you make it to a "1335," Daniel means that those who miss the Rapture and make it through the tribulation period will be blessed if they make it to the Pentecost following Christ's Second Coming. They will enter into the kingdom covenant.

Yearly Re-Dedication

What I find most fascinating is that the Essenes held a very solemn ritual every year to rededicate themselves to God and the coming New Covenant of the Age of Grace. I wish every Christian would take this to heart and consider repenting of sins committed during the year and rededicating their lives and family to God and His Word every Pentecost!

Summer Day of Remembrance

The summer Day of Remembrance always fell on Wednesday, Tammuz 1. Noah ordained this festival for the same purpose of gathering with family for feasting, repentance, and the study of prophecy. The summer Day of Remembrance specifically recalled the time when the waters of Noah's Flood were stopped.

> And on the new moon of the fourth month the mouths of the depths of the abysses beneath were closed. (Ancient book of Jubilees 6:24a)

All Days of Remembrance are for family gatherings, repentance, and studying prophecy.

New Wine

The Festival of the First Fruits of New Wine occurs on Sunday, Av 3, each year. Wine symbolizes the Holy Spirit.

The only Scripture that refers to this festival is in Judges 21. After the war between Benjamin and the other tribes, the tribes swore an oath to never give their daughters in marriage to anyone from the tribe of Benjamin. The tribe of Benjamin had to get wives from somewhere or they would cease to exist. The other tribes of Israel realized their rash oath and came up with a solution to correct their mistake. The Feast of New Wine was not only a celebration for the grape harvest, but also a time for weddings. On that day a couple could get married without parental consent.

> Then they said, Behold, there is a feast of the LORD in Shiloh yearly... Therefore they commanded the children of Benjamin, saying, Go and lie in wait in the vineyards; And see, and, behold, if the daughters of Shiloh come out to dance in dances, then come ye out of the vineyards, and catch you every man his wife of the daughters of Shiloh, and go to the land of Benjamin. (Judges 21:19–21)

This avoided the oath and allowed the Benjamites to marry. This is also a picture of the Messiah snatching away His bride at the Rapture of the church.

I think the First Fruits of New Wine uses the images of wine and marriage to teach the Holy Spirit indwelt believer needs to come to a realization that he or she needs to be completely dedicated to God. Paul says we have the first fruits of the Spirit now, but we are still waiting for the Resurrection / Rapture.

> And not only they, but ourselves also, which have the firstfruits of the Spirit, even we ourselves groan within ourselves, waiting for the adoption, to wit, the redemption of our body. (Romans 8:23)

The Jewish wedding ceremony symbolizes a total dedication, or entire sanctification, to only one spouse. Jesus is wholly sanctified to His bride, the church. We, His church, should be wholly sanctified to Christ.

> And the very God of peace sanctify you wholly; and I pray God your whole spirit and soul and body be preserved blameless unto the coming of our Lord Jesus Christ. (1 Thessalonians 5:23)

> And He said, "For this reason a man shall leave father and mother, and shall be joined to his wife, and the two shall become one flesh." So that they are no longer two, but one flesh. Therefore, what God has joined together, let not man separate. (Matthew 19:5–6 LITV)

New Wine is on Sunday, Av 3. Jesus went to a wedding in Cana and turned the water into wine on the Festival of New Wine. This cannot be a coincidence.

And the third day there was a marriage in Cana of Galilee; and the mother of Jesus was there. (John 2:1)

The washing of water by the Word, mentioned in Ephesians 5:26, and the marriage supper of the Lamb both show the concept of dedication.

The 144,000 are wholly dedicated to the Messiah and have no relationship with the daughters of the Babylonian harlot. They are a first fruits, not of the barley harvest but of the New Wine grape harvest.

These are they which were not defiled with women; for they are virgins. These are they which follow the Lamb whithersoever He goeth. These were redeemed from among men, being the firstfruits unto God and to the Lamb. (Revelation 14:4)

The Babylonian mystery religion drinks of the wine of God's wrath. This may seem like the opposite of dedication, but look at it this way. The nations are not wholly dedicated to the Messiah as His bride. They are wholly dedicated to Mystery Babylon or one of her daughters. This is why it is called spiritual fornication.

For all nations have drunk of the wine of the wrath of her fornication, and the kings of the earth have committed fornication with her, and the merchants of the earth are waxed rich through the abundance of her delicacies. (Revelation 18:3)

This dedication may also reflect on both Jews and Gentiles (Hebrew Roots and Noahides) becoming one new man in Christ.

For He is our peace, who hath made both one, and hath broken down the middle wall of partition between us; Having abolished in His flesh the enmity, even the law of commandments contained in ordinances; for to make in Himself of twain one new man, so making peace; And that He might reconcile both unto God in one body by the cross, having slain the enmity thereby. (Ephesians 2:14–16)

Conclusion

The Festival of New Wine teaches about our dedication to God, the marriage supper of the Lamb, the Jewish wedding ceremony, the Rapture of the church, and the new body of Christ being made of what were Jews and Gentiles.

New Oil

The Festival of the First Fruits of New Oil occurs on Sunday, Elul 22, every year. Oil is used in lamps to create light. Oil was also used to anoint kings, priests and temple utensils to make them holy. James 5:14 says the elders of the church are to anoint the sick with oil. James also refers to God as the "Father of lights" in connection to a First Fruits Festival.

> Every good gift and every perfect gift is from above and comes down from the Father of lights, with whom is no variableness nor shadow of turning. Of His own will He brought us forth with the Word of truth, for us to be a certain first fruit of His creatures. (James 1:17–18 MKJV)

Parables of Jesus

In Matthew 25 Jesus gives three parables, the ten virgins, the talents, and the judgment of the sheep and goats.

In the parable of the ten virgins, all ten virgins were expecting the bridegroom to come. The five wise had vessels of extra oil as well as in their lamps symbolizing that they were mature. The five foolish virgins never got around to buying any extra oil for their lamps, showing that they were not truly prepared for the Lord's coming. The oil in the lamps symbolizes letting our light shine with the Gospel and being prepared for His coming which requires we study prophecy.

In the parable of the talents, two are faithful servants who expanded the kingdom of God, and one did nothing to expand the kingdom. The two were rewarded but the one was punished.

In the parable of the sheep and the goats, the sheep were those who dedicated themselves to Messiah and followed His teachings, while the goats were those who were Christians in name only and refused to follow Christ's teachings.

Light of the Gospel

Compare how 2 Peter and the Testament of Levi describe light. The light of the Gospel comes from the sun of righteousness and it shines to all the Gentile nations.

> His star will arise in heaven, as a king shedding forth the light of knowledge in the sunshine of day, and He will be magnified in the world until His ascension. He will shine forth as the sun in the earth, and will drive away all darkness from the world under heaven... In His priesthood the Gentiles will be multiplied in knowledge on the earth and enlightened through the grace of the Lord. (Testament of Levi 18)

I believe Peter connects this priesthood of Gentiles, which is the Christian church, to the Festival of New Oil when he says:

> We have also a more sure word of prophecy; whereunto ye do well that ye take heed, as unto a light that shineth in a dark place, until the day dawn, and the day star arise in your hearts. (2 Peter 1:19)

The patriarchs teach that this synagogue of the Gentiles (the church) will have its own set of holy books (the New Testament). It will contain a series of epistles written from a Benjamite (the Apostle Paul) and his history (the book of Acts). These will give us the answers we need for the Age of Grace. The New Testament will continue to exist and be used throughout all the other ages.

> One will rise up from my seed in the latter times, beloved of the Lord, hearing His voice on the earth, enlightening with new knowledge all the Gentiles, bursting in on Israel for salvation with the light of knowledge, and tearing it away from them like a wolf, and giving it to the synagogue of the Gentiles. Until the consummation of the ages he will be in the synagogues of the Gentiles, and among their rulers, as a strain of music in the mouth of all; and he will be inscribed in the holy books, both his work and his word, and he will be a chosen one of God forever. (Testament of Benjamin 11)

Jesus said:

Ye are the light of the world. A city that is set on an hill cannot be hid. Neither do men light a candle, and put it under a bushel, but on a candlestick; and it giveth light unto all that are in the house. Let your light so shine before men, that they may see your good works, and glorify your Father which is in heaven. (Matthew 5:14–16)

The Apostle John said:

But if we walk in the light, as he is in the light, we have fellowship one with another, and the blood of Jesus Christ His Son cleanseth us from all sin. (1 John 1:7)

The process from the new birth to spiritual maturity is:
Born of the Spirit (First Fruits of Barley Harvest)

New nature given by the Holy Spirit (Pentecost, First Fruits of Wheat)

After maturing, totally commit your walk to Christ, and become one new body, neither Jew nor Greek but Christian (New Wine, First Fruits of Grapes).

Letting your light shine, witnessing (New Oil, First Fruits of Olives), God is now working through the Gentile Synagogue (Church) with the New Covenant and the New Testament holy books. We focus on prophecy.

Conclusion

The main idea of this festival of light is that we need the Word of God to grow to maturity. We specifically need to study prophecy focusing on the Rapture and the Millennial kingdom. The Festival of New Oil teaches us about the new Gentile church, the New Testament, spreading the Gospel, and later our physical glorification in the Rapture.

Wood Offering

The Festival of New Oil is Sunday Elul 22. The day after begins the weeklong wood offering. Each day two tribes were to bring a tithe of wood for the next year's sacrifices. This lasts from Monday, Elul 23 to Saturday, Elul 28.

Levi and Judah were to bring their offering on Monday Elul 23,
Benjamin and Joseph, on Tuesday,
Reuben and Simeon, on Wednesday,
Issachar and Zebulun, on Thursday,
Gad and Asher, on Friday,
Dan and Naphtali, on Saturday, the Sabbath.

Little is known about the wood offering. There might have been rituals that accompany the offerings of wood, but none are known. This holy day may or may not be prophetic.

Fall Day of Remembrance

The Fall Day of Remembrance always fell on Wednesday, Tishrei 1. This is the same day as the Feast of Trumpets. Noah ordained this feast for family gatherings including studies in prophecy and personal repentance before God. This Day of Remembrance commemorates when the waters of the Flood began to recede.

> And on the new moon of the seventh month all the mouths of the abysses of the earth were opened, and the waters began to descend into them. (Ancient Book of Jubilees 6:24b)

Feast of Trumpets

The Feast of Trumpets occurs on Wednesday, Tishrei 1, each year. One name for this festival is "Yom Teruah" which means "the day of the awakening blast." It is taken from Numbers 29:1.

> And in the seventh month, on the first day of the month, ye shall have an holy convocation; ye shall do no servile work: it is a day of blowing the trumpets [Yom Teruah] unto you. (Numbers 29:1)

The Hebrew for the words "day of blowing of trumpets" is literally Yom Teruah, the day of the awakening blast. *Teruah* is an awakening blast from the shofar that would be the signal for an army to wake up and prepare for the day's battle. *Teruah* is also translated "shout." The rabbis took this to mean this is the day of the resurrection of the dead.

The Last Trump

Another name for this festival is the festival of "the last trump." The rabbis taught this was to be the day of the Resurrection. The Apostle Paul said the Resurrection and Rapture happen at the same time.

In a moment, in the twinkling of an eye, at the last trump: for
the trumpet shall sound, and the dead shall be raised incorrupt-
ible, and we shall be changed. (1 Corinthians 15:52)

This festival may picture the Rapture / Resurrection of believers
prior to the seven-year tribulation period.

Day of Concealment ~ Yom HaKeseh

Another name for the Feast of Trumpets is "the Day of Concealment."
In Hebrew it is *Yom HaKeseh*. The term was taken from Psalm 81:3 by
the ancient rabbis.

Blow up the trumpet in the new moon, in the time appointed,
on our solemn feast day. (Psalm 81:3)

The Hebrew word *Keseh* is translated "time appointed" in this passage, but actually means to conceal. This is yet another picture of the
concealment of the church by the Rapture.

Day of the King ~ HaMelek

Rosh Hashanah is also called Yom HaMelek, or the Day of the King. It
is the time of Messiah's coronation and the beginning of His kingdom.
Compare this to passages like Daniel 7:13-14 and Revelation 5:1–14.

If a new king was to be crowned that year, the coronation would
occur on the festival of Rosh Hashanah. When this happened, Psalm 45
was read. A King always has his bride with him at his coronation.

Day of Remembrance ~ Yom HaZikkaron

Another title for this day is Yom HaZikkaron, which means "Day of
Remembrance." The rabbis took this name from Leviticus 23:24. It is

a memorial day. The word for memorial in this passage is *zikkaron* or remembrance.

> Speak unto the children of Israel, saying, In the seventh month, in the first day of the month, shall ye have a sabbath, a memorial of blowing of trumpets, an holy convocation. (Leviticus 23:24)

This is an ancient memory of the four "Days of Remembrance" commanded by Noah to his children. The Feast of Trumpets falls on the fall Day of Remembrance.

Days of Awe ~ Yamin Noraim

One interesting fact is that this festival is a two-day festival, which means the days between Trumpet and Yom Kippur (the third through the ninth) are called the Yamin Noraim, which means "the days of awe." This name is taken from the prophet Joel.

> For the day of the LORD is great and very terrible; and who can abide it? (Joel 2:11b)

The rabbis said that these terrible days were the same as the time of Jacob's trouble.

If the Rapture were to occur on this festival, since it is a two-day festival, no one could possibly know the exact day or hour it would occur!

Day of Atonement

The Day of Atonement occurs on Friday, Tishrei 10, each year. If we see Yom Teruah as the Rapture / Resurrection and the Yamin Noraim as the seven-year tribulation period, then Yom Kippur should teach on the Second Coming.

Ritual of the Two Goats

During the Festival of Yom Kippur there is a prophetic ceremony that involves two goats. Two nearly identical goats are selected and brought before the high priest. The high priest places his hands on one of the goats. Another priest brings out the Qalephi, a box containing two lots. One of the lots is randomly withdrawn by the high priest and placed with the first goat. The other is then withdrawn for the second goat. On one lot is engraved "for the Lord." The goat that randomly acquired the lot "for the Lord" is sacrificed for the sins of the people. This animal is a perfect representation of the Messiah dying for the sins of the world. The other lot is engraved with "for Azazel." This has commonly been translated "scapegoat," but Azazel actually is a proper name. Moses wrote about this ceremony in Leviticus 16, saying:

> And Aaron shall cast lots upon the two goats; one lot for the LORD, and the other lot for the scapegoat. And Aaron shall bring the goat upon which the LORD's lot fell, and offer him for a sin offering. But the goat, on which the lot fell to be the scapegoat, shall be presented alive before the LORD, to make an atonement with him, and to let him go for a scapegoat [to Azazel] into the wilderness. (Leviticus 16:8–10)

The Mishnah is a book written about AD 200. It contains the Oral Torah, or the exact details explaining how to perform the rituals described in the Old Testament. In Yoma 4.2 of the Mishnah, details are given concerning the ceremony of the two goats.

A scarlet-colored wool cord was specially created for this ceremony. One piece of this cord was tied to one of the horns of the Azazel goat. One piece of the cord was tied around the neck of the Lord's goat.

Leviticus describes the Azazel goat being sent into the "wilderness." But the Mishnah gives greater detail about that part of the ritual in Yoma 6. The two goats must be alike in appearance, size, and weight.

The "wilderness" that the Azazel goat was taken to was actually a ravine twelve miles east of Jerusalem. Between Jerusalem and this ravine were ten stations or booths. Since it was a High Holy Day, one could not travel very far. One priest took the Azazel goat from Jerusalem to the first booth. Then another priest took it from the second to the third booth. This continued until a priest took it from the tenth booth to the ravine. Anciently this ravine was called Beit HaDudo. It still exists in the Judean desert and is presently called Jabel Muntar. The Mishnah then says the priest took the crimson cord off of the goat and tied one piece to the large rock on the cliff of the ravine, and he tied the other piece back on to the horns of the goat. He then pushed the goat off the cliff. Before it would be halfway down the cliff, it was already torn into pieces.

If the ritual was properly done, the crimson cord would turn snow white. At that point the priest would signal the tenth booth, which would in turn signal the ninth, all the way back to the first booth, which would signal the high priest standing at the door of the sanctuary. When the high priest learned the crimson thread had turned white, he finished the ritual by quoting the prophet Isaiah.

"Come now, and let us reason together," saith the LORD, "though your sins be as scarlet, they shall be as white as snow; though they be red like crimson, they shall be as wool." (Isaiah 1:18)

After this a massive celebration began.

The Meaning of the Ritual

It has been speculated that the scapegoat represents Jesus taking away our sin. That is one possible interpretation. If the information given in the Mishnah is correct, another picture emerges. Two identical goats, one dedicated to God, the other dedicated to Satan. One goat represents the Messiah and the other represents the Antichrist. The only way to tell the difference between the Messiah and the Antichrist is to know the Lord's will by carefully studying the Word of God. At the Second

Coming, the Antichrist will be destroyed in Megiddo, in a battle called Armageddon.

The Rest of the Ritual

Now with the rejoicing in Azazel's death, the high priest moved forward with the rest of the ceremony. The high priest removed the innards of the bull and the goat whose blood had been sprinkled in the Holy of Holies and placed them in a receptacle. He twisted the bodies of the two animals and four priests carried the bodies out of Jerusalem on two poles to a place called "the place of the ashes... where the bull and goat were burned only after the Azazel goat had reached the wilderness. The high priest went into the Court of the Women and recited the eight benedictions: for the Torah, for the (sacrificial) service, for the thanksgiving, for the forgiving of sins, for the temple, for Israel, for Jerusalem, for the Kohanim (priests), and for other matters of prayer.

The high priest then returned to the roof of the Beit HaParvah (a chamber in the temple) to remove his linen garments. He then immersed himself in the bath and put on the golden garments. He washed his hands and feet before removing one set of garments and after putting on the other. Immediately, he went to the north side of the altar, where he offered up his ram and a ram for the people as burnt offerings.

The Day of Atonement is a perfect picture of the Second Coming and the destruction of the Antichrist!

Tabernacles

The Festival of Tabernacles occurs for seven days, between Wednesday, Tishrei 15, and Tuesday, Tishrei 21. Tabernacles is called the "Festival of Ingathering," because it begins with a great supper. The Israelites would take the second tithe and prepare a great feast. This happened every three years on the Festival of Tabernacles. See Deuteronomy 14 for details.

In the temple, seventy burnt offerings were given for the cleansing of all the Gentile nations (Numbers 29). Based on this passage the rabbis called this festival "The Festival of Nations."

Four Species
On the first day of Tabernacles, each man was to bring what is called the four species.
And ye shall take you on the first day the boughs [fruit] of goodly trees, branches of palm trees, and the boughs of thick [myrtle] trees, and willows of the brook; and ye shall rejoice before the LORD your God seven days. (Leviticus 23:40)

The Lulov is made with a tall palm branch in the center, a myrtle branch on one side, and a willow branch on the other side. These are bound together and held in the right hand. The fruit spoken of here is an etrog or yellow citron. It grows on a tree that produces fruit all year long. The fruit juice is often mixed with wine as an antidote for consuming poison.

The ritual consisted of holding the four species, the Lulov, in the right hand representing the Messiah, and the etrog upside down in the left hand, representing the Israelite and the world, backwards in sin. By the end of the ritual the etrog is right side up and joined in marriage to the Lulovim, creating the four species.

The Sukkah
Each Israelite family builds a tabernacle or tent, called a sukkah, out of the branches of palm, willow, myrtle, and other trees. They live in it for seven days.

And ye shall take you on the first day the boughs of goodly trees, branches of palm trees, and the boughs of thick trees, and willows of the brook; and ye shall rejoice before the LORD your God seven days. And ye shall keep it a feast unto the LORD seven days in the year. It shall be a statute forever in your generations: ye shall celebrate it in the seventh month. Ye shall dwell in booths seven days; all that are Israelites born shall dwell in booths: that your generations may know that I made the children of Israel to dwell in booths, when I brought them out of the land of Egypt: I am the LORD your God. (Leviticus 23:40–43)

Three Stars

One rabbinical requirement was that there be an opening in the roof of the sukkah large enough for the family members to see three stars. Genesis states we are to pay attention to the sun, moon, and stars for signs, seasons (*moedim*), and for days and years. If we use the proper calendar, we can accurately calculate the festivals and their future events. The star of Bethlehem is one example of a sign in the heavens.

Each day you are to have a meal with your family in the sukkah. An extra place is set for a guest. One night it is for Abraham, the next night for Isaac, then Jacob and so on. This rehearsal teaches us that in the millennium, mortals and immortals will dwell together.

Let us be glad and rejoice, and give honour to Him: for the marriage of the Lamb is come, and His wife hath made herself ready. And to her was granted that she should be arrayed in fine linen, clean and white: for the fine linen is the righteousness of saints. And he saith unto me, write, blessed are they which are called unto the marriage supper of the Lamb. And he saith unto me, These are the true sayings of God. (Revelation 19:7–9)

This great supper is the marriage supper of the Lamb and is in contrast to the feast of Leviathan.

The Feast of Leviathan

According to the Encyclopedia Judaica, Leviathan was anciently thought to be a seven-headed sea beast. It represents the Antichrist and his end time kingdom. The Feast of Leviathan is taken from Job 41.

Canst thou draw out leviathan with an hook? ...Shall the companions make a banquet of him? (Job 41:1, 6)

Those who follow Leviathan will be slaughtered in the Battle of Armageddon. Their flesh will be for the birds to feast on. This has also been applied to the Sheep and Goat Judgment of Matthew 25.

And I saw an angel standing in the sun; and he cried with a loud voice, saying to all the fowls that fly in the midst of heaven, Come and gather yourselves together unto the supper of the great God; that ye may eat the flesh of kings, and the flesh of captains, and the flesh of mighty men, and the flesh of horses, and of them that sit on them, and the flesh of all men, both free and bond, both small and great. (Revelation 19:17–18)

When the Egyptians were drowned in the sea, their bodies were left for the birds; likewise, the bodies of those destroyed in the battle of Armageddon will be left as food for the birds. While the church has the Marriage Supper of the Lamb, the unbelievers will take part in the Banquet of Leviathan.

Jesus says at the great trump the angels will gather the people, taking the sheep back to Jerusalem and the goats to where the eagles gather, or the Feast of Leviathan. See Matthew 24:28 and Luke 17:37.

Two men shall be in the field; the one shall be taken, and the other left. And they answered and said unto him, Where, Lord? And he said unto them, Wheresoever the body is, thither will the eagles be gathered together. (Luke 17:36–37)

House of the Water Pouring - Beit HaShoevah

Beit HaShoevah is a ritual that was performed every day during Sukkot. A group of priests would gather together and go out the Eastern Gate to the Mount of Olives and from there to a valley called Motzah. They would cut willow branches, each about twenty-five feet long. The priests would then make a procession back to the temple waving the willow branches. This would create the sound of a mighty rushing wind.

While this was going on, the high priest and an assistant would leave the temple, going out through the Water Gate down to the pool of Siloam also called Siloah. The high priest would fill a golden vessel with living water from the pool and take it back to the temple. The high priest timed his reentering through the Water Gate with the procession of priests carrying the willow branches returning through the Eastern Gate. This is a prophecy that when the Messiah returns, He will come through the Eastern Gate. At that time the shofar was blown and a single flute began to play. The man playing the flute is called "the pierced one." This was to signal both groups had returned and were about to enter the temple. At that moment another group of priests ascended the altar and began the additional animal sacrifices for that day of Sukkot.

Then the procession of priests would march around the altar seven times and lay the willow branches against the altar to form what looks like a sukkah over it. This canopy is called a "chuppah," or wedding canopy. Then the high priest with his golden vessel of living water, and his assistant with his silver vessel of sacred wine, would ascend the altar and pour both liquids together over the altar to cleanse it. At that moment the crowd witnessing this ritual would sing Isaiah 12:3.

And in that day Thou shalt say, O LORD, I will praise Thee: though Thou wast angry with me, Thine anger is turned away, and Thou comfortedst me. Behold, God is my salvation [Yeshua]; I will trust, and not be afraid: for the LORD JEHOVAH is my strength and my song; He also is become my salvation. Therefore with joy shall ye draw water out of the wells of salvation [Yeshua]. And in that day shall ye say, Praise the LORD, call upon His name, declare His doings among the people, make mention that His name is exalted. Sing unto the LORD; for He hath done excellent things: this is known in all the earth. Cry out and shout, thou inhabitant of Zion: for great is the Holy One of Israel in the midst of thee. (Isaiah 12:1–6)

Note that the word "salvation" here is "Yeshua"—the Hebrew name of Jesus.

The last day of Sukkot was called "the Great Day," Hoshana Rabbah. It was most likely at the time of the water pouring that Jesus stood up and called to the thirsty to come and drink.

In the last day, that great day of the feast, Jesus stood and cried, saying, If any man thirst, let him come unto Me, and drink. He that believeth on Me, as the scripture hath said, out of his belly shall flow rivers of living water. (But this spake He of the Spirit, which they that believe on Him should receive: for the Holy Ghost was not yet given; because that Jesus was not yet glorified. (John 7:37–39)

The ceremony of the Biet HaShoevah teaches about the Messianic Kingdom, the birth of the Messiah, the dedication of the temple, and the pouring of living water (water and wine) to cleanse the temple. Note Jesus' first miracle was to turn the water into wine; and He used the large stone pots that were designed for this ceremony to hold the sacred wine. Jesus turned normal water into sacred wine (or living water) showing that He was the fulfillment of this ceremony.

Zechariah predicted that all nations will be required to keep the Festival of Tabernacles, called the Festival of the Nations, during the Millennium.

And it shall come to pass, that every one that is left of all the nations which came against Jerusalem shall even go up from year to year to worship the King, the LORD of hosts, and to keep the feast of tabernacles. (Zechariah 14:16)

Winter Day of Remembrance

The winter Day of Remembrance always fell on Wednesday, Tevet 1.

> And on the new moon of the tenth month the tops of the mountains were seen, and Noah was glad. And on this account, he ordained them for himself as feasts for a memorial forever, and thus are they ordained. (Ancient Book of Jubilees 6:27–28)

Conclusion: Calendar Recreation?

Now that we have discovered how the ancient solar calendar works, we need to recreate it for daily use.

How to Determine New Year's Day

The first thing we need to do in any given year is determine when the spring equinox occurs. The spring equinox, Tekufah Nissan, is called the great sign of the start of a new year. Since we are used to the Gregorian calendar this is very easy to do. The spring equinox is almost always March 20. Once in a great while, towards the end or beginning of a century, it can fall on March 19. When writing a computer program, we would use the given calculations to determine exactly when the spring equinox occurs down to the hour and minute. But using the weekday and March 20 date as a rule of thumb, even that is not really necessary. Since we have determined that the seven-day week cycle is intact, we can just find New Year's the way it was originally designed.

The Wednesday closest to March 20 (the spring equinox) is New Year's Day, or Nisan 1. God's ways are so simple.

I have created the website dsscalendar.org. It is mobile friendly. When you go there on your phone, tablet, or PC, the first thing that you see is the Gregorian date, the Dead Sea Scroll date, and the modern Jewish date which we call the Pharisee date.

How Dsscalendar.org Works

On dsscalendar.org we created a php back end for the website. The webpage calculates the date you load the page and gets the Gregorian day of the week, day, month, and year. It then calculates the spring equinox for that year and the previous year. If the date you loaded the page is not past the spring equinox for the current year, it uses the previous year's equinox. It then calculates the closest Wednesday to whichever spring equinox it is using and begins the calendar year.

It first adds a number to the current year to find the current Dead Sea Scroll year, then displays the AD year and the AM Year. For instance, "2020 AD" and then "5945 AM." It then adds all the Gregorian and DSS dates and the Holy Days.

The whole php program is about two and a half pages of code. If we decide that the New Year should not be calculated as the closest Wednesday to the spring equinox, but instead, on one of the other two ways discussed in the chapter on leap years, we can easily change it. The part of the code to change the start of the New year is just five lines of code. Enjoy.

PART 2

ANCIENT TESTAMENTS
OF THE PATRIARCHS:
AUTOBIOGRAPHIES FROM
THE DEAD SEA SCROLLS

INTRODUCTION

The history of the Dead Sea Scrolls is very complex. We know that the Essenes kept an ancient library in Qumran. We also know that sometime before the Roman destruction of the Jerusalem Temple in AD 70, the Essenes sealed the scrolls of their library in jars for a future generation. Through the ages there were times when Bedouins sought to sell scrolls they found in caves near, or around, Jerusalem.

One such report was by the Syrian Patriarch in the eleventh century. He offered to buy any scrolls that were ancient copies of the books of the Bible. By the late 1700's, many such rumors abounded. One set of scrolls came to light. They were called the Testaments of the Twelve Patriarchs. These were supposedly the writings of the twelve sons of Jacob: Ruben, Simeon, Levi, Judah, Issachar, Zebulun, Dan, Naphtali, Gad, Asher, Joseph, and Benjamin. They were their last words to their children dealing mainly with morality; but also containing references to ancient prophecy.

Scholars had two major problems with these testaments. First, the prophecies were very focused on the Messiah and agreed wholeheartedly with Christian doctrine. Second, the story was that the original Hebrew version was in the hands of a private collector and only the retranslated Greek was available for scholars to study. With no original

111

Hebrew scrolls and messianic prophecies being too Christian-like, the Testaments of the Twelve Patriarchs were dubbed to be Christian fiction. They are still part of volume eight of the Ante-Nicene Fathers (ten volume set) that was produced in the late 1800's. All that changed with the official discovery of the Dead Sea Scrolls.

Between AD 1948 to 2016, twelve caves were found in Qumran containing many ancient scrolls that are pre-Christian. A forty-volume set of the Dead Sea Scrolls was produced entitled Discoveries in the Judean Desert. This set contains every photo, description, and translation of these scrolls. Fragments of five of the twelve sons of Jacob were found in the Dead Sea Scrolls: Levi, Judah, Naphtali, Joseph, and Benjamin. In this book, the portions of the twelve that were found in the Dead Sea Scrolls are underlined, so that you can see how much remains from the original Hebrew.

The Other Testaments

The legend found in the Talmud of the orthodox Jews and in the Essene community is that all of the patriarchs from Adam to Aaron (thirty-seven or more) were prophets and all wrote testaments for their posterity. Aaron started a new temporary priesthood that would exist until the time of what Elijah called the Messianic Age. We call this the church age. What is truly amazing is that not only do the Dead Sea Scrolls tell us of this legend, and contain five of the twelve testaments of the sons of Jacob, but they actually contain fragments of eight of the other testaments as well.

We have fragments of the testaments of: Enos (Adam's Grandson), Enoch, Lamech (Noah's Father), Noah, Abraham, Jacob, Levi, Judah, Naphtali, Joseph, Benjamin, Kohath (son of Levi, and father of Amram), Amram (father of Moses, Aaron, and Miriam), and Aaron.

The information given in these Dead Sea Scroll fragments is identical to the information given in the full Latin versions of the Testaments of the Twelve Patriarchs published in the late 1800's.

We have a modern English version of the Ancient Book of Enoch translated from the Ethiopic version (full book) compared to the fragments of Enoch found in the Dead Sea Scrolls.

When looking at a Dead Sea Scroll, it will have a title like 1Q21. The Testament of Levi is 1Q21. The "Q" in this designation means it was found in Qumran. The number "1" means it was found in cave one of the twelve caves. The "21" means it was the twenty-first scroll found in that cave.

The Book of Jubilees mentions the herbal medicine books of Noah and Shem (10:13), the books of Noah's fathers (12:27), the books of Enoch, Noah, and the forefathers (21:10), and the book of Amram (46:10). Jubilees 45:16 states that Jacob gave all of these books of the fathers to Levi. Jubilees 32:21-26 states that Jacob was buried with a copy of his testament. Maybe that and other testaments are buried with the patriarchs in the cave of Machpelah in Hebron.

Dead Sea Scroll Testaments

Enosh (4Q369)

Enoch (4Q201)

Lamech (1Q20, 4Q535)

Noah (1Q19, 1Q20)

Abraham (1Q20)

Jacob (4Q537)

Levi (1Q21)

Judah (3Q7, 4Q538-9)

Naphtali (4Q215)

Benjamin (1Q538)

Kohath (4Q542)

Amram (4Q543-549)

Aaron (4Q540, 4Q541)

5

ENOCH'S PROPHECIES

Most the prophecies given in these testaments are based, as they state, on older testaments we do not have. We do have the book of Enoch, which is often quoted in these testaments as authoritative. Before we begin our study of these testaments, we should take a moment to look at some of the prophecies given by Enoch. Here are the charts given on pages 10–12 of the Ancient Book of Enoch.

Biblical Doctrines Found in Enoch	Enoch	Bible
No flesh is righteous before the Lord	81:5	Rom. 3:10
Abortion is murder	98:5; 99:5	Ex. 21:22-23
God is omniscient and omnipotent	9:5	Jer. 23:24
Flood covered the entire earth	106:15	Gen. 7:19
Noah and family spent one year in the ark	106:15	Gen. 7:11; 8:14
Meditation (sorcery) blinds men to God	99:8	Rom. 1:21
Denying inspiration is calling God a liar	104:9	2 Tim. 3:16
All pre-flood men and giants perished	89:6	Gen. 7:4
Do not alter the Scripture	104:9	Rev. 22:18-19
Ignoring prophecy is a serious sin	108:6	Luk. 24:25
Book of Enoch not to be added to the Bible	104	Rev. 22:18
Doctrines About the Messiah	Enoch	Bible
Messiah is the Son of God	105:2	1 Jn. 5:5
Salvation hangs on the Messiah	40:5	Acts 4:12
Salvation by repentance and belief in His Name	50:2-3	Luk. 13:3
Salvation by believing on the Messiah's name	45:3; 48:7	Acts 4:12
Salvation by the righteousness of faith	39:6	Rom. 4:11
Messiah's name (Yeshua) is hinted at	5:7	Isa. 12:2-3
Messiah is called the "Word"	90:38	Joh. 1:1
Messiah is called the Son of Man	48:10	Mat. 9:6
Son of Man exists with God the Father eternally	48:6	2 Sam. 7:14
Messiah's shed blood is necessary for salvation	47:2,4	Mat. 26:28
Son of Man existed before any created thing	48:2-3, 6	Ps. 102:25-27
Messiah preserves the righteous	48:7	Jn. 17:12
Messiah will be a light unto the nations	48:4	Isa. 42:6

First Coming Prophecies	Enoch	Bible
Messiah born of a virgin	62:5	Isa. 7:14
Jews will deny the Messiah	48:10	Joh. 1:11
Elect One will resurrect from the dead	51:5	Joh. 21:14
Bible given to the righteous	104	2 Tim. 3:16
The Righteous One will resurrect	92:3	Joh. 21:14
The Righteous One will give eternal life	5:9; 92:4	Joh. 10:28
Man errs respecting time and the calendar	75:2, 82:5,9	Luk. 19:44
End Time Prophecies	**Enoch**	**Bible**
Angels will never crossbreed again	68:5	-
Corrupted Bibles will be created	99,104	Rev. 22:18-19
Jude's quote of Enoch	1:9	Jud. 1:14-15
Everyone will kneel before the Messiah	48:5; 57:3	Phil. 2:10
The Rapture (taking out of the midst) occurs	70:2	2 Thess. 2:7
Everyone will resurrect	62:5	Rev. 20:5
"Valley of dry bones" mentioned	90:4	Ezek. 37:4
Years will be shortened	80:2	Mat. 24:22
The Rapture and Resurrection are a mystery	103:2	1 Cor. 15:51
Rapture before the Tribulation to cause repentance	50:1-5	Dan. 12:3
Rapture mentioned as "the Mercy"		
Truth altered in the latter days	1:8; 5:5	Jud. 1:21
Iran will attack Israel, God sends confusion	104:10-13	Rev. 22:18-19
Days will be shortened	56:5-7	Ezek. 38-39
The moon will change its order	80:2	Mat. 24:22
There will be blood up to a horse's breast	80:4	Rev. 6:12-13
Millennium mortals and immortals dwell together	100:3	Rev. 14:20
There will be 7000 years of history	39:1	Rev. 20:4
	93	-

If we understand that the writers of the testaments reproduced in this volume were very familiar with these prophecies given by Enoch, we can better understand their writings.

6

The Testaments

Testament of Enos

4Q369
Fragment 1 Col 1

...all the mysteries. The angel of your peace will... until the guilty repent... all of the festivals in their periods because from old You have engraved Your marvelous... ...His judgement until the ordained time of judgement as recorded in the eternal commands. [My son,] Cainan was the fourth generation; Mahalalel, his son, was the fifth generation; Jared, his son, was the sixth generation; Enoch, his son, was the seventh generation...

Fragment 1 Col 2

You have divided Your name for his inheritance, so that he may establish Your name there. She [the holy city] is the glory of Your earthly kingdom. You will eternally watch over her and Your glory will manifest there. She will be an eternal passion throughout all generations to His seed. By Your righteous judgment, You will purify Him to be an eternal light. You have made Him a first-born son to You. He will be a prince and ruler of Your earthly kingdom. You have placed the crown of the heavens and the glory of the clouds upon Him." You have placed the angel of Your peace in His congregation and given Him laws of righteousness as a father does for his son. He loves You and He has your Spirit. Through them You establish Your glory.

Fragment 2

...and prison. Angels intercede and to fight against all lands... You judge and recompense them for their works...

Fragment 3

You rule all that is, and You give honor to whom You will. You hold all the dominions in Your hand, and call each one by name...

Fragment 4

times of dominion... in the generations...appointed times...

Fragment 5

Without you...

Commentary

Fragment 1, Column 1 has been classified as part of the Testament of Enos, partly because he begins a chronology with his son Cainan. God is sovereign and He has made unchangeable decrees that include true law, repentance (Teshuva), festivals for signs, and a future time of judgment.

Fragment 1, Column 2, seems to teach that the capital pre-flood city would be rebuilt afterwards and be the center for God's glory again.

It was first called Salem, but then was later renamed Jerusalem. It then describes either Abraham, who fathered the nation of Israel, or the Messiah, who came from that nation to bring salvation to all mankind.

Fragment 2 seems to be stating there are angels of countries that fight for control. God judges each situation, punishing some and forgiving others.

Fragments 3–5 are too small to really understand the complete context. They seem to indicate that God is in control and has decreed certain ages where certain powers rule, but ultimately God is always in control and evil will be judged in the Day of Judgment. There is also a mention of the Moedim, the appointed times.

Testament of Lamech

1Q20, cols. 0–5

The Testament of Lamech is found in 1Q20 which is commonly call the Genesis Apocryphon. It is fragmented but reproduced here. Enoch tells this same story in his testament, which is found in chapter 106-107 of the Ethiopic book of Enoch, also reproduced here. The Dead Sea Scroll is as follows:

Column 0

...and all of us from... so in each way we may consent in this adulterous act... all that you will... you will amplify anger and it will be unstoppable, for who is there...who... in the heat of anger... the simple, the humble, and the lowly shake and tremble... We are now imprisoned! ... to cease from your anger... by your anger...since we will leave the house of...the Great Holy One... Now your hand is ready to strike ...and to destroy all... because he ceased speaking when we were imprisoned... a fire that has appeared... before the Lord of Heaven... and attacking them from behind. And no longer... seek grace and mercy from the Lord of Eternity...before the Lord of Eternity.

Column 1

...descended, and with the women... and the mystery of iniquity[1] that... times, and the mystery that... we did not reveal... not... until the day... the mystery, whether they are all your sons, or... great... witchcraft, sorcery, and divinations... the earth, and I will begin... part of the deed up till now...which is upon dry ground, to establish... see, I have given all of them... and if... those who strike against... their strong bond... from... all flesh is cursed... the Lord, who sent messengers to you... to the earth, and to descend to strengthen the people ...teach what to do. Men of earth... he did not to them only but all flesh...

Column 2

It suddenly occurred to me that the conception could be from Watchers, or the seed from Holy Ones, or Nephilim. My mind wavered concerning the baby. Then I, Lamech, was so upset, I came to Batenosh,[2] my wife, and said to her... I swear by the Most High, the Mighty Lord, the King of all Ages... one of the sons of Heaven. So, you must tell the whole truth to me, no matter... you have to [truthfully] recount for me, no lies! Will you give birth to a son that is unique? Then Batenosh, my wife, started crying and pleading with me... she said, "My brother, my husband, you have to remember the time of our love, my pleasure... the heat of the moment, and my panting breath! I swear I have told you everything truthfully..." But I did not believe her. When Batenosh, my wife, saw that my demeanor had changed to anger, she calmed down and said to me, "My husband, my brother, my pleasure, I swear to you by the Great Holy One, the King of Heaven, that this baby is yours, yours! You are the father! I have not slept with any stranger, Watcher, nor son of Heaven. Why do I see sadness in your eyes and your doubt on your face, when I tell you the truth?" Then I, Lamech, ran to Methuselah my father and told him and asked him to ask his father Enoch what the dream actually means because he know the Watchers well and God makes everything known to him. Methuselah, my father, understood the importance of the dream and went to Enoch, his father, in the land of Parvain, which is called the "ends of the earth," to find out the truth. He said to Enoch, his father, "My father and my lord, I have come to you... do not to be angry that I came here to seek you..."

Column 3

For in the days of Jared my father... where the sons of Heaven dwelt... human houses... and upon... over all the earth... from my land to that sea... he will place all of it as one fruit. ...he called his people. Now go... truthfully, without lies... reaches by way of a spring to... he is the one who will divide the entire earth, and with... he made sure Methuselah, his son, understood... to him that in every sea... the Lord will give him an everlasting name... from her womb...

Column 4

Now... they will be the cause of much evil... for all ages... I passed judgment upon ... the name of the Great Holy One, and an end... them from the face of the earth...

Column 5

He wrote all of them in the scroll as a remembrance, all... "Methuselah, my son, this child... for when I, Enoch... not from the sons of Heaven, but from Lamech your son... he resembles... because of his appearance your son Lamech was afraid... Go, tell Lamech, your son, that the child is truly his, not from the sons of Heaven... He will be exalted on the earth, and be a judge over every man... that he lifted his face and his eyes shone like the sun, this means that...not the seed of a stranger... They will be caught and destroyed by their own impurity... they will act with much violence until they boil over, and every path of violence... make sure your son knows this mystery... what will occur in his days... blessing the Lord of All... When Methuselah understood the interpretation, and revealed it to Lamech, his son, the mystery... When I, Lamech, understood... rejoiced in the Lord...

Enoch's Account of Lamech's Dream

In the Ancient Book of Enoch 106–107, Enoch describes the same events.

Enoch 106—Lamech's Dream

After some time, my son Methuselah took a wife for his son Lamech, and she became pregnant by him and bore a son. 2His body was white as snow and red as the blooming of a rose, and the hair of his head was white as wool, and his eyes were beautiful. When he opened his eyes, they lit up the whole house like the sun, and the whole house was very bright. 3When he was taken from the hands of the midwife, he opened his mouth, and spoke to the Lord of Righteousness. 4His father Lamech was afraid of him, and fled, and came to his father Methuselah. 5He said unto him: "I have begotten a strange son, unlike a man, but resembling the sons of the angels of heaven; and his nature is different. He is not like us; and his eyes are as the rays of the sun, and his countenance is beautiful. 6It seems to me that he is not sprung from me but from the angels, and I fear that awful things will happen on the earth in his days."

Lamech Seeks Enoch's Interpretation

7"Now, my father, I am here to ask and implore you to go to our father, Enoch, and learn the truth from him, for his dwelling place is with the angels."

8When Methuselah heard the words of his son, he came to me at the ends of the earth, for he had heard that I was there, and he cried aloud. I heard his voice and I came to him. I said unto him, "Behold, here am I, my son. Why have you come to me?"

9He answered and said, "I have come to you because of a disturbing vision which has caused me great anxiety, 10and now, my father, hear me. Unto Lamech, my son, there was born a son, whose likeness and nature were unlike other men. His color was whiter than snow and redder than the bloom of a rose, and the hair of his head was whiter than white wool, and his eyes were like the rays of the sun, and when he opened his eyes he illuminated the whole house. 11When he arose in the hands of the midwife, he opened his mouth, and spoke to the Lord of heaven. 12His father Lamech was afraid and fled to me, and did not believe that the child sprang from him, because his likeness was like that of the angels of heaven. Behold, I have come to you that you may tell me the truth."

Enoch Interprets the Dream

13I, Enoch, answered and said unto him, "The Lord will do a new thing on the earth, and this I have already seen in a vision. I need to tell you that in the generation of my father Jared, some of the angels of heaven transgressed the word of the Lord. 14They committed sin and transgressed the law by uniting themselves with women. They committed sin with them, and have married some of them, and have begotten children by them. 15A great destruction will come over the whole earth, and there will be a flood of water and a great destruction for one year.[3] 16This son who was born unto you will be left on the earth; and his three children will be saved with him. When all mankind who are left on the earth will die, he and his sons will be saved. 17They who begot giants on the earth, not according to the Spirit, but according to the flesh, will suffer a great punishment on the earth, and the earth will be cleansed from all impurity.

18Now make known to your son Lamech that he who will be born is truly his son. Call his name Noah, for he will be left to you; and he and his sons will be saved from the destruction which will come upon the earth on account of all the sin and all the unrighteousness which will be consummated on the earth in his days. 19After that, there will be still more unrighteousness than that which was first committed on the earth; for I know the mysteries of the holy ones; for He, the Lord, has showed me and informed me, and I have read them in the heavenly tablets.

Enoch 107—The Flood Will Not Be the Complete End

I saw written on them that generation upon generation will transgress, till a generation of righteousness arises, and transgression is destroyed and sin disappears from the earth, and all manner of good comes upon it. 2Now, my son, go and tell your son Lamech that this son, which will be born, really will be his son, and that this is no lie." 3When Methuselah had heard the words of his father Enoch—for he had shown to him everything in secret—he returned with the interpretation and explained it to him and called the name of that son Noah; for he will comfort[4] the earth after all the destruction.

Commentary

Columns 0–1 are a retelling of the descent of the Watchers, their sin with the women of earth, and the race of Nephilim. The angels were to teach mankind to be godly; but they corrupted mankind instead, by teaching witchcraft, sorcery, divination, and other dark arts. God then judged the angels and sent the Flood of Noah to cleanse the earth for a new beginning.

In Column 2, Lamech has a fight with his wife about the dream he had concerning her pregnancy. He asked his father Methuselah to ask his grandfather Enoch to interpret the dream.

Columns 3–5 are Enoch's explanation to Methuselah about Noah.

Enoch's account of this from his book, chapters 106–107, are also given here for reference.

Testament of Noah

1Q20, cols. 6–18

The Testament of Noah actually starts on the last line of Col 5 which says:

"A copy of the book of the words of Noah…"

The rest of the testament is continued in Columns 6 through 18.

Column 6

From my birth my mother taught me in the ways of righteousness. My whole life I walked in the truth of the Holy One as He had instructed. I kept away from the paths of deceit which lead to eternal darkness. I studied the visions of truth and wisdom, praying ceaselessly, and avoided the paths of violence. Even after becoming an adult, I continued in righteousness, grew in wisdom… I married Emzera,[5] his daughter, and she bore me three sons… and daughters. Later I took three of the daughters of my brothers for wives for my sons, according to the marriage custom that the Lord of Eternity gave to Adam. After many years, about ten jubilees, after the time when my sons should have been married, the Lord appeared to me in a vision. He showed me the conduct of the sons of Heaven. I thought about this mystery a lot but did not tell anyone about the vision… the great Holy One sent the Watcher to instruct me. In the vision, he said, in a loud voice, "they are talking about you, Noah" … I considered their behavior and knew who would succeed. After two weeks… bore witness to all the blood shed by the Nephilim… I waited until… the daughters of men whom the holy ones made unclean by divination. I went and asked one of them… I, Noah, found grace, prominence, and righteousness in the eyes of the Lord… to cattle, wild animals, birds and even humans… the entire deed was very…

Column 7

"You will govern the entire earth; all that is upon it, including the mountains and the seas… forbid the worship of all the host of heaven; the sun, moon, stars, and the Watchers. …the great Holy One." Then I rejoiced at the words of the Lord of Heaven… He will make them pure by the blood upon… through you all humanity… this was my dream. So, I blessed the great Holy One, and gave thanks for the knowledge of what is to come. I made this known only to my family…

Column 8

…throughout the entire flood … the King of Heaven… in your week… everything occurring in its week. In the written account, its week… about three weeks… Then I went…

Column 9

… your father… not spare… My decrees are irrevocable…

Column 10[6]

Then I blessed the Lord of All, who kept me safe… I, Noah, spoke of these words to them… Now go, give praise and glory to the Creator… remember the instructions of our Lord, who is the King of all Ages forever and ever.

The ark rested on one of the mountains of Ararat, and the eternal fire… I atoned for the whole earth. First, I offered a male goat… afterward I burned the fat upon the fire. Second, I offered a thank offering consisting of ox, ram, and sheep. Then I poured out all of their blood on the base of the altar and, and burned all of their flesh on the altar. Third, I offered the young turtledoves (flesh and blood) with them upon the altar. Then I offered fine wheat flour, mixed together with oil containing incense, for their meal offerings. I said a blessing, and was putting salt on all of them, and the scent of my offering rose up to the heavens. Then the Most High blessed…

Column 11

I, Noah, was at the door of the ark when the waters receded… my sons and their sons… the mountains, valleys, wildernesses, and the coast-lands, all… Then I, Noah, went out and walked through the breadth and depth of the land… it had been reborn with grass, herbs, grain, and fruit trees with leaves. Then I blessed the Lord of Heaven, glory to Him! He showed His love for His creation by removing and obliterating all those who practiced violence, wickedness, and deceit, but rescued the righteous man… A heavenly one appeared to me and said, "Do not fear, Noah! I will be with you and all of your sons who will be like you, forever. Be fruitful and multiply, and fill the earth. Rule over all of them; over its seas and over its wildernesses, over its mountains and over everything that is in them. I now give everything to you and your sons for food; that of the vegetation and herbs of the land. But all blood you will not eat…"

Column 12

"I have now placed My bow in the clouds, and it is a sign from Me, in order to be… on the mountains of Ararat." After this, I left the mountain. My sons and I had to rebuild the cities, because the devastation was great. Then my sons had many sons and daughters after the flood. My oldest son Shem had a son, Arpachshad, two years after the flood.

All the sons of Shem, were: Elam, Asshur, Arpachshad, Lud, and Aram, with five daughters. The sons of Ham were: Cush, Mitzraim, Put, and Canaan, with seven daughters. The sons of Japheth were: Gomer, Magog, Madai, Javan, Tubal, Meshech, and Tiras, with four daughters. My sons and I began to plant crops. I planted a great vineyard on Mount Lubar, and in four years it produced great amounts of wine for me. I brought out all the wine when the first feast came.[7] On the first day of the first feast, in the first month... in the midst of my vineyard, I opened this vessel, and began to drink from it on the first day of the fifth year of the vineyard. On that day, I, my sons and grandsons, with all of our wives and daughters, gathered together at the altar. I blessed the Lord of Heaven, the Most High God, the great Holy One, who saved us from the destruction... which my fathers hid and... I laid down upon my bed, and my mind stirred...

Column 13—The Dream

"...to you, Noah, the king, ...and the decree... to all the forests with all the birds of heaven, the beasts of the field, the cattle of the land, and the creeping things of the dry ground... The stones and the clay were cutting down the forest to make it a place for themselves. Then, also, the gold, silver, brass, and iron, were cutting down the forest to make it a place for themselves. Then I watched as the sun, moon, and stars cut down part of the forest to make it theirs. Finally, the swarming things of the earth and water consumed it. When the water ceased, it ended... Then I saw that the olive tree had grown tall! It continued to grow for many hours, with beautiful fruit, a great amount of foliage. I wondered about this olive tree, with its abundance of leaves... everything tying ropes onto it. Then the winds of heaven blew violently against this olive tree, ripping off its branches and breaking it to pieces. First, a wind blew in from... west. It struck it, causing its leaves and fruit to fall from it, and scattered it to the winds. After this... and a northern wind from..."

Column 14

"...you were thinking about the tree with its upper branch separating and budding with much fruit and foliage... Understand that you are the great cedar tree that was standing before you on a mountain top in your dream. The shoots which emerged from it and grew equal to its height are your three sons... The first shoot that you saw adhering to the cedar trunk, with one branch separating from it and becoming an olive tree means the first son will not separate from you for all his days, and among his seed your name will be called.[8] From his division, all your sons [will be blessed] and from him, the first son, will come forth as a righteous planting [the nation of Israel] for all... standing fast forever. The second shoot adhering to the trunk of the cedar tree... The branch of the third shoot... brings the darkness, and a few of their boughs that enter into the midst of the boughs of the first one, represent two sons [Canaan and Nimrod] ... one south and one north of the land. As for their few boughs that enter into the midst of the boughs of the first one, the descendants of this shoot will invade his land by the coastlands of the Great Sea, and not... to understand the mystery, after your death... you will search... The mystery of... entering into it, and the first one... for himself above all their gods which... for himself... in an allotment in Amania, next to Elam [Iran]... the Great Sea [Mediterranean Sea] ... serve, first, exchanging his allotment for an allotment."

Column 15

"...of the Merciful One on all of those who multiply wickedness in your land and to the ends of the earth. You saw all of those crying out and turning away, because most them will be evil. The great warrior coming from the southern part of the land, with the sickle in His hand and the fire with Him, He will crush all... This one is the Mighty Lord who will come from the southern part of the land... the torches and the evil one.

Then He will throw all the rebellious ones into the fire and seal the pit. As to those who were plucked up…south."

"…four mighty angels chained away from all the peoples of the earth who will not have power over the agitated one [Antichrist] because of their conduct, their inadvertent error, and their undecidedness because of the great blasphemer [False Prophet] … He [Messiah] will couple this people to Himself. He will cut out a great mountain; and from it He will consecrate and separate between all the nations, those who serve Him and those who are entangled with… You, Noah, do not be amazed at this dream, and may no evil be added to it… I have revealed everything to you truthfully, as it is written concerning you. Some of your people will join you…" Then I, Noah, awoke. It was morning and I blessed the everlasting God. I quickly went to Shem, my son, and told him everything, that through him the Righteous One would come, and that he had to preserve the knowledge and become the next priest of the Most High God."

Column 16—Land of Shem and Japheth ~ Jubilees 8

…river, west until it reaches the sea that is between them; the source of the Ma'uk up to the Tina River. It runs through the entire length of the land of the north until it reaches its source in the Rafa mountain range. The boundary extends to the waters of the Great Sea until it reaches Gadir… This is the division that Noah gave to Japheth and his children as an eternal inheritance. Shem inherited the second portion, for himself and his children forever… where Tina River emerges, toward… the Me'at Sea, which reaches… the gulf of the Great Salt Sea. This boundary goes from the spring to the gulf… the gulf of the sea that faces Egypt…. Ham inherited the southern portion for himself and his children forever… Gihon River toward the south…

Column 17 – Divisions of Shem's and Japheth's Sons

Shem divided his portion between his sons. Elam inherited the area in the north, along the Tigris River, until it reaches the Erythrean Sea, to its source which is in the north. Asshur inherited the area toward the west, until it reaches the Tigris… Aram inherited the land between the two rivers until it reaches the peak of Mount Ararat, at this settlement. Lud… inherited the Mount Taurus. This portion continues west until it reaches Magog; everything along the… eastern gulf, in the north, touching this gulf… which is above the three portions in the south. Arpachshad… turns to the south; the entire land irrigated by the Euphrates, and all… the valleys and the plains that are between them, and the coastlands… Amana, which extends from Mount Ararat to the Euphrates… These are Shem's divisions. Japheth divided his portion between his sons. Gomer inherited the northern region that touches Tina River. After him lies the land of Magog, then the land of Madai, then the land of Javan, including all the islands and the gulf alongside Lud. Tubal inherited the land across the second gulf. Meshech inherited… Tiras inherited four islands, within the Great Sea that touches Ham's portion… These are the portions of Japheth that Noah gave him for allotments for his sons.

Column 18

This column was left blank.

Commentary

Columns 6–7 give an account of Noah's life and the visions he had about the fallen angels, the Nephilim, the genetic tampering, and the coming flood. After the flood, he is to rule all nations and forbid any form of idolatry. The middle of Column 7 reveals a descendant of Noah would cleanse all mankind though His blood.

Columns 8–9 are badly fragmented but seem to show Noah aboard the ark, waiting for the waters to recede, spending his time looking over the written prophecies handed down by his fathers. He mentions a prophecy of weeks and specifically his week. This sounds like the apocalypse of weeks given in the Ancient book of Enoch, 91-93. If so, we are missing some of the information.

Columns 10–12 relate Noah sacrificing after the flood. It records the names of his grandsons and the sacrifice he offered right before receiving the prophetic dream.

Columns 13–15 record the dream of Noah during the time referenced in Genesis 9:20–29. Noah sees himself as a great cedar tree. He is the king of the earth decreeing the Noahide laws for all nations. But the nations ignore him and one after another seek to conquer the world. Only Shem remains loyal to Noah and God, so Noah anoints him to be the new priest and a prophecy is given that "among his seed Your name will be called." This means the Messiah will be descended from Shem. Invasions come from the west (Canaan) and the North (Nimrod after he defeats Japheth's sons in a war). Column 15 advances into the end times with the Messiah bringing judgment from the southern part of the land and sealing all the rebels in the pit eternally.

Columns 16–18 recount the dividing of the earth between Noah's three sons and their subdivision of it. This same account appears in full in the Ancient Book of Jubilees 8-9.

Testament of Abraham

1Q20, cols. 19-22
Column 19

I called there on the name of God, saying, "You are God... King of Eternity." God spoke to me that night "... why wander? You have not reached the holy mountain." So, I traveled there. I went to the south around Moreh[9]... and continued until I came to Hebron. I built part of Hebron at that time and dwelt there for two years. A famine occurred over all this land; but, I heard that there was food in Egypt. I travelled toward the land of Egypt... until I reached the Carmon River, the last of seven streams that flow into the Great Salt Sea. I said to myself, "Now we are crossing into the land of the sons of Ham, the land of Egypt." The very first night we were in Egypt I had a dream.

In my dream, I saw a mountain with a cedar tree and a date palm, but they both had sprouted from the same root. Men came to cut down and uproot the cedar tree in order to separate it from the date palm. The date palm cried out, "Do not cut down the cedar, because we both grew from the same root." So, they left the cedar alone on account the date palm, and did not cut it down.

Then I awoke terrified, and I said to my wife, Sarai, "I have had a horrible dream, and I am really afraid." She said to me, "Tell me your dream, so that I understand." I told the dream, then said to her, "This dream warns that there are those in Egypt who will kill me to get to you, so this is the kindness that you must do for me: if anyone asks you who I am, tell them; ‹He is my brother.› In this way, you will protect me and my life will be spared. They will try to take you away from me, and even kill me if necessary." Sarai wept that night because of what I had said. When we entered Zoan, a district in Egypt, she was so concerned that no man should see her, that she concealed herself as best as she could. After five years, three men from the nobles of Egypt, servants of the Pharaoh of Zoan, were coming to me to hear my words of wisdom. They gave me gifts and asked advice about their personal lives, so I read to them out of the Book of Enoch...

Column 20

"...her face is irresistible and so beautiful; her forehead and soft flowing hair, her eyes, nose, every feature is prefect. She is a radiating beauty! And her breasts, oh, and her white complexion. Her arms and hands are perfect. Long, thin, and graceful hands and fingers. Her legs and feet are perfectly proportioned. She is more beautiful than any virgin or bride entering the bridal chamber. She is more beautiful than any woman I have ever seen; and in addition to that, she has great wisdom. Everything about her is absolutely prefect!" When the king heard everything Herqanos and his two companions said, he really wanted her.

He quickly sent someone to try to acquire her. When he saw her, he was completely dumbfounded by her beauty, and just had to have her for a wife. He also started to kill me, but Sarai told him that I was her bother, so I was spared because of her.

I, Abram, wept bitterly that night—I and Lot, my nephew, with me – when Sarai was forcefully taken away from me. I begged God for mercy that night. With tears running down my face, I prayed, "Blessed be the Most High God, Lord of all Ages, You are Lord and Ruler over all Creation. You rule over all the kings of the earth, and have the power to pass judgment on them. I cry out to You, my Lord. Pharaoh of Zoan, king of Egypt, has taken my wife away from me by force. Judge him for me. Reveal Your mighty hand to him and all his household. Please, do not let him defile my wife! This way they will all know that You, my Lord, are Lord over all the kings of the earth." I was so upset I just could not stop crying. But that night, the Most High God sent a spirit that caused a disease to afflict him and his entire household. He was not able to have sexual relations with her. The affliction was ongoing and after two years the disease grew much worse. So, he sent for all the wise men of Egypt, the magicians and physicians, to try to heal him and his household of this affliction. Not only could they not heal them, but they became infected as well and they all fled.

Then Herqanos came to me and asked if I would come lay hands on him and pray that he be healed. He asked this because he had seen this occur in a dream. But Lot interrupted him saying, "Abram, my uncle, cannot pray over the king while he holds his wife, Sarai, captive! Go tell the king to send Sarai back to her lawful husband. Only then can Abram pray over him.[10] If he hurries he might survive." When Hyrqanos heard what Lot said, he went and told the king, "The afflictions troubling my lord, the king, are due to Sarai. She is the wife of Abram. If you send Sarai back to her husband, the affliction of this putrid spirit will vanish."

So, the king called for me. When I came before him he said, "What have you done to me? Why did you tell me Sarai was your sister when she was really your wife? That is why I took her to be my wife! Here is your wife. Take her, go. Get out of Egypt! But before you go, pray over me and my household, so that this evil spirit will leave." I laid my hands on his head and prayed for his healing. Immediately the evil spirit left, and he and his household were restored to full health.

That same day the king gave me many gifts and swore an oath to me that he never had sexual relations with Sarai, or defiled her in any way. He gave her gold, silver, clothes of fine linen and purple, and a hand-maid named Hagar. He then appointed an escort to take us back to the border of Egypt. Now I, Abram, left Egypt with a tremendous amount of flocks, silver, and gold. Lot, my brother's son, came with me. Lot had also acquired many flocks and took an Egyptian wife.

Column 21

I stopped at each of my former encampments until I arrived at Bethel, the place where I had built the altar. I then rebuilt it and offered up a burnt offering and a meal offering to the Most High God. There, I called on the name of the Lord of the Ages. I praised God, blessed Him, and thanked Him for all the flocks and wonderful things that He gave to me, and because He had kept me safe and returned me to this land in peace.

Later, Lot separated from me due to the behavior of our shepherds. I added to the flocks that he possessed and he left with them and headed toward the Jordan Valley. When he came to the city of Sodom, he bought a house there. He lived in Sodom while I was living in Bethel. I did not like that fact that Lot, my brother's son, was on his own.

Then God appeared to me in a dream, saying, "Go up to Ramat-

Hazor, north of Bethel, where you now live. Lift up your eyes and look to the east, west, south, and north. The entire land that you view from there I will give to you and to your descendants for all ages."

In the morning I went up to Ramat-Hazor and I viewed the Land from its high point. I could see from the River of Egypt to Lebanon and Senir, and from the Great Sea to Hauran, and all the land of Gebal up to Kadesh, and the entire Great Desert east of Hauran and Senir, up to the Euphrates. He told me, "I will give all of this land to your descendants, as an inheritance for all ages. I will make them as numerous as the dust of the earth, uncountable. Go and walk the length and width of the land and see how great it is. I will give it to you and your descendants after you for all time."

So, I, Abram, surveyed the land. I traveled the circuit beginning at the Gihon River, and along the Sea to Mount Taurus. Then I traversed along the shore of the Great Salt Sea and alongside Mount Taurus to the east, through the entire breadth of the land, until I came to the Euphrates River. I journeyed along the Euphrates until I reached the Erythrean Sea, to the east, and went along that sea until I came to the gulf of the Red Sea, which joins the Erythrean Sea. I went through the south until I reached the Gihon River. Then I safely returned home to find all of my people were well. We moved from there to the Oaks of Mamre, which are slightly northeast of Hebron.

I built an altar there and offered a burnt offering and a meal offering to the Most High God. I ate and drank there with all my household. Then I sent an invitation to Mamre, Arnem, and Eshkol, three Amorite brothers, friends of mine, and they ate and drank with me.

Fourteen years earlier, Chedarlaomer, the king of Elam, Amraphel, the king of Babylon, Arioch, the king of Cappadocia, and Tiral, the king of Mesopotamian Goiim, came and waged war with Bera, the king of Sodom; Birsha, the king of Gomorrah; Shinab, the king of Admah; Shemiabad, the king of Zeboiim; and with the king of Bela. This battle was fought in the Valley of Siddim. The king of Elam and those with him were victorious over the king of Sodom and his allies. Chedarlaomer imposed tribute on them. They submitted to his authority and taxes for twelve years. They rebelled in the thirteenth year and in the fourteenth year Chedarlaomer amassed his army and went by way of the desert, destroying and plundering from the Euphrates River on. They destroyed the Rephaim in Ashtera, the Karnaim and the Zamzumim in Amman, the Emim, in Shaveh-Hakerioth, and the Hurrians in the mountains of Gebal. Then they came to El-Paran, in the desert. After camping there for a while they destroyed Ein-[Dina] in Hazazon-Tamar.

Now the king of Sodom, allied with the kings of Gomorrah, Admah, Zeboiim, and Bela, met Chedarlaomer's forces in battle in the Valley of Siddim. Chedarlaomer crushed the resistance. The king of Sodom fled, the king of Gomorrah and many others were killed. The king of Elam plundered all the goods of Sodom and Gomorrah, including Lot, Abram's nephew, with all of his belongings.

Column 22

While Abram was eating and drinking with his friends Arnem, Eshkol, and Mamre, one of the shepherds Abram had given to Lot escaped and came to Abram who was living in Hebron. He told Abram about the battle and that Lot had been captured along with all his property, but Lot was still alive. He told Abram that Chedarlaomer had taken captives, plundered, destroyed, and murdered all the way through the Great Valley; and now his army was heading for Damascus. Abram wept for his nephew Lot. After he got himself together, he chose out of his servants three hundred and eighteen seasoned warriors. Arnem, Eshkol, and Mamre joined him. They followed the trail, and found the army resting in the Valley of Dan.

Abram's men attacked them at night from all four sides, killing them all through the night. He crushed the army, but many fled. Abram caught up to the remnant in Helbon, just north of Damascus. There he freed all their prisoners and gave everyone back their belongings. Lot, his nephew, was freed and got back all his property.

When the king of Sodom heard that Abram had brought back all the captives of his people and all their property, he went up to Salem, which is Jerusalem, to meet him. Abram was encamped in the Valley Shaveh, also called the Valley of the King – the Valley of Bet-Hakerem.

King Melchizedek of Salem brought out food and drink for Abram and all his men. He was the priest of the Most High God. Melchizedek blessed Abram, saying, "Blessed be Abram by the Most High God, the Lord of heaven and earth! Blessed be the Most High God, who delivered your enemies into your hands!" Then Abram gave him a tenth of all the property of the king of Elam and his allies to Melchizedek.

Then the king of Sodom came to Abram and said, "My lord, Abram, give me my citizens out of the prisoners whom you rescued from the king of Elam. You may take all the spoils."

Then Abram said to the king of Sodom, "I raise my hands and swear to the Most High God, the Lord of heaven and earth, that I will take none of the spoil that belonged to you. I do not want you to be able to say 'Abram is wealthy because he took my property as a spoil,' excluding the food my men have eaten and the portion of the three men who fought alongside me. Only they have authority to give you their portions. So Abram returned all the captives along with all the property to the king of Sodom. Every last one of the captives were freed and sent home.

After this, God appeared to Abram in a vision, and said to him, "Ten years have gone by since you left Haran; two years here, seven in Egypt, then one more after you returned from Egypt. Take an inventory of your possessions. They have more than doubled since you left Haran. Do not fear. I am with you, and will support and strengthen you. I will protect you from those who are stronger than you. Your wealth and property will increase enormously." Abram said, "My Lord God, I have great wealth and property, but what good are they if I die childless? One of my household servants, Eliezer of Damascus, will inherit all I have." But He said, "Eliezer will not receive your inheritance, but your biological child…"

Commentary

It is interesting to see God warn Abraham about Pharaoh taking Sarah for himself with deadly force. We should take warnings seriously but use good judgment.

Testament of Jacob

4Q537
Fragment 1

"...your descendants. All just and upright men will survive..., absolutely no deceit or debauchery is to be found... Now, take the tablets and read everything..." ... and all my troubles and all that was to happen to me over the one hundred and forty-seven years of my life. Again, he said to me, "Take the tablet from my hands..." So, I took the tablets from him...and I saw written in them that you would leave there on that day... corrupted before the Most High God.

Fragment 2

...and how the temple will be and how their priests will dress, and... their purification rites; how they will offer sacrifices on the altar; and how they will eat a part of their sacrifices as their food, in the whole land... who will leave the city and from under the walls; and where they will... before me a land of two quarter parts and...

Fragment 3

...of the land, and you will eat its fruit and all that is good, and you will live... to go insane and err, and to go in the path of the error of... your wickedness, until finally you will be to Him a...

Commentary

The fragments of the Testament of Jacob seem to be saying that Jacob saw in a dream that his descendants would be enslaved in a foreign country and leave on a specific day (as Abraham had prophesied). They would enter the Promised Land, and some of them would become priests and work in a magnificent temple with underground passages holding amazing relics. The rituals those priests would perform were described to him. But, in time, the priesthood would become corrupt.

This testament of Jacob is described in Jubilees:

21. And he saw in a vision of the night, and behold an angel descended from heaven with seven tablets in his hands, and he gave them to Jacob, and he read them and knew all that was written therein which would befall him and his sons throughout all the ages. 22. He showed him all that was written on the tablets, and said unto him, "Do not build this place, and do not make it an eternal sanctuary, and do not dwell here; for this is not the place. Go to the house of Abraham your father and dwell with Isaac your father until the day of the death of your father. 23. For in Egypt you will die in peace, and in this land you will be buried with honor in the sepulcher of your fathers, with Abraham and Isaac. 24. Fear not, for as you have seen and read it, thus will it all be; and write down everything as you have seen and read." 25. And Jacob said: "Lord, how can I remember all that I have read and seen?" He said unto him: "I will bring all things to your remembrance." 26. He went up from him, and he awoke from his sleep, and he remembered everything which he had read and seen, and he wrote down all the words which he had read and seen. (Ancient book of Jubilees 32:21-27)

Testament of Reuben

Concerning Thoughts

1. Reuben's Sin

The copy of the testament of Reuben and what things he charged his sons before he died in the hundred and twenty-fifth year of his life. When he was sick two years after the death of Joseph, his sons and grandsons gathered together to visit him. He told them, "My children, I am dying, and will go to my fathers." When he saw there Judah, Gad, and Asher, his brothers, he said to them, "Raise me up so I can tell you and my children what is in my heart." They got him up, then he kissed them, and said, tearfully, "Listen to me, your father, and follow my commands. I call the God of heaven to witness my words to you. Do not walk in the ignorance of youth and fornication like I did. I defiled the bed of my father, Jacob. For this, God gave me a disease in my loins that lasted seven months. If Jacob, our father, had not prayed for me, I know I would have died. I was thirty years old when I sinned in the sight of the Lord, and for seven months I was deathly sick; and I repented for seven years purposing in my heart before the Lord not to drink wine or strong drink nor eat meat or pleasant food, mourning over my sin. Such a great sin should never be seen in Israel."

2. The Eight Gifts

"Learn this lesson, my children. The time of my repentance has taught me that every man is born with eight gifts from God, but Belial twists them into seven errors, which are mainly done in youth.

Life, by which man's whole being is created;
Sight, which arouses desire;
Hearing, which brings learning;
Smell and taste, which is given by breath;
Speech, which brings knowledge;

Taste, which turns food and drink into strength;

Reproduction and sexual desire, with which, through love of pleasure, sin also enters in. Therefore, it is the last in order of creation, and the first of youth, because it is filled with ignorance, which leads the young as a blind man to a pit.

Dreams, which create entrancement of man's nature, and the image of death.

3. The Eight Sins

"When these eight gifts are mingled with error they create:

Fornication, which dwells in our nature and senses;

Gluttony and drunkenness;

Fighting, in the liver and the gall;

Deceit and trickery, that through over-aggressiveness a man may seem fair;

Arrogance, that a man may be stirred up and become high-minded;

Lying with jealousy, to deceive or hide the truth;

Injustice, which brings theft. When combined with other errors beings craft;

Dreams with error and fantasy, which destroys a young man by darkening his mind from truth, God's law, and the warnings of his fathers.

"My children, love truth and it will preserve you. Listen to my counsel. Do not take a woman just for her outward beauty, privately associate with a married woman, or meddle in a woman's affairs. For if I had not seen Bilhah bathing in a private place, I would not have committed this great sin. I could not stop seeing her nakedness in my mind. I couldn't sleep. I just had to have her. So, when Jacob and Isaac went away, and we were at Gader, near Bethlehem Ephratha, Bilhah was drunk, and asleep naked in her tent. I went in to her tent and saw her lying naked, I committed the sin, then left her lying there asleep. An angel of God revealed my sin to my father, Jacob, and he came and mourned over me, and touched her no more.

4. Fornication

"Pay no attention to the beautiful women, and do not even be involved with them; but walk with the Lord with a pure heart and in fear. Work, study, and focus on your flocks, until the Lord gives to you the wife He wants you to have, so that you will not suffer as I did. Until my father's death I was never bold enough to look him in the eye, or stand up to my brothers, because of my reproach. Even now my conscience bothers me because of my sin. My father forgave me; he prayed for my forgiveness and healing. From that point on, I was protected, and I never committed that sin again. Therefore, my children, observe all my commands, and you will not fall into sin. Fornication destroys the soul, separates you from God, and entices you into idolatry, because it deceives your mind and understanding and will lead you to Hell before your time. Belial has destroyed many through fornication; even noble elderly men have ruined their lives because of it. Joseph kept himself from every woman, and purged his thoughts from all fornication. He found favor before the Lord and men. For the Egyptian woman did many things unto him, and called for magicians, and offered him love potions, but he purposed in his soul not to allow the evil desire. Therefore, God kept him from death. If fornication does not overcome your mind, neither will Belial overcome you.

5. Modest Dress

My children, ungodly women hurt you, not by strength, but by subtle enticement. They hide who they really are and make you see what they want you to see. They cannot overcome you by strength, so they overcome you by craft. An angel of God told me that fornication overcomes ungodly women more than men. They devise schemes to seduce men; they deceive a man's mind through their adornment, instill poison by the glance of their eye, and capture him by their actions. Therefore, flee fornication, my children. Command your wives and daughters not to adorn their heads and faces; because every woman who acts deceitfully in these things is destined for everlasting punishment. This is how they seduced the Watchers before the flood; they appeared constantly in their presence this way until the watchers fell for them. They changed their form into that of men and came to the women. The ungodly women planned for this to happen because they desired heavenly husbands. Then they gave birth to Nephilim.

6. Levi's Priesthood

"Beware of fornication; and if you wish to have a pure mind, guard your senses against every woman. Command your wives and daughters not to keep company with men, so that they will also keep their minds pure.[11] Even if they do not fornicate, constant meetings are an incurable disease to women, and an everlasting reproach of Belial to men. He who is wise and godly will not fall into fornication; neither will he who controls his desires fall into jealousy. Therefore, you will be jealous against the sons of Levi, and will seek to be exalted over them; but you will fail, because God will avenge them. You will die an evil death. For the Lord made Levi, Judah, Dan, Joseph, and me rulers over you. Therefore, I command you to obey Levi, because he will know the law of the Lord, and will create ordinances for judgment and sacrifice for all Israel until the time of Messiah, the High Priest whom the Lord has declared. I adjure you by the God of heaven to be truthful to each other; and humbly submit to Levi, that you may receive his blessing. For he will bless Israel; and specially Judah, because the Lord chose him to rule over all the people. We will worship his Seed, because He will die for us in wars visible and invisible, and will be among you an everlasting king."

7. Reuben's Death

Reuben died after giving these commands to his sons; and they placed him in a coffin until they brought him up from Egypt, and buried him in Hebron in the double cave where his fathers are.

Commentary

Reuben 6 gives a prophecy that Levi would obtain the priesthood until the Messiah arises from the tribe of Judah. This Messiah will be a man, but also God incarnate. He will die for us and yet rule forever. He will be worshiped as God incarnate by all true believers. The Apostle Paul described a law which was added until Messiah came, in Galatians 3:16-17. Reuben teaches here the "temporary law" was that which was the ordinances for judgment and sacrifice created by Levi and the priesthood.

Testament of Simeon

Concerning Envy

1. Simeon
The copy of the words of Simeon, what things he spoke to his sons before he died, in the hundred and twentieth year of his life, in the year in which Joseph died. For they came to visit him when he was sick, and he strengthened himself and sat up and kissed them, and said to them:

2. Simeon's Heart
Listen, my children, to what is on my heart. I was Jacob's second son. My mother, Leah, called me Simeon, because the Lord heard her prayer.[12] I became very strong. I took unnecessary risks because I was afraid of nothing. I allowed myself to become hard-hearted, stubborn, and uncompassionate because the Most High endowed me with bravery. I became jealous of my brother Joseph simply because my father loved him. I allowed the Prince of Deceit to so overwhelm my mind with jealousy that I decided to kill my own brother. I never once thought about how it would affect my father, Jacob. God delivered him from me. When I went to buy ointment for the flock and Reuben went to Dotham for other supplies our brother, Judah, sold him to the Ishma-

elites. Reuben was grieved, for he wished to restore Joseph safe to his father.[13] But I was furious with Judah because he let Joseph live. I was so wrathful I plotted against Judah and God punished me. I lost the use of my right hand. That brought me to my senses and I repented for seven days. I prayed that the Lord would restore the use of my hand and keep me from falling back into the sin of envy and all foolishness. I knew this was the punishment for my envy against my bother Joseph.

3. Flee Envy
My children, guard yourselves against the deceit of envy. It takes over your mind so that you cannot eat, drink, or do any good. Envy destroys the one who envies, but the one who is envied always flourishes. After praying and fasting, I realized envy is only overcome by the by the fear of God. If you flee to the Lord, envy ceases and your mind rests. You are able to sympathize with the one you envied and become one of those who love him.

4. Avoid Jealousy and Envy
When we went down into Egypt, and he bound me as a spy, I knew that I deserved it, and I did not grieve. Joseph was a good man, and had the Spirit of God within him. Compassionate and pitiful, he did not bare any malice against me. He loved me and the rest of his brothers.

My children, avoid all jealousy and envy. Live a devoted life with a good heart, so that God will bless you like He did Joseph. Joseph never brought up the incident. Instead he loved us and gave us great riches. Love each other and forsake envy because it ruins both the soul and body. It turns anger to war and puts you in a frenzy so that you cannot sleep. It destroys your wisdom, gnaws at your soul, stresses the body, and brings confusion. You actually begin to look like your body has been poisoned.

5. Be Righteous and Study Prophecy
Joseph was so good looking because he did not poison his body with wicked intentions. You can always see this in a person's face. My children

be righteous before God and you will find favor with both God and men. Do not fornicate; it is the mother of all evils. It separates you from God, and pushes you toward Belial. I have seen in the writing of Enoch that your sons will be corrupted by fornication and will attack Levi with the sword. But Levi will win the war of the Lord, and will conquer all of you. Levi and Judah will always produce the true kings and priests and rule over you as our father Jacob has prophesied.

6. Prophecy will be Fulfilled!

I have foretold you all these things to make myself clear about the sin of your souls. If you forsake envy and stubbornness, you will flourish like a rose, like the cedars of Lebanon, and you will be holy forever, and will branch afar off. Then the seed of Canaan, Amalek, the Philistines,[14] the Hittites, and all the cursed seed of Ham will perish. Then the world will rest from war and Shem will be glorified, because the Lord God, the Mighty One of Israel, will appear upon earth as man, and save the seed of Adam. Then all the deceitful, wicked, spirits will be trampled underfoot, and no longer rule over man. Then will I arise [at the Resurrection] in joy, and will bless the Most High because of His marvelous works, because God hath taken a body and eaten with men and saved men.

7. The Messiah

My children, obey Levi, and in Judah will you be redeemed. Do not rebel against these two tribes, for from them will arise the salvation of God. For the Lord will raise up from Levi as it were a Priest,[15] and from Judah as it were a King, who is both God and man. So, He will save all the Gentiles and Israel. Therefore, I command you these things, in order that you also may command your children, that they may observe them throughout their generations.

8. Simeon's Death and Burial

Simeon finished speaking, and died, being a hundred and twenty years old. They laid him in a wooden coffin and took his remains to be buried in Hebron about the time of the Egyptian war (with the Philistines). They did this secretly because the bones of Joseph and his brothers were guarded in the treasure-house of Egypt; for the sorcerers told them that when the bones of Joseph leave Egypt there would be such a great darkness throughout all the land that a man will not be able to see his brother even with a lamp.

9. The Wait till Moses

The sons of Simeon mourned for their father according to the law, and they continued living in Egypt until the day of their departure by the hand of Moses.

Commentary

Simeon 5 teaches that Enoch predicted a civil war in Israel and stated that Jacob was a prophet.

Simeon 6 teaches that Levi has the priesthood and Judah has the kingship. In time, the Canaanites will be wiped out and the Messiah (the God-man) will come to earth and bring salvation for all mankind. After this, the resurrection will occur.

Simeon 7 also mentions that the Messiah will be both God and man.

Testament of Levi

Concerning the Priesthood and Arrogance

1. Levi

The copy of the words of Levi to his sons, including his commands and prophecies. He was in good health when he called them to him, for it had been shown to him that he should die. When they were gathered together he said to them:

2. Levi's First Dream

I, Levi, was born in Haran. When I was young my father moved us to Shechem. When I was about twenty, Simeon and I took vengeance on Hamor for our sister Dinah. One day we were feeding our flocks in Abel-Maul, and the spirit of understanding of the Lord came upon me, and I understood that all men corrupt their way, and that righteousness had retreated behind walls and iniquity ruled. I grieved for mankind, and I prayed to the Lord that I might be saved.

Then I fell asleep, and I beheld a high mountain. It was Aspis in Abel-Maul. The heavens opened, and an angel of God said to me, "Levi, enter." I travelled into the first and then into the second heaven. There was a body of water between them. When I came to the third heaven it was far brighter than the first two, and its height was without bounds. I asked the angel, "why is the third heaven brighter than the first two?" The angel replied, "You will see four other heavens brighter than these, without comparison. For you will stand before the Lord, be His minister, reveal the redeemer of Israel,[16] and His mysteries to men. The Lord will appear among men through you and Judah, saving them out of every race. Serving the Lord will be your portion in life.

3. Seven Heavens Explained

"Listen concerning the seven heavens.[17] The lowest is darker because it is near all the iniquities of men. The second has fire, snow, and ice, ready for the day of the Lord, when the righteous judgment of God is poured out in vengeance on the wicked. In the third are the hosts of the armies which are ordained for the day of judgment, to work vengeance on the spirits of deceit and of Belial. The top four heavens are holy, for in the highest of all dwells the Great Glory, in the holy of holies, far above all holiness. In the sixth are the angels of the presence of the Lord, who minister and make propitiation to the Lord for all the sins the righteous committed in ignorance; and they offer to the Lord a reasonable sweet-smelling savor, and a bloodless offering. In the fifth heaven are the angels who bear the answers to the angels of the presence of the Lord. And in the fourth heaven are thrones and dominions, in which hymns are ever offered to God. Therefore, whenever the Lord looks upon us, all of us tremble. The heavens, the earth, and the abysses tremble in the presence of His majesty; but the sons of men who do not regard these things, sin, and provoke the Most High.

4. Levi Forgiven, and the Messiah's Coming

Understand that the Lord will execute judgment upon the sons of men; because when the rocks are rent,[18] the sun quenched, the waters dried up, the fire trembling, all creation troubled, the invisible spirits melting away, and the grave spoiled in the suffering of the Most High, unbelieving men will continue in their iniquity. Therefore, they will be judged. The Most High has heard your prayer. Your sins are forgiven, and you will become a son to Him, a servant and minister of His presence. You will shine the light of knowledge to Jacob, a sun to the seed of Israel. You and all your seed will be blessed until the Lord visits all the heathen in the tender mercies of His Son, even forever. Nevertheless, your sons will lay hands upon Him to crucify Him. Therefore, you have been given counsel and understanding to instruct your sons about Him, because he who blesses Him will be blessed, but they that curse Him will perish."[19]

5. The Command to Destroy Shechem

Then the angel opened the gates of heaven, and I saw the holy temple, and the Most High upon a throne of glory. He said to me, "Levi, I have given you the blessings of the priesthood until I will come and sojourn in the midst of Israel." Then the angel brought me to the earth, and gave me a shield and a sword, and said, "Take vengeance on Shechem because of Dinah, and I will be with you, because the Lord has sent me." In the dream, I destroyed the sons of Hamor, like the heavenly tablets recorded that I would. I asked the angel to tell me his name, so I could call on him in the day of tribulation. He said to me, "I am the angel who intercedes for the children of Israel, that He not totally destroy them, because every evil spirit attacks them." Then I awoke from the dream and blessed the Most High and the angel who intercedes for the children of Israel and all the righteous.

6. Destruction of Shechem

When I came to my father, I found a brazen shield. Therefore, the name of the mountain is called Aspis. It is near Gebal, on the right side of Abila; and I kept these things in my heart. I suggested to my father and my brother, Reuben, that he should bid the sons of Hamor to be circumcised. I was indignant because of the abomination which they had done in Israel. First, I killed Shechem and then Simeon killed Hamor. After that, our brothers came and attacked the city with the edge of the sword. Our father heard it and was very angry, and he was grieved that they were put to death after they were circumcised. He still blessed us, but it was a sin because we did this without his knowledge, and he was sick all that day. But I knew that this was the proper sentence that God passed on Shechem; for they had tried to do to the same thing to Sarah as they did to Dinah our sister, but the Lord hindered them. Not only that, but they persecuted Abraham our father when he lived near there by shamefully harassing his flocks, shepherds, and Jeblae, his servant, who was born in his house. This is what they did to all strangers, taking away their wives by force, and exiling the men. But the wrath of the Lord hit them suddenly and completely.

7. Jacob's Anger Soothed

I said to my father, "Sir, please do not be not angry. The Lord will destroy all the Canaanites and give the entire land to your descendants. From this day forward Shechem will be called a city of those who are without understanding; for as a man mocks a fool, we mocked them, because they wrought folly in Israel by defiling our sister." We took our sister and went back to Bethel.

8. Second Vision—The Three Priesthoods

After seventy days, while at Bethel, I dreamed again like the former dream. I saw seven men in white raiment saying to me, "Arise,[20] put on the robe of the priesthood, the crown of righteousness, the breast-plate of understanding, the garment of truth, the diadem of faith, the crown of miracles, and the ephod of prophecy." Each one of them gave me one of these things. I put them on and then they said, "From now on you are a priest of the Lord, you and your seed forever." The first anointed me with holy oil, and gave to me the rod of judgment. The second washed me with pure water, and fed me with bread and wine, the most holy things, and dressed me with a holy and glorious robe. The third clothed me with a linen garment like an ephod. The fourth put around me a purple girdle. The fifth gave me a branch of rich olive. The sixth placed a crown on my head. The seventh placed on my head a diadem of priesthood, and filled my hands with incense, so that I served as a priest to the Lord. They said to me, "Levi, your seed will be divided into three branches,[21] for a sign of the glory of the Lord who is to come.

The first will be he who has been faithful; no portion will be greater than his.

The second will be in the priesthood.

The third—a new name will be called over Him, because He will arise as King from Judah, and will establish a new priesthood, after the fashion of the Gentiles, to all the Gentiles.[22] His appearing will be unutterable, as of an exalted prophet of the seed of Abraham our father.

Every desirable thing in Israel will be for you and for your seed, and everything fair to look upon will you eat, and the table of the Lord your seed will apportion, and some of them will be high priests, judges, and scribes; for by their mouth will the holy place be guarded." When I awoke, I understood that this dream was like the former dream. I hid this also in my heart, and did not tell anyone.

9. Levi Learns the Priesthood

After two days Judah and I went up to Isaac after our father; and my grandfather blessed me according to all the words of the visions which I had seen. He would not come with us to Bethel. When we came to Bethel, my father Jacob had a vision concerning me, that I should become a priest unto the Lord; and he rose up early in the morning, and paid tithes of all to the Lord through me. We came to Hebron to dwell there, and Isaac continually taught me the law of the Lord, even as the angel of God showed to me.[23] He taught me the law of the priesthood, of sacrifices, whole burnt-offerings, first-fruits, free-will offerings, and thank-offerings. Every day he instructed me, and prayed for me before the Lord. He told me, "Take heed, my child, of the spirit of fornication;[24] for this will continue, and will by your seed pollute the holy things. Therefore, while yet you are still young, take a wife, without blemish, nor yet polluted, nor of the race of the Philistines or Gentiles. Before entering into the holy place, bathe; and when you offer the sacrifice, wash; and again, when you finish the sacrifice, wash. Of twelve evergreen trees, offer up the fruits to the Lord, as Abraham taught me. Of every clean beast and clean bird offer a sacrifice to the Lord. Of every firstling and of wine offer first-fruits. Every sacrifice you will salt with salt."[25]

10. Levi to His Children

My children, observe my commands. I have explained to you what I have learned from my fathers. I am clear from all your ungodliness and transgression which you will do in the end of the ages against the Savior of the world, acting ungodly, deceiving Israel, and raising up against it great evils from the Lord. You will deal lawlessly with Israel, so that Jerusalem will not endure your wickedness; but the veil of the temple will be rent, so as not to cover your shame. You will be scattered as captives among the heathen, and will be for a reproach, for a curse, and for a trampling under foot. For the house which the Lord will choose will be called Jerusalem, as is contained in the book of Enoch the Righteous.

11. Levi's Children

Therefore, I took Melcha as a wife when I was twenty-eight years old. She called our firstborn son Gersham, because we were sojourners in our land. Gersham means "sojourning." But I saw that he should not inherit the blessing of the firstborn. Kohath was born in my thirty-fifth year, towards the east. Later, in a vision, I saw him standing high above all the congregation. Therefore, I called his name Kohath, which means, beginning of majesty and instruction. Thirdly, she bore Merari, in the fortieth year of my life[26]; and since his mother bare him with difficulty, she called him Merari, which means "my bitterness," because he also died. Jochebed was born in my sixty-fourth year,[27] in Egypt, for I was renowned then in the midst of my brothers.

12. Levi's Grandchildren

Gersham took a wife, and she gave birth to Lomni and Semei. The sons of Kohath were Amram, Isaar, Chebro, and Ozel. The sons of Merari were Mooli and Homusi. In my ninety-fourth year Amram took Jochebed my daughter to him to wife, for they were both born on the same day. Eight years old was I when I went into the land of Canaan, and eighteen years when I slew Shechem. At nineteen years, I became priest, and at twenty-eight years I took a wife. At forty years, I went into Egypt. Behold, you are my children and grandchildren. In my hundred and eighteenth year Joseph died.

13. Simplicity

Now, my children, I command you that you fear our Lord with your whole heart, and walk in simplicity according to all His law. Instruct your children so that they will understand all their life, reading unceasingly the law of God; for everyone who will know the law of God will be honored, and will not be a stranger wherever he goes. He will gain more friends than his forefathers did. Many men will desire to serve him, and to hear the law from him. Work righteousness, my children, upon the earth, that you may find treasure in heaven, and sow good things in your souls, that you may find them in your life. For if you sow evil things, you will reap all trouble and affliction. Get wisdom in the fear of God with diligence; for though there will be a captivity, cities destroyed, and lands, gold, silver, and every possession will perish, no one can take your wisdom from you! Ungodliness leads to blindness and sin. The wise will make friends of his enemies even in a foreign country. If a man teaches and practices these things, he will rule with kings, as Joseph our brother did.

14. The Corruption of the Levitical Priesthood

Now, my children, I have learned from the writing of Enoch that at the last you will deal ungodly, laying your hands on the Lord in all malice. Your brothers will be ashamed because of you, and all the Gentiles will mock you. Our father, Israel, will be pure from the ungodliness of the priests who will lay their hands upon the Savior of the world. Pure is the heaven above the earth, and you are the lights of the heaven as the sun and the moon. What will all the Gentiles do if you are darkened in ungodliness? You will bring a curse upon our race for whom the light of the world came, which was given among you for the lighting up of every man. You will desire to slay Him, teaching commandments contrary to the ordinances of God. The offerings of the Lord you will rob, and from His portion you will steal. Before you sacrifice to the Lord, you will take the choicest parts, in despitefulness eating them with harlots. Amid excesses you will teach the commandments of the Lord. The women that have husbands you will pollute, and the virgins of Jerusalem you will defile. With harlots and adulteresses you will be joined. The daughters of the Gentiles you will take for wives, purifying them with an unlawful purification; and your union will be like unto Sodom and Gomorrah in ungodliness. You will be prideful because of the priesthood, lifting yourselves up against men. Not only so, but being puffed up also against the commands of God, you will scoff at the holy things, mocking in despitefulness.

15. Roman Expulsion

Therefore, the temple which the Lord will choose will be desolate in uncleanness, and you will be captives throughout all nations. You will be an abomination among them, and you will receive reproach and everlasting shame from the righteous judgment of God. All who see you will flee from you. Were it not for God's promises to Abraham, Isaac, and Jacob, our fathers, not one from my seed should be left upon the earth.

16. Enoch's Prophecy

I have also learned in the book of Enoch that for seventy weeks you will go astray, will profane the priesthood, pollute the sacrifices, corrupt the law, and ignore the words of the prophets. In perverseness, you will persecute righteous men, hate the godly, and abhor the words of the faithful. The man who renews the law in the power of the Most High you will call a deceiver.[28] At last, as you suppose, you will slay Him, not understanding His resurrection, wickedly taking upon your own heads the innocent blood.[29] Because of Him will your holy places be desolate, polluted even to the ground, and you will have no place that is clean; but you will be among the Gentiles a curse and a dispersion, until He will again look on you, and in pity will take you to Himself through faith and water.[30]

17. Jubilees

Because you have heard concerning the seventy weeks, hear also concerning the priesthood. In each jubilee, there will be a priesthood.

In the first jubilee, the first who is anointed into the priesthood will be great, and will speak to God as to a Father. His priesthood will be filled with the fear of the Lord, and in the day of his gladness will he arise for the salvation of the world.

In the second jubilee, he who is anointed will be conceived in the sorrow of beloved ones. His priesthood will be honored, and will be glorified among all.

The third priest will be held fast in sorrow;

and the fourth will be in grief, because unrighteousness will be laid upon him exceedingly, and all Israel will hate each one his neighbor.

The fifth will be held fast in darkness, likewise also the sixth and the seventh.

In the seventh there will be such pollution as I am not able to express, before the Lord and men, for they will know it who do these things. Therefore, they will be in captivity and for a prey, and their land and their substance will be destroyed. In the fifth week they will return into their desolate country, and will renew the house of the Lord.

In the seventh week the priests will come, worshippers of idols, contentious, lovers of money, proud, lawless, lascivious, abusers of children and beasts.[31]

18. Messiah's Priesthood

After the Lord punishes them, He will raise up to the priesthood a new Priest, to whom all the words of the Lord will be revealed. He will execute a judgment of truth upon the earth in the fullness of days. His star will arise in heaven, as a king shedding forth the light of knowledge in the sunshine of day, and He will be magnified in the world until His ascension. He will shine forth as the sun in the earth, and will drive away all darkness from the world under heaven, and there will be peace in all the earth. The heavens will rejoice in His days, the earth will be glad, and the clouds will be joyful. The knowledge of the Lord will be poured forth upon the earth, as the water of seas; and the angels of the glory of the presence of the Lord will be glad in Him. The heavens will be opened, and from the temple of glory will the sanctification come upon Him with the Father's voice, as from Abraham, the father of Isaac. The glory of the Most High will be uttered over Him, and the Spirit of understanding and of sanctification will rest upon Him in the water. He will give the majesty of the Lord to His sons in truth for evermore; and there will none succeed Him for all generations, even forever. In His priesthood the Gentiles will be multiplied in knowledge on the earth and enlightened through the grace of the Lord. In His priesthood all sin will come to an end, the lawless will rest from evil, and the just will rest in Him. He will open the gates of paradise, and will remove the threatening sword against Adam. He will give to His saints to eat from the tree of life, and the Spirit of holiness will be on them. Belial will be bound by Him, and He will give power to His children to tread upon the evil spirits. The Lord will rejoice in His children, and will be well pleased in His beloved forever. Then Abraham, Isaac, and Jacob will be joyful, and I will be glad, and all the saints will put on gladness.

19. Levi's Death
My children, you have heard everything. Choose for yourselves darkness or light; either the law of the Lord or the works of Belial. We swore to our father that before the Lord we will walk according to His law. Our father said, "The Lord and His angels are witnesses, as I am and you also, concerning your oath." We said, "We are witnesses." Levi ceased giving charge, laid down, and died, after he had lived a hundred and thirty-seven years. Then they laid him in a coffin, and afterwards buried him in Hebron, beside Abraham, Isaac, and Jacob.

Commentary

Levi 4 teaches that the Son of God will bring salvation but the sons of Levi will destroy (crucify) Him.

Levi 5 states that Levi has the priesthood until the Messiah comes.

Levi 8 teaches there will be three priesthoods. The Messiah, a descendant of Judah, will fashion a new Gentile-type priesthood.

Levi 10 predicts that at the end of the age the Messiah will come and the Levites will turn on Him, the veil in the temple will be torn in two. That chapter also teaches that Enoch prophesied about the Jerusalem temple.

Levi 14 says Enoch taught that the priests will turn on the Messiah.

Levi 16 reveals Enoch taught a seventy-weeks prophecy.

Levi 17 maps out the priesthood's fall into corruption in jubilee periods, starting with the Maccabees renewal to its complete corruption under the Romans. See the chapter on the Prophecy Outline for details.

Levi 18 mentions the Messiah's priesthood, ascension, baptism, spiritual gifts, and sanctification.

Testament of Judah

Concerning Fortitude, and Love of Money, and Fornication

1. Judah

The copy of the words of Judah, which he spoke to his sons before he died: they gathered together around him, and he said, "I was my father's fourth son. My mother named me Judah, saying, 'I give thanks to the Lord, because He has given a fourth son to me.' I was swift and active in my youth, and obedient to my father in everything. I honored my mother and my mother's sister. When I grew up, my father, Jacob, prayed over me, saying, 'You will be a king, and prosper in all things.'

2. Judah's Strength and Cunning

"The Lord showed me favor in all my works both in the field and at home. When I saw that I could run with the hind, then I caught it, and prepared meat for my father. I seized upon the roes in the chase, and all that was in the plains I outran. A wild mare I outran, and I caught it and tamed it. I killed a lion, and plucked a kid out of its mouth. I took a bear by its paw, and rolled it over a cliff. If any beast turned upon me, I killed it like a dog. I encountered the wild boar, and overtaking it in the chase, I tore it. A leopard in Hebron leaped upon the dog, and I caught it by the tail, and flung it from me, and it was dashed to pieces in the coasts of Gaza. A wild ox feeding in the field I seized by the horns; and whirling it round and stunning it, I cast it from me, and killed it.

3. Canaanite Wars

"When the two kings of the Canaanites came in warlike array against our flocks, and many people with them, I, by myself, rushed upon King Sur and seized him; and I beat him upon the legs, and dragged him down, and killed him. The other king, Taphue, I killed as he sat upon his horse, and so I scattered all the people. King Achor, a man of giant stature, hurling darts before and behind as he sat on horseback, I killed; for I hurled a stone of sixty pounds, and cast it upon his horse, and killed him. I fought with Achor for two hours, and I killed him. I split his shield in two, and chopped off his feet. As I stripped off his breastplate, behold, eight of his companions began to fight with me. I used my garment as a sling and killed four of them. The rest fled. Jacob, my father, killed Beelisa, king of all the kings, a giant in strength, twelve cubits high. Fear fell on them, and they ceased from making war with us. Therefore, my father had no care in the wars when I was among my brothers. For he saw in a vision concerning me, that an angel of might followed me everywhere that I should not be overcome.

4. War in Hebron

"In the south, we faced a greater war than that in Shechem. I joined in the battle with my brothers, and pursued a thousand men. I killed two hundred of them and four kings. I went up against them on the wall, and killed two other kings; and so, we freed Hebron, and took all the captives of the kings.

5. Areta, Thaffu Destroyed

"On the next day, we departed to Areta, a strong, walled, and inaccessible city that threatened us with death. Therefore, Gad and I approached on the east side of the city, and Reuben and Levi on the west and south. Those who were upon the wall thought that we were alone, and charged down upon us. Our brothers secretly climbed up the wall on both sides by ladders, and entered into the city, while the men did not know it. We took it with the edge of the sword. We set fire to the tower, and took both it and those who had taken refuge there. As we were departing, the men of Thaffu set upon our captives. We and our sons fought with them even to Thaffu. We killed them, and burnt their city, and spoiled all the things that were in it.

6. Jobel and Machir Destroyed

"When I was at the waters of Chuzeba, the men of Jobel came to battle against us, and we fought with them. We killed their allies from Selom, and we allowed them no means of escaping or of coming against us. The men of Machir came on the fifth day to carry away our captives. We attacked them, and overcame them in fierce battle, for they were a mighty host in themselves. We killed them before they had gone up the side of the hill. When we came to their city, their women rolled stones on us from the brow of the hill on which the city stood. Simeon and I hid ourselves behind the town, and seized the heights, and utterly destroyed the whole city.

7. More Canaanite Wars

"The next day we were told that the cities of the two kings with a great host were coming against us. Therefore, Dan and I feigned ourselves to be Amorites, and went as allies into their city. In the middle of the night our brothers came, and we opened the gates for them. We destroyed all the men and their substance, and we took for a spoil all that was theirs. We knocked down three of their walls. We drew near Thamna, where all the hostile kings took refuge. Having been injured I was angry, and chased them to the top of the hill. They shot stones and darts at me. If Dan my brother had not helped me, they would have been able to kill me. Therefore, we fiercely attacked them, and they all fled. Going around another way, they sought out my father, and he made peace with them. Therefore, we did them no harm, but made a truce with them, and restored to them all the captives. I built Thamna, and my father built Rhambael. I was twenty years old when this war happened, and the Canaanites feared me and my brothers.

8. Judah's Wife and Children

"Moreover, I had many cattle, and the chief of my herdsmen was Hirah the Adullamite. When I went to him, I saw Barsan, king of Adullam, who made us a feast. He entreated me, and gave me his daughter Bathshua for a wife. She bore me Er, Onan, and Shelah. The Lord struck two of them and they died childless, but Shelah lived, and you are his children.

9. Esau Slain

"For eighteen years after we came from Laban in Mesopotamia we and our father lived in peace with his brother Esau and his sons. After this, in the fortieth year of my life, Esau came against us with many strong people. He fell by the bow of Jacob,[32] and was taken up dead in Mount Seir. As he went above Iramna he was slain. We pursued the sons of Esau. They had a city with walls of iron and gates of brass. We could not enter it, so we encamped around it, and besieged them. When they did not open to us after twenty days, I set up a ladder in the sight of all. With my shield on my head I climbed up, assailed with stones of three talents' weight. I climbed up, and killed four mighty men. The next day Reuben and Gad entered in and killed sixty others. Then they asked for terms of peace. Being aware of our father's purpose, we received them as tributaries. They gave us two hundred cors of wheat, five hundred baths of oil, and fifteen hundred measures of wine, until we went down into Egypt.

10. Tamar

"After these things, my son Er took to wife Tamar, from Mesopotamia, a daughter of Aram. Now Er was wicked, and he doubted concerning Tamar, because she was not of the land of Canaan. On the third night, an angel of the Lord killed him, because he had not known her, according to the evil craftiness of his mother, for he did not wish to have children from her. In the days of the wedding feast I espoused Onan to her. He also in wickedness refused to know her, though he lived with her a year. When I threatened him, he lay with her, but he did the way his mother told him, and he also died in his wickedness. I wanted to give Shelah to her also, but my wife, Bathshua, would not allow it; for she hated Tamar, because she was not of the daughters of Canaan, as she herself was.

11. Shelah

"I knew that the race of Canaan was wicked, but the thoughts of youth blinded my heart. When I saw Bathshua pouring out wine, in the drunkenness of wine was I deceived, and I fell in love with her. While I was away, she went and took for Shelah a wife from the land of Canaan. When I realized what she had done, I cursed her in the anguish of my soul, and she also died in the wickedness of her sons.

12. Judah sleeps with Tamar

"After these things, while Tamar was a widow, she heard after two years that I was going up to shear my sheep; then she decked herself in bridal array, and sat by the gate of the city. For it is a law of the Amorites, that she who is about to marry sit in fornication seven days by the gate. I therefore, being drunk at the waters of Chozeb, recognized her not by reason of wine; and her beauty deceived me, through the fashion of her adorning. I turned aside to her, and said, I would enter in to you. She said to me, 'What will you give me?' I gave her my staff, and my girdle, and my royal crown; and I lay with her, and she conceived. I then, not knowing what she had done, wished to slay her; but she secretly sent my pledges, and put me to shame. When I called her, I heard also the secret words which I spoke when lying with her in my drunkenness; and I could not slay her, because it was from the Lord. For I said, in case by accident she did it in subtlety, and received the pledge from another woman: but I came near her no more till my death, because I had done this abomination in all Israel. Moreover, they who were in the city said that there was no bride in the city, because she came from another place, and sat for a while in the gate, and she thought that no one knew that I had gone in to her. After this, we came into Egypt to Joseph, because of the famine. I was forty-six years old, and I lived there seventy-three years.

13. Greed, Pride, and Fornication

"Now, my children, in whatever things I command you, listen to your father, and keep all my sayings to perform the ordinances of the Lord, and to obey the command of the Lord God. Do not walk after your lusts, nor in the thoughts of your imaginations in the haughtiness of your heart. Do not glory in the works of the strength of youth, for this also is evil in the eyes of the Lord. For since I also gloried that in wars the face of no beautiful woman ever deceived me, and upbraided Reuben my brother concerning Bilhah, the wife of my father, the spirits of jealousy and of fornication arrayed themselves within me, until I sinned with Bathshua the Canaanite, and Tamar who was espoused to my sons. I said to my father-in-law, 'I will counsel with my father, and so will I take your daughter.' He showed me a boundless store of gold in his daughter's behalf, for he was a king. He decked her with gold and pearls, and caused her to pour out wine for us at the feast in womanly beauty. The wine led my eyes astray, and pleasure blinded my heart; and I loved her, and I fell, and transgressed the commandment of the Lord and the commandment of my fathers, and I married her. The Lord rewarded me according to the thought of my heart, insomuch that I had no joy in her children.

14. Deception of Alcohol

"My children, do not be drunk with wine; for wine turns the mind away from the truth, kindles the passion of lust, and leads the eyes into error. Fornication uses wine to create fantasies for the mind. These two take away man's power of self-control. If a man drinks to a state of drunkenness, his mind becomes filled with filthy thoughts of fornication, and if the woman is present, he sins without a second thought. Such is wine, my children. A drunkard respects no one. It also made me err, so that I was not ashamed of the multitude in the city, I turned aside unto Tamar in front of them all, and I sinned, and I uncovered the covering of the shame of my sons. After I was drunk with wine, I disobeyed God's commandment and took a Canaanite wife. Therefore, my children, whoever drinks wine lacks discretion. Here is discretion: drink only as long as you can be decent; if you go beyond this point, the wine deceives your mind and works evil. It makes the drunkard talk filthily, transgress, and not be ashamed. It even causes him to glory in his dishonor, believing he has done well.

15. Fornication Enslaves
"He who fornicates, and uncovers his nakedness, has become the servant of fornication, and cannot escape its power, as I also was uncovered. For I gave my staff, the symbol of my tribe; my girdle, the symbol of my power; and my crown, which is the glory of my kingdom. Then I repented of these things, and took no wine or flesh until my old age, nor did I behold any joy. An angel of God showed me that women eternally bear rule over kings and beggars alike. They take away the king's glory, and the valiant man's strength, and they take from the beggar even the little that keeps him from poverty.

16. Moderation
"Therefore, my children, observe moderation in wine; for it brings out four evils: lust, wrath, rioting, and greed. If you drink wine in gladness, with humility, and with the fear of God, you will live. If you do not drink with humility, and the fear of God leaves you, then comes drunkenness, and pride sets in. Even if you never drink, guard yourselves lest you sin in words of outrage, fighting, or slander, transgressing the commandments of God; or you will perish before your time. Moreover, drunkenness causes you to divulge the mysteries of God and men to unbelievers, just as I revealed the commandments of God and the mysteries of Jacob, my father, to the Canaanite, Bathshua, to whom God forbade to declare them. Wine is also a cause of war and confusion.

17. Judah's Charge
"I charge you, therefore, my children, not to love money, nor to gaze upon the beauty of women; because, for the sake of money and beauty,

I was led astray to Bathshua the Canaanite. I know that because of these two things my descendants will fall into wickedness. Even wise men among my sons they will mar, and will cause the kingdom of Judah to be diminished, which the Lord gave me because of my obedience to my father. For I never disobeyed a word of Jacob my father; I did everything he commanded. Abraham, my great-grandfather, blessed me that I should be king in Israel, and Isaac further blessed me in like manner. I know that from me will the kingdom be established.

18. The Books of Enoch

"I have also read in the books of Enoch, the Righteous, [the books of Enoch and his fathers'] what evils you will do in the last days. Guard against fornication and the love of money. Listen to your father, for these things separate you from the law of God, blind the understanding of the soul, teach arrogance, and take away your compassion. They rob your soul of all goodness, bind you in troubles, take away your sleep, devour your flesh, and hinder the sacrifices of God. They cause you to forget the blessing, ignore the prophets, and trouble you with ungodliness. You cannot serve these two passions and obey the commandments of God, because they blind your soul, and make those who walk in the daytime like they were walking in the night.

19. Guard Against Your Weaknesses

"My children, the love of money leads to idolatry; because, when money leads men astray they talk about false gods, and it causes them to fall into madness. For the sake of money, I lost my children, and only through repentance, humbling my soul, and the prayers of Jacob my father, I found forgiveness. The God of my fathers, who is pitiful and merciful, pardoned me, because I did it in ignorance. The Prince of Deceit blinded me, and I was ignorant in my humanity, being corrupted in sins; and I learned of my own weakness while thinking myself unconquerable.

20. Truth or Error

"Learn therefore, my children, that two spirits wait upon man — the spirit of truth and the spirit of error. Among them stands the understanding of the mind. Truth and error are written on the hearts of men, and the Lord knows each one. There is no time that the works of men can be hidden from Him. Each man must decide deep within his own heart whether to be true or not. The Spirit of Truth testifies all things, and accuses all. He who sins is destroyed by his own heart, and cannot raise his face unto the Judge.

21. Obey Levi

"My children, love Levi, that you may live. Do not rebel against him, or you will be utterly destroyed. The Lord gave me the kingdom, and him the priesthood, and He set the kingdom beneath the priesthood. He gave me the things upon the earth; but to him, the heavenly things. As the heaven is higher than the earth, so is the priesthood of God higher than the kingdom upon the earth. The Lord chose him above you, to draw near to Him, and to eat of His table and first-fruits, even the choice things of the sons of Israel, and you will be to them as a sea. For as on the sea, just and unjust are tossed about. Some are taken into captivity while others are enriched, so also will every type of man be in you. Some are in jeopardy and taken captive, and others will grow rich by means of plunder. Those who rule will be as great sea-monsters, swallowing up men like fishes. They will enslave free sons and daughters. They will plunder houses, lands, flocks, and money. With the flesh of many they will wrongfully feed the ravens and the cranes; and they will go further in evil, advancing in greed. There will be false prophets like tempests, and they will persecute all righteous men.

22. Judah's Seed is King Forever

"The Lord will bring divisions on them, one against another, and there will be continual wars in Israel. Among men of another race will my kingdom be brought to an end, until the salvation of Israel will come, until the appearing of the God of Righteousness, that Jacob and all the Gentiles may rest in peace. He will guard the might of my kingdom forever: for the Lord swore to me with an oath that the kingdom should never fail from me, and from my seed, for all days, even forever.

23. Sins of His Children

"I am much grieved, my children, because you will sin against the kingdom with lewdness, witchcraft, idolatry, and by seeking those who have familiar spirits. You will make your daughters singing girls and harlots for divinations and demons of error, and you will be mingled in Gentile pollution. For these things, the Lord will bring on you famine, pestilence, death by the sword, avenging siege, dogs for rending enemies to pieces, revilings of friends, destruction, blindness, children slaughtered, wives carried off, and possessions plundered. The temple of God will be in flames and your land desolated. You will be enslaved among the Gentiles, and they will make some of you eunuchs for their wives. Whenever you return to the Lord with humility of heart, repenting and walking in all the commandments of God, then will the Lord visit you in mercy and love, bringing you out of the bondage of your enemies.

24. The Messiah

"After these things will a star arise to you from Jacob in peace, and a man will rise from my seed, like the Sun of Righteousness, walking with the sons of men in meekness and righteousness, and no sin will be found in Him. The heavens will be opened above Him, to shed forth the blessing of the Spirit from the Holy Father. He will shed forth a spirit of grace on you. You will be to Him sons in truth, and you will walk in His commandments, the first and the last. This is the Branch of God Most High, and this is the well-spring unto life for all flesh. Then the scepter of my kingdom will shine forth, and from your root a stem will arise. In it will arise a rod of righteousness to the Gentiles, to judge and to save all that call upon the Lord.

25. The Resurrection

"After these things will Abraham, Isaac, and Jacob arise unto life. I and my brothers will be chiefs, even your scepter in Israel: Levi first, I the second, Joseph third, Benjamin fourth, Simeon fifth, Issachar sixth, and so all in order. The Lord blessed Levi with the Angel of the Presence; me with the powers of glory; Simeon with the heaven; Reuben with the earth; Issachar with the sea; Zebulun with the mountains; Joseph with the tabernacle; Benjamin with the lights of heaven; Dan with the fatness of earth; Naphtali with the sun; Gad with the olive; Asher... There will be one people of the Lord, and one tongue. There will no more be a spirit of deceit of Belial, for he will be cast into the fire forever. Those who have died in grief will rise in joy. Those who have lived in poverty for the Lord's sake will be made rich, and those who have been in want will be filled. Those who have been weak will be made strong, and those who have been put to death for the Lord's sake will awake in life. The hearts of Jacob will run in joyfulness, and the eagles of Israel will fly in gladness; but the ungodly will lament, and sinners all weep, and all the people will glorify the Lord forever.

26. Judah's Death

"My children, observe the whole law of the Lord, for there is hope for all those who follow His way correctly. Today I die, a hundred and nineteen years old. Let no one bury me in costly apparel, nor tear open my bowels, for this is what kings do. Carry me up to Hebron with you."

Judah, when he had said these things, fell asleep; and his sons did according to all that he commanded them, and they buried him in Hebron with his fathers.

Commentary

Judah 21 warns that false prophets will arise and persecute the righteous.

Judah 22 says the Messiah is from Judah's line and will bring salvation.

Judah 23 sees a vision of the temple of God in flames, and the nation of Israel desolated.

Judah 24 teaches that the Messiah is a star of Jacob, a branch, and a rod of the Gentiles. Compare this to Numbers 24:17.

Judah 25 teaches that there will be a future Resurrection.

Testament of Issachar

Concerning Simplicity

1. Issachar

The record of the words of Issachar. He called his sons, and said to them, "My children, listen to Issachar, your father; you who are beloved of the Lord. I was the fifth son born to Jacob, even the hire of the mandrakes.[33] For Reuben brought in mandrakes from the field, and Rachel met him and took them. Reuben wept, and at his voice Leah, my mother, came out. These mandrakes were sweet-smelling apples which the land of Aram produced on high ground below a ravine of water. Rachel said, 'I will not give them to you. They will be for my children.' There were two apples; and Leah said, 'Isn't it enough that you have taken the husband of my virginity. Will you also take these?' Rachel said, 'I will give you Jacob for tonight and you give me your son's mandrakes.' Leah said to her, 'Don't boast or be prideful; for Jacob is mine, and I am the wife of his youth.' But Rachel said, 'How so? He was espoused to me first. He served our father fourteen years for me! It is not my fault that our father was a deceiver and that deception has increased upon the earth. If it was not for deception, you would have never seen the face of Jacob. You are not his wife, but a pawn our father used. He also deceived me, and sent me away that night. If I had been there, the deception would not have happened.' Rachel said, 'Take one mandrake, and for the other you will hire him from me for one night.' Jacob knew Leah, and she conceived and bare me, and on account of the hire I was called Issachar.

2. Rachel's Mandrakes

"Then an angel of the Lord appeared to Jacob, saying, 'Rachel will bear two children; for she has refused the company of her husband, and has chosen continency.' If my mother, Leah, had not given up the two apples for the sake of his company, she would have borne eight sons. Because of the mandrakes, the Lord visited Rachel and she bore two sons and Leah only bore six. God knew that for the sake of children she wished to company with Jacob, and not just for pleasure. For she went further, and on the morrow too gave up Jacob that she might receive also the other mandrake. Therefore, the Lord listened to Rachel because of the mandrakes; for though she desired them, she ate them not, but brought them to the priest of the Most High who was at that time,[34] and offered them up in the house of the Lord.

3. Simplicity of life

"When I grew up, I walked in uprightness of heart, and I became a husbandman for my parents and my brothers. I brought in fruits from the field in their season. My father blessed me, for he saw that I walked in simplicity. I was not a busybody, malicious, nor slanderous. I never spoke against anyone, nor did I criticize anyone, but walked in simplicity. Therefore, when I was thirty years old I married, for my labor wore away my strength, and I was never a womanizer. I was content in my work and sleep, and my father always rejoiced in my simplicity. Out of my produce I offered first-fruits to the Lord by the hands of the priests,[35] then to my father, and then took for myself. The Lord increased His benefits twofold in my hands; and Jacob knew that God blessed my simplicity, for I helped the poor and distressed out of the good things of the earth in simplicity of heart.

4. The Righteousness of Simplicity

"Listen, my children. Walk in simplicity of heart, for it brings all that is well-pleasing to the Lord. The simple do not covet gold, defraud his neighbor, long after many dainties, delight in varied apparel, nor desire long life for himself.[36] Instead, he waits for the will of God, and the spirits of error have no power against him. He does not allow his mind to be corrupted by lust, envy, jealousy, or greed. He walks in righteousness and sees everything in simplicity, not focusing on the malice from the errors of the world. He does not learn to pervert any of the commandments of the Lord.

5. Seek God's Blessing

"My children, keep God's law, live in simplicity, and walk without guile. Do not curiously pry into your neighbor's business. Instead, love the Lord and your neighbor. Have compassion on the poor and weak. Work hard and offer gifts unto the Lord with thanksgiving; for the Lord blessed me with the first-fruits of the earth, as He blessed all the saints from Abel even until now. The portion God gave you is the fatness of the earth, whose fruits are raised by toil; for our father Jacob blessed me with blessings of the earth and of first-fruits. The Lord glorified Levi and Judah among the sons of Jacob; for the Lord made choice of them. He gave the priesthood to one, and the kingdom to the other. Therefore, obey them, and walk in the simplicity of your father; for unto Gad has it been given to destroy the temptations that are coming upon Israel.

6. The End Times

"My children, I know that in the last times your sons will forsake simplicity. Their lives will be filled with greed and malice. They will forsake the commandments of the Lord, will cleave unto Belial. They will leave simplicity, follow wickedness, and will be dispersed among the Gentiles, serving their enemies. Teach your children what awaits them, so that if they sin, they may quickly return to the Lord; for He is merciful, and will deliver them even to bring them back into their land.

7. Issachar's Last Days

"I am a hundred and twenty-two years old, and I never committed a sin unto death. I have not known any woman except my wife. I never committed fornication, got drunk, or coveted anything that was my neighbor's. Guile never entered in my heart nor did a lie ever pass through my lips. If any man grieved, I wept with him, and I shared my bread with the poor. I never ate alone. I moved no landmark in all my days. I was godly and truthful. I loved the Lord with all my strength and every man like they were my own children. My children, if you do these things, every spirit of Belial will flee from you, malicious men will not rule over you, and you will subdue every wild beast. God will be with you. Walk among men in simplicity of heart."

Issachar commanded them that they should carry him up to Hebron, and bury him there in the cave with his fathers. He stretched out his feet and died, the fifth son of Jacob, in a good old age. With every limb sound, and with strength unabated, he slept the eternal sleep.

Commentary

Issachar 6 predicts a dispersion from the land.

Testament of Zebulun

Concerning Compassion and Mercy

1. Zebulun

The record of Zebulun, which he instructed his children in the hundred and fourteenth year of his life, thirty-two years after the death of Joseph. He said to them, "Listen to me, my sons. I, Zebulun, am a good gift to my parents. For when I was born, our father had greatly increased in both flocks and herds, when with the streaked rods he had his portion. My children, I know throughout my life I sinned in my thoughts. I do not remember actually committing a sin, except the sin of ignorance which I committed against Joseph; for I helped my brothers and did not tell my father what had happened. I cried secretly, because I was afraid of my brothers. They had all agreed together, that if anyone should declare the secret, he should be slain with the sword. But when they wished to kill him, I pleaded with them to not be guilty of this iniquity.

2. Joseph Sold

"Simeon and Gad came against Joseph to kill him. Joseph fell upon his face, and said unto them, 'Pity me, my brothers, have compassion for the sake of Jacob our father. Do not kill me. I am innocent. I have not sinned against you. If I have sinned, then punish me, but do not kill me. Think of what it will do to Jacob, our father.' When I heard him say those words, I pitied him and began to weep. My heart melted, and I became sick to my stomach. Joseph also wept, and I wept with him. My heart pounded, and I trembled. When Joseph saw them coming against him to kill him, he fled behind me, begging them. Reuben said, 'My brothers, let us not kill him, but let us cast him into one of these dry pits which our fathers dug.' The Lord kept those wells dry in order to preserve Joseph's life, because after he was sold to the Ishmaelites, water sprung up from them.

3. Law of Enoch

"I had no share in the money obtained for Joseph. But Simeon, Gad, and six of our brothers took the money, and bought sandals for themselves, their wives, and their children, saying, 'We will not eat of it, for it is the price of our brother's blood, but will tread it down under foot, because he said that he was king over us, and so let us see what his dreams mean.' It is written in the law of Enoch, that whosoever will not raise up seed to his brother, his sandal will be unloosed, and they will spit into his face. Joseph's brothers did not wish him to live, and the Lord loosed unto them the sandal of Joseph. For when they came into Egypt, they were unloosed by Joseph's servants before the gate, and so made subject to Joseph in the Egyptian way. Not only that, but they were spit upon also, falling down before him immediately, and so they were put to shame before the Egyptians. After this, the Egyptians heard all the evils which we had done to Joseph.

4. Joseph Sold

After these things, they brought forth food. For two days and nights I tasted nothing, through pity for Joseph. Judah did not eat with them, but watched the pit; for he was afraid that Simeon and Gad would go back and kill him. When they saw that I did not eat, they set me to watch him until he was sold. He remained in the pit three days and three nights, and so was sold starving. When Reuben heard that while he was away Joseph had been sold, he rent his clothes about him, and mourned, saying, 'How will I look in the face of Jacob, my father?' He took the money, and ran after the merchants, but could not find them; for they left the main road. Reuben did not eat that day. Dan came up to him, and said, 'Don't worry; I have figured out what to say to our father Jacob. Let us kill a kid of the goats, and dip in it the coat of Joseph; and we will say, "Look and see if this is your son's coat." For they stripped Joseph of the coat his father gave him and put slave's clothes on him before they sold him. Now Simeon had the coat, and would not give it up, wishing to rend it with his sword; for he was angry that Joseph lived, and that he had not killed him. We all rose up together against him, and said, 'If you do not give it up, we will say that you alone did this wickedness in Israel,' and so he gave it up, and they did as Dan had said.

5. Sin Causes Sickness

"Now, my children, I bid you to keep the commands of the Lord. Show mercy to your neighbor, and have compassion towards all, not just men, but also animals. For this thing's sake, the Lord blessed me. When all my brothers were sick, I escaped without sickness, for the Lord knows each person's heart. Therefore, have compassion, because whatever a man does to his neighbor, the Lord will do to him. The sons of my brothers were sick and dying because of Joseph, because they did not show mercy in their hearts; but my sons were preserved without sickness, as you know. When I was in Canaan, by the seacoast, I caught spoil of fish for Jacob, my father; and when many were drowned in the sea, I survived unhurt.

6. Sailing and Fishing

"I was the first who made a boat to sail upon the sea, for the Lord gave me understanding and wisdom therein. I let down a rudder behind it, and stretched a sail on an upright mast in the midst; and sailed along the shores. I caught fish for the house of my father until we went into Egypt. Through compassion, I gave of my fish to every stranger. If any man were a stranger, or sick, or aged, I boiled the fish and dressed them well, and offered them to all men as every man had need, bringing them together and having compassion upon them. Therefore, the Lord granted me to catch many fish; for he that imparts unto his neighbor, receives much more from the Lord. For five years I caught fish, and gave to every man whom I saw, and brought sufficient for all the house of my father. In the summer, I caught fish, and in the winter, I kept sheep with my brothers.

7. Showing Mercy

"Now I will declare unto you what I did. I saw a man in distress and nakedness in wintertime, and had compassion upon him. I secretly gave him a garment from my house. Do the same from which God has given to you. Impartially show compassion and mercy to all men, and give to every man with a good heart. If you have nothing to give at that time, at least show him mercy. When I had nothing to give, I walked with them, listened, and gave them advice.

8. Compassion and Mercy

"Show compassion to everyone with mercy, so the Lord will be compassionate and merciful to you. God will show compassion in the last days and will dwell with all those who practice mercy. If you have no compassion on your neighbor, God will have no compassion for you. When we went down into Egypt, Joseph bore no malice against us. When he saw me, he was filled with compassion. Take his example. Forsake malice, love one another, and plan no evil for your brother; for this breaks unity, divides families, and troubles the soul. Whoever bears malice cannot show mercy.

9. Two Kingdoms and Two Captivities

"Consider a river that can move trees and rocks. If it is divided into many small streams, the earth just dries them up. So will you be if you become divided. Do not divide yourselves into two heads, for everything which the Lord made has only one head. He gave pairs of shoulders, hands, and feet, but all the members are subject unto the one head. I have learned by the writing of my fathers, that in the last days you will depart from the Lord, and be divided in Israel. You will follow two kings, work every abomination, and worship every idol. Your enemies will lead you captive, and you will dwell among the nations with all infirmities, tribulations, and anguish of soul. After these things, you will remember the Lord, and repent. He will lead you back, for He is merciful and full of compassion, not imputing evil to the sons of men because they are flesh. The spirits of error deceive them in all their ways. After these things the Lord Himself will arise to you.[37] The light of righteousness, healing, and compassion will be in His wings. He will redeem all captivity of the sons of men from Belial, and every spirit of error will be trodden down. He will bring back all the nations to zeal for Him, and you will see God in the fashion of a man whom the Lord will choose. Jerusalem is His name. With the wickedness of your words will you provoke Him to anger again, and you will be cast away, even unto the time of consummation.

10. Zebulun's Death

"My children, do not grieve over my death. I will arise once more in your midst, as a ruler in the midst of his sons. I will rejoice in the midst of my tribe, as many as have kept the law of the Lord, and the commandments of Zebulun their father. But the Lord will destroy the ungodly with everlasting fire throughout all generations. I am quickly going to my rest, as did my fathers. Fear the Lord your God with all your strength, all the days of your life."

When he had said these things, he fell calmly asleep, and his sons laid him in a coffin. Afterwards they carried him up to Hebron, and buried him with his fathers.

Commentary

Zebulun 3 states that the law of Enoch contains the Mosaic ritual of the brother-in-law.

Zebulun 9 teaches that Israel will split into two kingdoms. They will have two captivities (which were the Babylonian and Roman). The Writings of the Fathers, teach that the Messiah starts His ministry in the land of Zebulun, and that the Messiah is both God and man.

Zebulun 10 teaches that there will be a Resurrection.

Testament of Dan

Concerning Anger and Lying

1. Dan's Hatred

The record of the words of Dan, which he spoke to his sons in his last days. In the hundred and twenty-fifth year of his life he called together his family, and said, "Listen to my words, sons of Dan. I know in my heart, that throughout my whole life, God has been pleased with truth and just dealing. Lying and anger are evil; because they teach man all kinds of wickedness. My children, I confess that in my heart I rejoiced concerning the death of Joseph, a true and good man. I rejoiced at the selling of Joseph, because our father loved him more than us. I became jealous and vain because I was his son, too. A satanic spirit caused me to hate Joseph so much I wanted to kill him with a sword. With Joseph gone, my father would love me in the way he did him. This spirit of anger so consumed me that I thought of nothing else but to kill him. But the God of Jacob, our father, kept him from me. I never found him alone. I thank God for not allowing it or there would be two less tribes in Israel.

2. Hatred and Envy

"My children, I am dying, and I tell you the truth: unless you avoid lying and anger, and embrace love, truth, and patience, you will perish. There is blindness in anger, my children, and no angry man trusts anyone to tell the truth. He treats his father and mother as enemies, and his brother like he does not know him. Even if his brother is a prophet of the Lord, he disobeys him. He will not regard a righteous man, and he ignores his friends. Anger surrounds him with nets of deceit, blinds his natural eyes, and darkens his mind through lies. He sees what he wants to see. He only sees his own hatred, all because of envy.

3. Wrath of the Rich and Poor

"My children, anger tricks you. It takes over your body and masters your soul. It uses you to do all manner of sin. Your mind justifies what you have done because you refuse to see it as sin. A rich man's anger is threefold: it comes through his servants, his influence in the courts, and his direct anger. A poor man's anger is twofold: his direct anger, and his manipulation and lies behind the scenes. Through both, Satan works through cruelty and lying.

4. How to Avoid Being Attacked with Anger

"Understand the vanity of anger. At first, it only attacks by words. If agitated, it attacks with deeds which then afflict the mind and create bitterness. Therefore, when anyone speaks against you, do not show anger. If any man praises you, do not show pride. If you do, it may stir up another's anger against you. It will only cause you trouble. If you fall into some loss, remember God is in control and your anger about it will only lead to bitterness, making everything much worse. Bitterness always leads to two things: anger and lying. They work hand in hand, causing the Lord to depart and Belial to rule over you.

5. Last Days Prophecy

"My children, observe the commandments of the Lord, and keep His law. Depart from anger, hate, and lying, and the Lord will dwell with you, and Belial will flee from you. Speak truth to each other, and you will not fall into lust and confusion. Instead, you will have the peace of God, and no war will prevail over you. Love the Lord and each other with a true heart all your life. For I know that in the last days you will depart from the Lord, and will provoke Levi unto anger, and will fight against Judah; but you will not prevail against them. An angel of the Lord will guide them both and by them Israel will stand. When you depart from the Lord, you will walk in all kinds of evil, working the abominations of the Gentiles and going astray with ungodly women. The spirits of error will work in you with all malice. I have read in the book of Enoch the Righteous that your prince is Satan. All the spirits of fornication and pride will be subject unto Levi, but they will lay a snare for the sons of Levi to cause them to sin before the Lord. My sons will draw near unto Levi and sin with them in all things. The sons of Judah will be covetous, plundering other men's goods like lions. Therefore, you will be led away with them into captivity, and there you will receive all the plagues of Egypt, and all the malice of the Gentiles. When you return to the Lord, you will obtain mercy, and He will bring you into His sanctuary, calling peace upon you. There will rise unto you from the tribes of Judah and of Levi the salvation of the Lord. He will make war against Belial, and He will give the vengeance of victory to our coasts. He will take the captivity from Belial, even the souls of the saints, and will turn disobedient hearts unto the Lord. He will give everlasting peace to those who call upon Him. The saints will rest in Eden, and the righteous will rejoice in the New Jerusalem, which will be to the glory of God forever and ever. No longer will Jerusalem endure desolation, nor Israel be led captive. The Lord will be in the midst of her, dwelling among men, even the Holy One of Israel reigning over them in humility and in poverty. He who believes on Him will reign in truth in the heavens.

6. The Savior

"My children, fear the Lord, and guard against Satan and his spirits. Draw close to God, and to the Angel that intercedes for you, for He is a mediator between God and man[38] for the peace of Israel. He will stand up against the kingdom of the enemy. Therefore, the enemy is eager to destroy all that call upon the Lord. For he knows that in the day Israel believes, the kingdom of the enemy will be destroyed. The very angel of peace will strengthen Israel, so that it will not fall into extreme evil. It will be in the time of the iniquity of Israel, that the Lord will depart from them, and will go after those who do His will, for unto none of His angels will it be as unto him. His name in every place of Israel, and among the Gentiles will be Savior.[39] Therefore, keep from every evil work, anger, and all lying. Love truth and patience. Teach your children everything I told you so that the Father of the Gentiles may receive you. He is true and patient, meek and lowly, and teaches by His works the law of God. Depart from unrighteousness, and hold on to the righteousness of the law of the Lord. Bury me near my fathers."

7. Dan's Death

When he had said these things, he kissed them, and slept the long sleep. His sons buried him in Egypt, and later they carried up his bones to the side of Abraham, Isaac, and Jacob. Nevertheless, as Dan had prophesied to them that they should forget the law of their God, and should be alienated from the land of their inheritance, and from the race of Israel, and from their kindred, so also it came to pass.

Commentary

Dan 5 states that there will be a rebellion against Levi and Judah. Enoch wrote that Satan becomes the prince over the rebels. Eventually there will be a New Jerusalem in the eternal age.

Dan 6 predicts the great diaspora and the church age. Eventually Israel will accept the Messiah. Dan calls God the Father of the Gentiles.

Testament of Naphtali

Concerning Natural Goodness

1. Naphtali

The record of the testament of Naphtali, what things he ordained at the time of his death in the hundred and thirty-second year of his life. When his sons were gathered together in the seventh month, the fourth day of the month, while he was still in good health, he made them a feast. After he awoke the next morning, he said to them, "I am dying," but they did not believe him. He blessed the Lord, and affirmed that after the previous day's feast he would die. He began then to say to his sons, "Listen, my children. I was born from Bilhah. Because Rachel dealt craftily, and gave Bilhah in place of herself to Jacob, she bore me upon Rachel's lap. Therefore, I was called Naphtali. Rachel loved me because I was born upon her lap. When I was of young and tender form, she was used to kiss me, and say, 'I hope I have a son just like you!' Joseph turned out just like me in many ways, just as Rachel prayed. Now my mother was Bilhah, daughter of Rotheus, the brother of Deborah, Rebecca's nurse, and she was born on the same day with Rachel. Rotheus was of the family of Abraham, a Chaldean, God-fearing, free-born and noble. He was taken captive, and bought by Laban, who gave him Aena his handmaid for a wife. She bore a daughter, and called her Zilpah, after the name of the village in which he had been taken captive. Next, she bore Bilhah, saying, "My daughter is eager after what is new," for immediately after she was born she was eager for the breast.⁴⁰

2. Find Your Calling

"Since I was swift on my feet like a deer, my father Jacob appointed me for all errands and messages, and as a deer he gave me his blessing.⁴¹ As the potter creates clay vessels designed for different purposes, so the Lord designs a body for the unique spirit it is to contain. Differences from one body to another are by design, not chance. As the potter knows what each vessel can and cannot do, so the Lord knows each person. He knows how much good and evil they are capable of, and when they can turn evil. God knows everything about every one of His creations and man is created in His image. Man's work depends on his strength, his mind, his purpose, what he practices, and what is in his heart. This can be known by observing his speech, desires, dreams, his soul, and his patterns of life. By observing these, you can know if he belongs to the Lord or Belial. You can see and hear the division between light and darkness in men and women. No group or race is superior to another. Everyone has five senses, minds, and hearts with all the same emotions. My children, practice righteousness in the fear of God, and do nothing out of its proper order. Remember an eye cannot hear, neither can darkness do the works of light.

3. Do not Change God's Word
"Do not corrupt yourselves by excess, or deceive yourselves with empty words.[42] If your mouth is silent and your heart is pure, you will be able follow the will of God, and resist the will of the devil. The sun, moon, and stars do not change their order. Do not try to change the law of God into what you want it to be. Nations went astray, deserted the Lord, changed their order, and worshipped stones and wood, following spirits of error. Do not be like them, my children. Recognize that the Lord created all things, and only He is to be worshipped. Do not become like Sodom, who changed the order of their nature, in the same manner as the Watchers changed the order of their nature. They are the cause of the Flood and the desolation of the earth.

4. Prophecy
"These things I say, my children, for I have read in the holy writing of Enoch that you also will depart from the Lord, walking in the wickedness of the Gentiles, and the iniquity of Sodom. The Lord will bring captivity upon you. There you will serve your enemies, and you will be covered with all affliction and tribulation, until the Lord has consumed

you all. After that, when you are few, you will return and acknowledge the Lord your God. He will bring you back into your own land, according to His abundant mercy. After you return to the land of your fathers, you will again forget the Lord and deal wickedly. The Lord will scatter you upon the face of all the earth until the compassion of the Lord will come, a Man working righteousness and showing mercy unto all who are afar off, and who are near.

5. Vision of the Sun and Moo¡n

"In the fortieth year of my life, I saw in a vision the sun and the moon standing still on the Mount of Olives, at the east of Jerusalem. Isaac, my grandfather, said to us, 'Run and lay hold of them, each one according to his strength; and he that seizes them, his will be the sun and the moon.' Then we all ran together, and Levi laid hold of the sun, and Judah outran the others and seized the moon, and they were both lifted up with them.[43] When Levi became as a sun, a certain young man gave to him twelve palm branches. Judah was bright as the moon, and under his feet were twelve rays. Levi and Judah ran, and laid hold of one another. There was a bull on the earth, having two great horns, and an eagle's wings upon his back. We wanted to seize him, but could not. Joseph outran us, and took him, and ascended on high with him. I saw, for I was there, and behold, a holy writing appeared to us. It had written on it: Assyrians, Medes, Persians, [Elamites, Gelachæans,] Chaldeans, Syrians, will possess in captivity the twelve tribes of Israel.[44]

[Aramaic Version adds this to the end of chapter 5.]

Joseph stretched out his staff and hit Judah, his brother. Judah said, 'Brother, why are you hitting me?' Joseph said, 'Because you have in your hand twelve staves [rays]. I have only one. Give me ten and there will be peace.' Judah refused. Joseph then beat him and took ten staves by force. Only two were left with Judah. Joseph then said to his ten brothers, 'Why follow Judah and Levi? Follow after me.' His brothers immediately left Levi and Judah and all that was left was Judah, Levi, and Benjamin. When Levi saw this, he descended from the sun saddened. Joseph said to Benjamin, his brother, 'Benjamin, you are also my bother. Come with me.' But Benjamin refused. That night a storm arose and separated Joseph from his brothers, so that no two were left together.

6. Second Dream

"After seven months, I saw our father, Jacob, standing by the Sea of Jamnia, and we, his sons, were with him. Then there came a ship sailing by, [full of dried flesh[45]], without sailors or pilot. There was written upon the ship the name of Jacob. Our father said to us, 'Let us board our ship.' When we had gone on board, there arose a fierce storm, and a strong wind. Our father, who was holding the helm, flew away from us. We, being tossed with the wind, were carried over the sea. The ship was filled with water and beaten about with a mighty wave, so that it was nearly broken in pieces. Joseph fled away upon a little boat. We all were divided on twelve boards, and Levi and Judah were together. We were all scattered far away. Then Levi, clothed with sackcloth, prayed for us all unto the Lord. When the storm ceased, immediately the ship reached the land, as though in peace. Then Jacob our father came, and we all rejoiced together.

7. Jacob's Interpretation

"I told my father these two dreams. He said to me, 'These things must be fulfilled in their season, after Israel has endured many things.' Then my father said to me, 'I believe that Joseph is alive, for I see that the Lord always numbers him with you.' Then, weeping, he said, 'You live, Joseph, my child, but I cannot behold you, and you cannot see Jacob, your father.' We all wept when he said these things. My heart broke, wanting to tell him that Joseph had been sold, but I feared my brothers.

8. Proper Order

"My children, I have shown to you the last times, and all that will come to pass in Israel. Charge your children to be united with Levi and Judah.

For through Judah will salvation arise to Israel, and Jacob will be blessed through him. For through his tribe God will be seen dwelling among men on the earth, to save the race of Israel. He will gather together the righteous from the Gentiles. If you work what is good, my children, both men and angels will bless you. God will be glorified through you among the Gentiles, and the devil will flee from you. The wild beasts will fear you, and the angels will cling to you. If a man raises a child well, he is kindly remembered. So God remembers those who do good. Whoever does evil is cursed by man and angels, and God is dishonored among the heathen through him. The devil makes him his own peculiar instrument. Every wild beast will master him, and the Lord will hate him.

"The commandments of the law are twofold, and must be fulfilled through prudence. For instance, there is a season for a man to embrace his wife, and a season to abstain from her for prayer. So then, there are two commandments, and unless they be done in the proper order, they bring about sin. It is the same with the other commandments. Pursue godly wisdom, prudence, the understanding of the order of the commandments, and the laws of every work, that the Lord may love you."

9. Naphtali's Death
After he charged them with these words, he exhorted them that they should bury him in Hebron, with his fathers. When he ate and drank with a merry heart, he covered his face and died. His sons obeyed everything that Naphtali, their father, had commanded.

4Q215 (often referred to as the Time of Righteousness)

Fragment 1
"They will be hunted, afflicted, and oppressed by the trial of the pit but the elect of righteousness will forgive all their iniquity because of His mercy and His pious ones will refine them.[46] When the age of wickedness is complete, all unrighteousness will pass away. The time of righteous-

ness is coming, and the earth will be full of the knowledge and glory of God. In this age of peace, the true laws and the righteous testimony will instruct those in the ways of God and in His mighty deeds forever. Every tongue will bless Him. Everyone will bow down to serve Him with one mind.[47] For He knew their deeds before they were created and divided their borders for the work of righteousness in their generations. For the dominion of righteousness is coming and He will raise up the throne of the ... and very high. Insight, prudence, and sound wisdom are proved by His holy design.[48]

Fragment 2

"...His holiness. He established them for ...

...He created them to renew...

...from his/its days, the darkness...

...for his appointed time ... darkness...

...for appointed times before ...

...host...

Fragment 3

"...To destroy earth in His anger and to renew it...

...Source of their knowledge because ..."

Commentary

Naphtali 4 states that Enoch predicted the tribe of Naphtali would be drawn to the sin of Sodom, which in chapter 3 is related to the sin of the Watchers. There will be two expulsions.

Naphtali 5 reveals a prophecy very similar to one given by the prophet Gad.[49] The sun is depicted as God's priesthood on earth, governed by Levi, and the moon is depicted as God's kingdom on earth, led by Judah. Israel would be oppressed by seven kingdoms: Assyrians, Medes, Persians, Chaldeans [Babylonians], Syrians and two others. See the prophecy outline for details.

Naphtali 8 teaches the Savior will come from the linage of Judah and will be both God and man. Righteous Gentiles will flock to Him.

In 4Q215 fragment 1, Naphtali says in the age of peace the Messiah will teach "the true laws of God," implying that the Levites perverted the laws of God and rejected the Messiah.

Testament of Gad

Concerning Hatred

1. Gad

The record of the testament of Gad, and what things he spoke to his sons, in the hundred and twenty-seventh year of his life, saying: "I was the seventh son born to Jacob, and I was valiant in keeping the flocks. I guarded the flock at night. Whenever any wild beast came against the fold, I pursued and killed it. Joseph had been feeding the flock with us for about thirty days, but he was young and could not stand the heat. He got sick. He returned to Hebron to his father, who made him lie down, because he loved him. Joseph told our father that the sons of Zilpah and Bilhah were slaying the best of the beasts, and devouring them without the knowledge of Judah and Reuben. He had seen that I delivered a lamb out of the mouth of the bear, and I put the bear to death. I killed the lamb, because I did not think it would live, and we ate it. He told our father. I was angry with Joseph for that until the day that he was sold into Egypt. The spirit of hatred was in me, and I did not want to see or even hear Joseph. He rebuked us to our faces for having eaten of the flock without Judah. Whatever he told our father, he believed him.

2. The Sin of Hatred

"My children, I confess now my sin, that I often wished to kill him, because I hated him, and felt no mercy towards him. I hated his dreams even more. If I had the chance, I would have killed him. Therefore,

Judah and I sold him to the Ishmaelites for thirty pieces of gold.[50] We hid ten and showed the twenty to the brothers. I was bent on his destruction but my greed saved him. The God of my fathers delivered him from my hands, so I could not work iniquity in Israel.

3. Avoid Hatred at all Costs

"My children, listen to the words of truth. Walk in righteousness, and all the law of the Most High. Do not be led astray by hatred, for it causes all kinds of evil. The person who hates cannot see any righteousness in the person he hates. He only sees his hatred, evidenced by his slander and arrogance toward him. It blinds his soul. This happened to me because of my hatred toward Joseph.

4. Hatred and Envy

"My children, fear hatred. It works iniquity against the Lord Himself. It will not listen to His command to love his neighbor. It sins against God. If a brother stumbles, he is immediately slandered to all men, and rushed to judgment to be punished and slain. If he is a servant, his master accuses him severely and, if possible, kills him. Hatred worsens through envy. Just as love would pardon those condemned to die, hatred would slay the living, even those with a minor offence. Satan uses hatred along with impulsiveness to kill; but the spirit of love works with the law of God in patience, producing salvation.

5. Overcoming Hatred

"Hatred is evil, because it is always found with lying, dishonesty, and exaggeration. It brings darkness rather than light, calls the sweet bitter, and teaches slander, war, and violence. It fills the heart with the deadly poison of every evil. I say this to you from experience. Flee hatred, and cling to the love of the Lord. Righteousness casts out hatred. Humility destroys hatred. He who is just and humble is ashamed to do wrong, being reproved not by another, but by his own heart, because the Lord views his intent. He does not speak against any man, because the fear of the Most High overcomes hatred. Fearing to offend the Lord, he will not do any wrong to anyone, not even in thought. These things I finally learned, after I repented concerning Joseph. For true godly repentance destroys unbelief, drives away the darkness, enlightens, gives knowledge to the soul, and guides you to salvation. Those things you cannot learn from man, you learn through repentance. God punished me with a disease of the heart. If Jacob, my father, had not prayed for me I surly would have died. The sins of a man are the same things that destroy him. Just as I showed no mercy toward Joseph for eleven months, I suffered mercilessly just as long.

6. The Power of Forgiveness

"My children, put away hatred. Love one another in thought, word, and deed. I spoke kindly of Joseph when I was with my father, but privately hatred darkened my mind to the point I wanted to kill him. Love each other. And if a man sin against you, talk to him gently. Do not foster the poison of hatred or guile. If he confesses and repents, forgive him. If he denies it, do not argue with him, in case he swears, and you sin twice. Do not rebuke him publicly because it may cause others to hate you, or gossip about you, causing great sin. If he denies it but is convicted in his heart, do not speak of it any further. For he who denies but repents will do you no more harm. Instead, he will honor, respect, and be at peace with you. If he continues in his wrongdoing, forgive him from the heart, and give the vengeance to God.

7. Envy

"If a man prospers more than you, do not envy, but pray that he increases even more. This attitude will benefit you greatly. If he is further exalted, do not envy him but remember that we all die. Instead, praise God for what He has done. Focus on the things of the Lord, and your mind will rest and be at peace. If a man becomes rich by dishonesty, like Esau, do not be jealous, but wait on the Lord. The Lord will take his riches away or punish him if he does not repent. If he continues in sin, he will suffer eternal punishment. The poor who are free from envy, and thank the Lord for all things, are truly rich among men, because jealousy does not control them. Therefore, put away hatred, and love one another with a pure heart.

8. Gad's Death

"Teach your children these things, so that they honor Judah and Levi, for from them will the Lord raise up a Saviour to Israel. I know that eventually your children will depart from them, and walk in wickedness, mischief, and corruption before the Lord."

When he had rested for a little while, he told them, "My children, obey your father, and bury me near my fathers." Then he fell asleep in peace. After five years, they carried him up, and laid him in Hebron with his fathers.

Commentary

Gad 8 reveals that the Savior will come from the tribe of Judah.

Testament of Asher

Concerning Hypocrisy in Vice and Virtue

1. Asher

The record of the testament of Asher, what things he spoke to his sons in the hundred and twentieth year of his life. While he was still in health, he said to them: "My children, listen to me, I want to tell you what is right in the sight of God. God has given two ways to the sons of men, two different mindsets, or lifestyles, and they lead to two different eternities. The two ways are good and evil; and we each have two natures. Therefore, if the soul takes pleasure in good, all his actions are righteous. If he sins, he immediately repents, because his mind is focused on righteousness, he rejects evil, and this uproots the sin. If the soul focuses on evil, his actions begin to be evil. He drives away the good, and becomes increasingly evil. Belial rules over him and even the good he does perverts to evil because the poison is in his heart.

2. Evil that appears to be godly[51]

"There are those who speak good for the sake of the evil, which only brings trouble.

1. A man who shows no compassion upon a truly repentant sinner. This looks like righteousness, but is actually sin.

2. A man who chooses to live with, or even die for, an evil person because he loves him. This has an appearance of righteousness, but is actually sin.

3. There is a compassion that conceals evil in the name of mercy. It may seem good, but it only brings more evil. That kind compassion turns mercy into sin.

4. One person steals, cons, plunders, and defrauds, but pities the poor. He seems both good and evil, but in reality, he is only evil. When he defrauds his neighbor, he provokes God, and swears falsely against the Most High. Even though he pities and refreshes the poor, he sets aside the law of God defiling his soul. He may appear to be good, but in reality, he kills many and pities few.

5. Another person commits adultery and fornication, but abstains from meats. His fasting only works evil, and he perverts many through his power and wealth. The fornication turns his fasting into sin.

"Such men are like swine or hares;[52] only half clean, but in truth they are unclean, God's heavenly tablets have declared.

3. The Hypocrite

"My children, do not be like the hypocrite, practicing both good and wickedness. Instead, hold fast only to what is good, for God rests in goodness and all men desire it. Flee wickedness. Destroy the devil by your good works. The hypocrites do not serve God, but their own lusts, pleasing Belial and other men like themselves.

4. Godliness that Appears to be Evil

"Hypocrites consider godly, single-minded men to be in error.

1. They say putting a murderer to death is evil, but in reality, it is a good work, because it uproots and destroys evil from the land.

2. They do not understand that it is not hypocritical to show mercy on a truly repentant adulterer and thief, but punish the unrepentant sinner, both are acts of righteousness because he follows the Lord's example, in that he refuses evil that appears to be good, and that which is obviously evil.

3. They also think it hypocritical to strive against those who carouse, but the righteous know that by tolerating sinners, they will pollute their souls and defile their own speech. It is a righteous act to both refrain from these actions and forcibly stop others from doing them. Such men are like stags and hinds, because in a wild condition they seem to be unclean, but they are altogether clean. They walk in a zeal for God, and abstain from what God also hates and forbids by His commandments, and they ward off the evil from the good.

5. The Single-minded

"My children, you see how that there are two sides to all things. One opposes the other, and one is hidden by the other. Death succeeds to life, dishonor to glory, night to day, and darkness to light; and all things are under the day, and just things under life. Everlasting life also awaits death. Nor may it be said that truth is a lie, nor right, wrong; for all truth is under the light, even as all things are under God. All these things I proved in my life, and I wandered not from the truth of the Lord. I searched out the commandments of the Most High, walking single-mindedly with all my strength unto that which is good.

6. Live a Righteous Life

"My children, remember the commandments of the Lord. Single-mindedly follow the truth, for the hypocrites receive twofold punishment. Hate the spirits of error that strive against men. Keep the law of the

Lord, and do not practice evil with good. Practice only good, and keep all of the commandments of the Lord. Conduct your lives by Him and rest in Him. Your actions will show if you are righteousness and whom you follow: the angels of God or the angels of Satan. If the soul dies troubled, it is because it was tormented by the evil spirits it served through its lusts and evil works. If the soul dies quietly and with joy, it is because God's peace has comforted him in life.

7. Recognize the Messiah

"My children, do not become as Sodom who perished forever because they did not recognize the angels of the Lord. I know that you will sin, and you will be delivered into the hands of your enemies. Your land will be made desolate, and you will be scattered unto the four corners of the earth. You will be disregarded in the Dispersion as useless water, until the Most High will visit the earth. He will come as man, eating and drinking with men, and in peace He will break the head of the dragon through water. He will save Israel and all nations, God speaking in the person of man. Therefore, teach these things to your children, so they will not disobey Him; for I have read in the heavenly tablets that you truly will disobey Him, and act ungodly against Him, not giving heed to the law of God, but to the commandments of men. Therefore, you will be scattered as Gad and Dan, my brothers, who will not know their own lands, tribe, or tongue; but the Lord will gather you together in faith through the hope of His tender mercy, for the sake of Abraham, Isaac, and Jacob."

8. Asher's Death

When he had said these things to them, he charged them, saying: "Bury me in Hebron." Then he fell into a peaceful sleep, and died. After this his sons did as he had charged them, and they carried him up and buried him with his fathers.

Commentary

Asher 7 predicts an expulsion to all nations. The Messiah is God incarnate appearing on earth, who will bring salvation for Israel and the Gentiles.

Testament of Joseph

Concerning Sobriety

1. Joseph

The record of the testament of Joseph: when he was about to die, he called his sons and his brothers together, and said to them: "My children and brothers, listen to Joseph, the beloved of Israel, your father. I have seen in my life envy and death, and I have not wandered in the truth of the Lord. My brothers hated me; but the Lord loved me. They wished me dead; but the God of my fathers guarded me. They threw me into a pit; but the Most High brought me back up. I was sold for a slave; but the Lord set me free. I was taken into captivity; but His strong hand comforted me. When I was hungry, the Lord Himself nourished me. When I was sick and alone, God was with me. When I was in prison, the Savior showed me favor and released me. Amid slanders, He rescued me and exalted me above all envy and guile.

2. Joseph's Trials

"Potiphar, the chief cook[53] of Pharaoh, entrusted to me his house, and I struggled against a shameless woman urging me to transgress with her; but the God of Israel, my father, guarded me from the burning flame. I was cast into prison, beaten, and mocked; but the Lord granted me to find pity in the sight of the keeper of the prison; for He will, in no wise, forsake those who fear Him, neither in darkness, nor bonds, nor tribulations, nor in necessities. For God is not a man. He cannot be ashamed, afraid, weak, or thrust aside. In every situation, He is there to comfort. He only departs for a little while to try your soul. In ten temptations He showed me approved, and in all of them I endured; for endurance is a mighty charm, and patience gives many good things.

3. Joseph and the Egyptian Woman
"How often did the Egyptian threaten me with death! How often did she give me over to punishment, and then call me back, and threaten me when I would not company with her! She said to me, 'You will be lord of me, and all that is mine, if you will give yourself unto me, and you will be as our master.' Therefore, I remembered the words of the fathers of my father Jacob, and I entered into my chamber and prayed unto the Lord; and I fasted in those seven years, and I appeared to my master as one living delicately, for they that fast for God's sake receive beauty of face. If one gave me wine, I drank it not. I fasted for three days, and took my food and gave it to the poor and sick. I sought the Lord early, and wept for the Egyptian woman of Memphis, for she troubled me unceasingly, and at night she came to me under the pretense of visiting me. At first, because she had no male child, she feigned to count me as a son. I prayed unto the Lord, and she bare a male child. Therefore, for a time she embraced me as a son, and I knew it not. Last of all, she sought to draw me into fornication. When I perceived it, I sorrowed even unto death. When she had gone out I came to myself, and I lamented for her many days, because I saw her guile and deceit. I declared unto her the words of the Most High, if perhaps she would turn from her evil lust.

4. Egyptian Woman's False Conversion
"How often she fawned upon me with words as a holy man, with guile in her talk, praising my chastity before her husband, while desiring to destroy me when we were alone. She lauded me openly as chaste, and in secret she said unto me, 'Do not be afraid of my husband; for he is convinced you are chaste, so that even should one tell him concerning us, he would never believe him.' For all these things, I lay upon the ground

in sackcloth, and I besought God that the Lord would deliver me from the Egyptian. When she prevailed nothing, she came again to me under the plea of instruction, that she might know the word of the Lord. She said unto me, 'If you want me to abandon my idols, just tell me, and I will persuade my husband to depart from his idols, and we will walk in the law of your Lord.' I said unto her, 'The Lord does not want those who reverence Him to live in uncleanness, nor does He take pleasure in those who commit adultery.' She held her peace, longing to accomplish her evil desire. I gave myself yet more to fasting and prayer, that the Lord should deliver me from her.

5. The Threat of Murder

"At another time she said unto me, 'If you will not commit adultery, I will kill my husband, and so can I lawfully take you to be my husband.' When I heard this, rent my garment, and said, 'Woman, reverence the Lord, and do not this evil deed, lest you be utterly destroyed; for I will declare your ungodly thought unto all men.' She therefore, being afraid, begged me not to tell her wickedness to anyone. She departed, soothing me with gifts, and sending to me every delight of the sons of men.

6. Egyptian Woman Tries Drugs

"She sent me food sprinkled with enchantments. When the eunuch who brought it came, I looked up and beheld a terrible man giving me with the dish, a sword, and I perceived that her scheme was for the deception of my soul. When he had gone out I wept, nor did I eat any of her food. After one day she came to me and observed the food, and said unto me, 'What is this? Why have you not eaten the food?' I said unto her, 'It is because you filled it with death. How said you, "I come not near to idols but to the Lord alone"? Now therefore know that the God of my father has revealed your wickedness to me by an angel, and I have kept it to convict you, if perhaps you may see it and repent. But that you may learn that the wickedness of the ungodly has no power over those who reverence God in chastity,' I took it and ate it before her, saying, 'The

God of my fathers and the angel of Abraham will be with me.' She fell upon her face at my feet, and wept; and I raised her up and admonished her, and she promised to not to do this iniquity again.

7. The Threat of Suicide

"But because her heart was set upon me to commit lewdness, she sighed, and her countenance fell. When her husband saw her, he said unto her, 'Why is your countenance fallen?' She said, 'I have a heartache, and my spirit is grieved.' So, he comforted her. Then she rushed in to me while her husband was right outside, and said unto me, 'I will hang myself, or cast myself into a well or over a cliff, if you will not consent to me.' When I saw the spirit of Belial was troubling her, I prayed unto the Lord, and said unto her, 'Why are you troubled, disturbed, and blinded in sins? Remember that if you kill yourself, Sethon, your husband's concubine, your rival, will beat your children, and will erase all memory of you.' She said unto me, 'Then you do love me; this alone is sufficient for me, that you care for my life and my children. I have expectation that I will enjoy my desire.' She did not realize that it was because of my God I said this, not because of her. If anyone falls into the passion of a wicked desire, they become enslaved by it. She was so enslaved by her desire that she mistook any kind word from me as a sign that her wicked desire might soon be fulfilled.

8. Prison is the Answer to Joseph's Prayer

"I declare unto you, my children, that it was about the sixth hour when she departed from me; and I knelt before the Lord all that day, and continued all the night. About dawn I rose up weeping, and praying for a release from the Egyptian. At last, then, she laid hold of my garments, forcibly dragging me to have an affair with her. When, therefore, I saw that in her madness she was forcibly holding my garments, I fled away naked. She falsely accused me to her husband, and the Egyptian cast me into the prison in his house. The next day, he had me scourged and sent to the prison house. When, therefore, I was in fetters, the Egyptian woman fell sick from her vexation. I sang praises unto the Lord while I was in the abode of darkness, and with glad voice rejoiced and glorified my God only because by a pretext I had been rid of the Egyptian woman.

9. Wicked Woman Visits Joseph in Prison

"How often she had sent unto me, saying, 'Consent to fulfil my desire, and I will release you from your bonds, and free you from the darkness of the prison!' Not even in thoughts did I incline unto her. For God loves those who in a den of darkness fast with chastity, rather than those who in secret chambers live delicately without restraint. Whosoever lives in chastity, and desires also glory, and if the Most High knows that it is expedient for him, He bestows this also upon him, even as upon me. How often, though when she was sick, did she come down to me at odd times, and listened to my voice as I prayed! When I heard her groanings, I held my peace. For when I was in her house she used to bare her arms, breasts, and legs, so I might fall before her; for she was very beautiful, splendidly adorned for my deception. The Lord guarded me from her devics.

10. Patience, Fasting, and Prayer

"You see, my children, how great things come through patience with prayer and fasting. If you, therefore, practice sobriety and purity in patience and humility of heart, the Lord will dwell among you, because He loves sobriety. Wherever the Most High dwells, even though a man falls into envy, slavery, or slander, the Lord who dwells in him, for his sobriety's sake, not only delivers him from evil, but also exalts and glorifies him, even as me. For in every way the man is guarded, whether in deed, or in word, or in thought. My brothers, know how my father loved me, and I was not exalted in my heart. Although I was a child, I had the fear of God in my thoughts. For I knew that all things should pass away, and I kept myself within bounds, and I honored my brothers. Through fear of them I held my peace when I was sold, and revealed not my family to the Ishmaelites, that I was the son of Jacob, a great and mighty man.

11. The Fear of God

"Do you also, therefore, have the fear of God in your works, and honor your family? For everyone who follows the law of the Lord will be loved by Him. When I came to the Indocolpitæ with the Ishmaelites, they asked me, and I said that I was a slave from their house, that I might not put my brothers to shame. The eldest of them said unto me, 'You are not a slave, even your appearance shows that.' He threatened to kill me, but I said that I was their slave. Now when we came into Egypt, they strove concerning me, which of them should buy me and take me. Therefore, it seemed good to all that I should remain in Egypt with a merchant of their trade, until they should return bringing merchandise. The Lord gave me favor in the eyes of the merchant, and he entrusted to me his house. The Lord blessed him because of me, and increased him in silver and gold, and I was with him three months and five days.

12. God and Your Reputation

"About that time the Memphian wife of Potiphar passed by with great pomp, and cast her eyes upon me, because her eunuchs told her concerning me. She told her husband concerning the merchant, that he had become rich by means of a young Hebrew, saying, 'They say that men have indeed stolen him out of the land of Canaan. Now therefore execute judgment with him, and take away the youth to be your steward; so, the God of the Hebrews will bless you, for grace from heaven is upon him.'

13. Joseph in Egypt

"Potiphar was persuaded by her words, and commanded the merchant to be brought, and said unto him, 'What is this that I hear, that you steal people out of the land of the Hebrews, and sell them for slaves?' The merchant therefore fell upon his face, and besought him, saying, 'I beseech you, my lord, I know not what you say.' He said, 'From where then is your Hebrew servant?' He said, 'The Ishmaelites entrusted him to me until they should return.' He believed him not, but commanded him to be stripped and beaten. When he persisted, Potiphar said, 'Let the youth be brought.' When I was brought in, I did obeisance to the chief of the eunuchs — for he was third in rank with Pharaoh, being chief of all the eunuchs, and having wives and children and concubines. He took me apart from him, and said unto me, 'Are you a slave or free?' I said, 'A slave.' He said unto me, 'Whose slave are you?' I said to him, 'The Ishmaelites'.' Again he said to me, 'How did you become their slave?' I said, 'They bought me out of the land of Canaan.' But he did not believe me, and said, 'You lie,' and he commanded me to be stripped and beaten.

14. Memphian Woman Tries to Obtain Joseph

"Now the Memphian woman was looking through a window while I was being beaten, and she sent unto her husband, saying, 'Your judgment is unjust; for you punish a free man who has been stolen, as if he were a transgressor.' When I gave no other answer though I was beaten, he commanded that I should be kept in guard, until, said he, 'the owners of the boy should come.' His wife said unto him, 'Why do you detain in captivity this noble child, who ought rather to be set at liberty, and wait upon you?' For she wished to see me in desire of sin, but I was ignorant concerning all these things. Then he said to his wife, 'It is not the custom of the Egyptians to take away that which belongs to others before proof is given.' This he said concerning the merchant, and concerning me, that I must be imprisoned.

15. Joseph with the Ishmaelites

"Now, after twenty-four days the Ishmaelites came. Having heard that Jacob my father was mourning for me, they said to me, 'Why did you say that you were a slave? We have learned that you are the son of a mighty man in the land of Canaan, and your father grieves for you in sackcloth.' I would have wept again, but I restrained myself, that I should not put my brothers to shame. I said, 'I do not know; I am a slave.' Then they took counsel to sell me, so that I would not be found in their hands. For they feared Jacob, lest he should work upon them a deadly vengeance. For it had been heard that he was mighty with the Lord and with men. Then the merchant said to them, 'Release me from the judgment of Potiphar.' They therefore came and asked for me, saying, 'He was bought by us with money.' And he sent us away.

16. Joseph Bought

"Now the Memphian woman pointed me out to her husband, that he should buy me; 'for I hear,' she said, 'that they are selling him.' She sent a eunuch to the Ishmaelites, and asked them to sell me; and since he was not willing to traffic with them, he returned. When the eunuch had made trial of them, he made known to his mistress that they asked a large price for their slave. She sent another eunuch, saying, 'Even if they demand two minæ of gold, do not to spare the gold; only buy the boy, and bring him here.' He gave them eighty pieces of gold for me, and told his mistress that a hundred had been given for me. When I saw it I held my peace, that the eunuch should not be punished.

17. Forgive Those Who Wrong You

"My children, you see what great things I endured that I should not put my brothers to shame. Do you also love one another, and with patience hide one another's faults? For God delights in the unity of families, and in the purpose of a heart approved unto love. When my brothers came into Egypt, and learned that I returned their money unto them, and did not accuse them, instead I comforted them, and after the death of Jacob I loved them all the more. And everything that he commanded I did very abundantly, then they marveled. For I did not allow them to be afflicted even to the smallest matter; and all that was in my hand I gave to them. Their children were my children, and my children were as their servants. Their life was my life, all their suffering was my suffering, and all their sickness was my infirmity. My land was their land, my counsel their counsel, and I did not exalt myself among them in arrogance because of my worldly glory, but I was among them as one of the least.

18. Walk in the Ways of the Lord

"If you walk in the commandments of the Lord, my children, He will exalt you there, and will bless you with good things forever and ever. If anyone seeks to do evil to you, pray for him, and you will be redeemed of the Lord from all evil. You see that through patience I took a wife, even the daughter of my master. A hundred talents of gold were given me with her; for the Lord made them to serve me. He gave me also beauty as a flower above the beautiful ones of Israel. He preserved me to old age in strength and in beauty, because I was like in all things to Jacob.

19. Joseph's Visions

"Hear also, my children, the visions which I saw. There were twelve deer feeding, and the nine were divided and scattered in the land, likewise also the three. I saw that from Judah was born a virgin wearing a linen garment, and from her went forth a Lamb, without spot, and on His left hand there was a lion. All the beasts rushed against Him, and the Lamb overcame them, destroyed them, and trampled them under foot. Because of Him, the angels, men, and all the earth rejoiced. These things will take place in their season, in the last days. Therefore, my children, observe the commandments of the Lord, and honor Judah and Levi. From them will rise unto you the Lamb of God, by grace saving all the Gentiles and Israel. For His kingdom is an everlasting kingdom, which will not be shaken; but my kingdom among you will come to an end as a watcher's hammock, which after the summer will not appear.

20. Joseph's Death

"I know that after my death the Egyptians will afflict you, but God will undertake your cause, and will bring you into that which He promised to your fathers. But carry my bones up with you; for when my bones are taken up, the Lord will be with you in light, and Belial will be in darkness with the Egyptians. Carry up Zilpah, your mother, and lay her near Bilhah, by the hippodrome, by the side of Rachel."

When he had said these things, he stretched out his feet, and slept the long sleep. All Israel and Egypt mourned him with a great lamentation, for he felt for the Egyptians even as his own family, and showed them kindness, aiding them in every work, counsel, and matter.

4Q539

4Q539 is five very small fragments of the Testament of Joseph. Phrases like "my uncle Ishmael" are readable.

Commentary

Joseph 19 reveals that the Messiah will be virgin-born.

Testament of Benjamin

Concerning a Pure Mind

1. Benjamin

The record of the words of Benjamin, which he set forth to his sons, after he had lived a hundred and twenty years. He kissed them, and said, "As Isaac was born to Abraham in his hundredth year, so also was I to Jacob. Since Rachel died in giving me birth, I had no milk. Therefore, I was nursed by Bilhah her handmaid. Rachel remained barren for twelve years after she gave birth to Joseph. She prayed to the Lord with fasting for twelve days, and she conceived and bare me. Our father loved Rachel dearly, and prayed that he might see two sons born from her; which is why I was called the son of days, which is Benjamin.

2. Benjamin and Joseph

"When I went into Egypt, and Joseph my brother recognized me, he asked me, 'What did they tell my father when they sold me?' I said unto him, 'They dabbled your coat with blood and sent it, and said, 'Is this the coat of your son?' He said to me, 'When the Ishmaelites took me, one of them stripped off my coat, gave me a girdle, scourged me, and told me to run. As he went away to hide my garment, a lion met him and killed him; and so, his partners were afraid, and sold me to their companions.'

3. Godliness Protects from Evil

"My children, love the Lord God of heaven, and keep His command-ments, and be followers of the good and holy man Joseph. Let your mind focus on what is good, as I do. He that focuses on good sees all things correctly. Fear the Lord, and love your neighbor. Even if the spir-its of Belial allure you into troublesome wickedness, yet it will have no dominion over you, just as it did not over Joseph my brother. How many men wished to kill him, and God shielded him! He who fears God and loves his neighbor cannot be afflicted by Belial's spirit of the air, being shielded by the fear of God. Neither can he be ruled over by the device of men or of beasts, for he is aided by the love of the Lord which he has towards his neighbor. Joseph even asked our father Jacob to pray for our brothers, that the Lord would not impute to them the evil that they devised concerning Joseph. Thus, Jacob cried out, 'My child Joseph, you have touched the heart of your father Jacob.' He embraced him, and kissed him for two hours, saying, 'In you will be fulfilled the prophecy of heaven concerning the Lamb of God, even the Savior of the world. He will be delivered up spotless for transgressors. He will be sinless, yet put to death for ungodly men in the blood of the covenant, for the salvation of the Gentiles and of Israel. He will destroy Belial, and them that serve him.

4. Godly Men

"My children, you know what happens to a godly man. Follow his compassion with a good mind, that you also may wear crowns of glory. The good man does not have a dark eye. He shows mercy to all men, even though they are sinners, even though they devise evil against him. So, he who does good overcomes the evil, being shielded by Him who is good. He loves the righteous as his own soul. If anyone is glorified, he does not envy him. If anyone is enriched, he is not jealous. If anyone is valiant, he praises him. He trusts and praises the sober-minded. He shows mercy to the poor. He helps the weak. He sings the praises of God. He protects those who fear God, like a shield. He aides those who love God, but warns and turns away those who reject God. He loves those who have the grace of God, like his own soul.

5. The Power of Forgiveness

"If you have a good mind, my children, then wicked men will be at peace with you. The profligate will reverence you and turn to good. The covetous will not only stop being greedy, but start giving to those who are afflicted. If you do well, the unclean spirits will flee from you. Even beasts will flee from you in dread. Darkness flees from those who reverence good works. When anyone injures a holy man, they repent because the holy man forgives him and holds his peace. If anyone betrays a righteous soul, the righteous man, though praying, may be humbled for a little while. Yet, not long afterwards he appears far more glorious, as Joseph my brother did.

6. The Godly Mind

"The mind of the good man is not under the power of the deceit of the spirit of Belial, for the angel of peace guides his soul. He does not gaze passionately on corruptible things, nor hoard riches for his own pleasure. He does not delight in pleasure, hurt his neighbor, pamper himself with food, or err in pride, for the Lord is his portion. The good mind does not dwell on the glory or dishonor of men. He does not practice guile, lying, fighting, or reviling. The Lord dwells with him and lights up his soul, and he rejoices with all men. The good mind is not hypocritical. It does not bless and curse, insult and honor, or spread sorrow and joy. It does not make peace and cause trouble, speak hypocritically and truthfully, or bring poverty and wealth. It only has one temperament: pure and uncorrupt, concerning all men. It has no trouble seeing and hearing the truth, for in everything the Lord watches his soul, and keeps his mind clean so that he will not be condemned by God or men. But every work of Belial is hypocritical, and cannot be straight.

7. Sin Caused by not Trusting God

"My children, flee Belial's temptation to sin, for it brings a sword to those who obey, and the sword causes seven evils. When the mind first conceives sin, it brings envy, ruin, tribulation, exile, need, panic, and destruction. Cain received seven judgments by God, for in every hundred years the Lord brought one plague upon him. When he was two hundred he began to suffer and when he was nine hundred he was destroyed for Abel his righteous brother's sake. Cain was judged seven hundred years, and Lamech, seventy times seven.[54] All those who are like Cain in their envy and hatred will always be punished in the same way.

8. The Pure Mind

"Therefore, my children, flee all wrong-doing, envy, and hatred of family, and cleave to goodness and love. He who has a pure mind in love does not think about fornicating with a woman because he has no defilement in his heart, and the Spirit of God rests in him just as the sun is not defiled by shining over dung and mire, but rather it dries up both and drives away the stench. So also, the pure mind, constrained among the defilements of the earth, rather edifies others and suffers no defilement itself.

9. Rebellion Against the Messiah

"The words of the righteous Enoch teach that even your descendants will practice evil. They will commit fornication like the fornication of

Sodom, and all but a few will perish, and will multiply inordinate lusts with women; and the kingdom of the Lord will not be among you, for immediately He will take it away. Nevertheless, the temple of God will be built in your portion, and will be glorious among you. For He will take it, and the twelve tribes will be gathered together there, and all the Gentiles, until the Most High will send forth His salvation in the visitation of His only-begotten One. He will enter into the front of the temple, and there will the Lord be treated with outrage, and He will be lifted up on a tree. The veil of the temple will be rent, and the Spirit of God will descend upon the Gentiles as fire poured forth. He will rise from the grave, and will ascend from earth into heaven. I know how lowly He will be upon the earth, and how glorious in the heaven.

10. The Inheritance

"Now when Joseph was in Egypt, I longed to see him face to face; and through the prayers of Jacob my father I saw him, while awake in the daytime, in his full and perfect shape. Know therefore, my children, that I am dying. Work truth and righteousness to your neighbors, judge righteously, and keep the law of the Lord and His commandments. These things I teach you instead of an inheritance. Give them also to your children for an everlasting possession; for so did Abraham, Isaac, and Jacob. These things they gave us for an inheritance, saying, 'Keep the commandments of God until the Lord will reveal His salvation to all nations.' Then you will see Enoch, Noah, Shem, Abraham, Isaac, and Jacob, rising on the right hand in gladness. Then we will also rise, each one over our tribe, worshipping the King of Heaven, who appeared upon the earth in the form of a man of humility. All those who believed on Him on the earth will rejoice with Him; and then will all men arise, some unto glory and some unto shame. The Lord will judge Israel first, even for the wrong they did unto Him; for when He appeared as a deliverer, God in the flesh, they did not believe Him. Then He will judge all the Gentiles, as many as did not believe Him when He appeared on earth. He will reprove Israel among the chosen ones of the Gentiles, even as He reproved Esau among the Midianites, who deceived their brothers, so that they fell into fornication and idolatry. They were alienated from God, and became as those who were not children in the portion of them that fear the Lord. But if you walk in holiness in the presence of the Lord, you will dwell in hope again with me, and all Israel will be gathered unto the Lord.

11. Prophecy of the Apostle Paul

"I will no longer be called a ravening wolf on account of your ravages, but a worker of the Lord, distributing food to them that work what is good. One will rise up from my seed in the latter times, beloved of the Lord, hearing His voice on the earth, enlightening with new knowledge all the Gentiles, bursting in on Israel for salvation with the light of knowledge, and tearing it away from them like a wolf, and giving it to the synagogue of the Gentiles. Until the consummation of the ages he[55] will be in the synagogues of the Gentiles, and among their rulers, as a strain of music in the mouth of all; and he will be inscribed in the holy books, both his work and his word, and he will be a chosen one of God forever; and because of him my father Jacob instructed me, saying, 'He will fill up that which lacks from your tribe.'"

12. Benjamin's Death

When he finished his words, he said: "I charge you, my children, carry up my bones out of Egypt, and bury me at Hebron, near my fathers." So, Benjamin died a hundred and twenty-five years old, in a good old age, and they placed him in a coffin. In the ninety-first year of the departure of the children of Israel from Egypt, they and their brothers brought up the bones of their fathers secretly in a place which is called Canaan; and they buried them in Hebron, by the feet of their fathers. They returned from the land of Canaan, and lived in Egypt until the day of their departing from the land of Egypt.

Commentary

Benjamin 3 predicts that the Messiah would be sinless, and bring salvation to the whole world by being put to death by godless men.

Benjamin 9 predicts the temple will be built in the tribe of Benjamin. The temple ceases when the Messiah brings His salvation. The Messiah will be crucified and the veil of the temple will be rent.

Benjamin 10 teaches the Messiah will be God in flesh and that all men will resurrect.

Benjamin 11 describes the apostle Paul and his written works making up most of what we call the New Testament.

Testament of Kohath

4Q542
Fragment 1

"…and God of gods for all the centuries. He will make His light shine upon you and you will know His great name. …you will know Him, because He is the God of the centuries, the Lord of all creation, and the Ruler of all, to deal with them as He wishes. He will create great joy and gladness for you and your sons in the generations of truth forever. Now, my sons, be careful with the inheritance which has been given to you by our fathers. Do not give your inheritance to foreigners or your heritage to half-breeds, or you will become foolishly humiliated in their eyes. They will scorn you when they go from being residents among you to being chiefs over you. Hold on to the words of our righteous fathers: Abraham, Jacob, Levi, and my words. Be holy and pure from all corruption. Hold on to the truth and walk in uprightness. Do not be double-minded, but have a pure heart and a truthful and good spirit. It will give a good name to me, joy to Levi, gladness to Jacob, rejoicing to Isaac, and honor to Abraham; if you keep and carry on the inheritance which your fathers gave you in truth, justice, uprightness, perfection, purity, and holiness. You must keep the priesthood in every way that I have commanded you and according to all that...

Fragment 2

"...I have taught you in truth. Now, and for all time, the word of truth will come on you and eternal blessings will rest on you and will be... will remain throughout all generations and there will be no more... from your punishment, and you will rise to make judgement on... and to see the sins of all the sinners of the world... in the fire, in the abyss, and in all the caverns in order to... in the time of justice; and all the wicked will vanish. Now, Amram, my son, I command you and your descendants... given to Levi my father, which he in turn gave to me along with all my writings as witness. You must take care of them. They are for you and your descendants and in them is great worth. It is important that they be carried on with you.

Fragment 3

"... to read and... his sons... men and life...upon them and... darkness and... and light, but... and I... the stones were heavy... will be great in number because of fornication. Those who... very great, because very few..."

Commentary

Fragment 1 of the Testament of Kohath seems to be saying that God would bless his children, specifically the descendants of his grandson Levi, the priests. Even though the Levitical priests did not inherit land, they inherit something. The inheritance that Kohath is referring to is most likely the testaments of their fathers: all the books and prophecies from Adam down to Kohath. The Talmud testifies that these books were given to Levi and his descendants to keep for all generations. The idea that some might try to kill the Messiah before He was fully grown probably lead to the tradition that these writings should be kept secret in order to protect Him.

Fragment 2 seems to state that the priesthood will bring in the ever-lasting kingdom but some of the priests would be wicked. Levi and the righteous priests will rise and judge those who transgressed. This sounds like the apostle Paul when he said we would "judge the angels." Kohath then tells his descendants how important it is to preserve the written records of the fathers. Levi gave them to him and he now hands them over to Amram for his posterity.

Fragment 3 is so badly fragmented that all we can glean from it is that fornication is very evil. He may have been telling of a dream about God destroying fornicators with giant falling stones, a type of wrath from heaven.

Testament of Amram

4Q543–4Q549
4Q543

...copy of the book of the words of the vision of Amram, son of Kohath, son of Levi, all that he explained to his sons on his deathbed. He was one hundred and thirty-seven years old when he died, which was the one hundred and fifty-second year of Israel's exile in Egypt. He should ... "...to call Uzziel, his youngest brother, and he gave his thirty-year-old daughter, Miriam, to him for a wife. He gave a wedding feast lasting seven days. He ate, drank, and rejoiced during the feast. When the days of the wedding feast were over, he called for Aaron, his son, who was about twenty years old, and told him, 'Son, call the messengers, your brothers from the house of ...'

4Q544

"Kohath went there to stay, dwell, and build ... many of the sons of my uncle together with... since the work was very great and would continue until our dead would be buried there... In the year when I began, news of a war brewing worried me. I allowed those of our company who wanted to return to Egypt to go and I went on to finish the work and to bury them. They did not help in finishing the tombs of our fathers. My father Kohath, and my wife, Jochebed, left me to stay and build, and provide them with all their needs from the land of Canaan. We dwelt in Hebron while we were building. A war broke out between the Philistines and the Egyptians. When the Philistines defeated the Egyptians with the help of the Canaanites, they closed off the border of Egypt. It was impossible for Jochebed, my wife, to come here to Canaan from Egypt for forty-one years. We could not return to Egypt either. We could not even... the Egyptian and Canaanite / Philistine War... During all this time, I was separated from Jochebed, my wife, who was in Egypt ... I in Canaan ... for she was not with me. I did not take another wife... Women... All I ever thought about was returning to Egypt in peace to see the face of my wife.

4Q545

"I had a dream where I saw two Watchers. They were arguing about me, saying... it became a heated argument about me. I asked them why... They answered me, 'We have been made masters of the earth and rule over all the nations of men.' Then they asked me, 'Which one of us do you choose ...' I looked closely at one of them and he looked frightening, like a serpent, and he wore multi-colored clothes, but he was extremely dark... I looked at the other and... his face looked like an adder covered with... both together, and over his eyes...

4Q546

"...this Watcher, 'Who is he?' He answered me saying, 'This Watcher... and his three names are Belial, Prince of Darkness, and Melkiresha[56] I said: 'My Lord, what rule ...' He said to me... '... and all of his paths and all of his works only lead to darkness, and he is... in darkness... He rules over all darkness ... and I rule over all light and all...'

4Q547

"... and I will explain to you your names... that he wrote for Moses, and also about Aaron... I will explain to you the mystery of His worship. He is a holy priest to the Most High God. Also, all of his seed will be holy throughout their generations, eternally... The seventh of the men of (God's) good will he will be called and he will be said ... and will be chosen as a priest forever..."

4Q548

"...I declare the true path to you. I will instruct you... the sons of light will teach truth, and all the sons of darkness will teach deceit. By their knowledge all the sons of light will... but the sons of darkness will be removed... Every wicked fool will flee to the darkness but every righteous sage will seek the light. For all the sons of light will be drawn to the light, but all the sons of darkness will be drawn to death and destruction... They will explain the light to the people..."

Commentary

4Q543 stated that Miriam, the sister of Moses, was married at the age of 30. From the Bible, we know she married Hur.

4Q544 tells that Kohath and a team of cousins went to build the sepulchers at the cave of Macpelah. This is where Sarah and Abraham are buried. A war broke out and the border of Egypt and Canaan was closed for forty-one years. Amram was separated from Jochebed, his wife, all this time. This same thing happened to many Germans while the Berlin wall was up the 28 years, from 1961 to 1989. This story is significant because a legend in the Talmud says Amram divorced his wife. We see here that he never did. Although this error in the Talmud is very understandable under this circumstance, it shows that not everything in the Talmud is true.

4Q545–4Q546 related a dream Amram had about Watchers who were fighting over him for domination of the nations of earth.

4Q547 seems to be teaching the Talmudic legend that all the names of the patriarchs, from Adam through Aaron, are themselves prophetic. He goes further stating that there is a prophetic mystery in the worship rituals and the generations. He then seems to be saying that the seventh from Adam (Enoch) would preserve the teachings for all time. This is either referring to the book of Enoch and/or the writings his forefathers (Adam through Jared).

4Q548 teaches godly people will be drawn to the truth of God's word and desire to study and understand and teach others about Him. Evil people will try to convince others they are righteous, but their deeds will expose them because they have no love for Scriptures.

Testament of Aaron

AARON A – 4Q540-4Q541
Column 1, Fragment 2
"...words... and according to the will of... to me. Once more he wrote... I spoke about them in parables... was close to me. Therefore, ... was far away from me... The vision will be profound... the fruit...

Column 1, Fragment 6
"... deep things... those who do not understand. He wrote... and he calmed the great sea... Then the books of wisdom will be opened... by his word...

Column 2
"... God... You will receive the afflicted... will bless their burnt offerings and You will establish for them a foundation of Your peace... your spirit, and you will rejoice in your God. Now I am speaking to you in parables... rejoice. Behold, wise men will understand the visions and comprehend the deep mysteries, which is why I speak in parables. The Greek... [non-God fearer] will never understand. But the knowledge

of wisdom will come to you, for you have received... you will acquire...
Pursue wisdom and continue to seek her. Let her become a part of you.
Behold, you will make many glad and give them a place...

Column 4

"... His wisdom will be great. He will make atonement for all the children of His generation. He will be sent to all the sons of His [generation]. His word will be as the word of heaven, and His teaching will be in accordance with the will of God. His eternal sun will burn bright. The fire will be kindled in all the corners of the earth. It will shine into the darkness. Then the darkness will vanish from the earth and the deep darkness from the dry land. They will speak many words against Him. There will be numerous lies. They will invent stories about Him. They will say shameful things about Him. He will overthrow His evil generation and there will be great wrath. When He arises, there will be falsehood and violence, and the people will wander astray in His days and be confounded.

Column 5, Fragment 1

"I saw one... I saw seven rams... Some of his sons will walk... They will be gathered to the heavenly beings...

Column 5, Fragment 5

"...and those who are grieved about... your judgment but you will not be guilty... the scourging of those who afflict you... your complaint will not fail and all... your heart...

Column 6

"God will right all the errors... He will reveal and judge sins... Learn fully why Jonah wept. ...will not destroy the weak by wasting away or by crucifixion... Let not the nail touch him. Then you will raise up for your father a name of rejoicing and for all your brothers a firm foundation.

You will understand and rejoice in the eternal light and you will not be one whom God hates."

Commentary

Columns 1 and 2 seem to be about a dream where Aaron needs to be schooled in God's wisdom (from the books of his fathers) to understand the parables in dreams and visions. Those who do not try to study prophecy will never get to a place where they can understand the things of God.

Column 4 seems to continue with a description of the Messiah. When He comes, Aaron's descendants will turn on Him with lies and violence. Those who reject Messiah will wander in confusion.

Column 5 seems to be a part of a vision where Aaron's descendants are divided into seven categories. Some walk in a godly manner and others do not. The godly will be "gathered" to heaven.

Column 6 continues teaching about Messiah. God will right all the errors through Him by crucifixion. If you do not want to be hated by God, accept Him and have no part in His crucifixion.

7

PROPHECY OUTLINE

Messiah is the Son of God (L4)

Messiah is God incarnate (S6,7; Z9; N8; As7; B10)

Levi's priesthood is only until Messiah (R6; L4,5; B9)

Levi's ordinances and sacrifices are only until Messiah (R6)

Tribes rebel against Judah and Levi (R6; D5)

Messiah is the seed of Judah (R6; Ju24; G8)

Messiah is virgin-born (Jo19)

We worship the Messiah (R6)

Messiah is an everlasting King (R6; Jo19)

Messiah dies for us (R6)

Physical resurrection (S6; Ju25; Z10; B10)

Messiah brings salvation (S6; L4; As7; Jo19; B3)

Levites crucify the Messiah (L4,16; Aa4,6; B9)

There will be two expulsions (L15; Z9; N4; As7)

Messiah resurrects (L16)

Messiah ascends (L18)

Messiah creates a new priesthood (L18; Aa4)

Book of Enoch mentioned (L16; Ju18; Z3; N4; B9)

The Writings of the Fathers existed (Z9; K2)

Messiah appears in Zebulun (Z9)

New Jerusalem mentioned (D5)

Old Jerusalem mentioned (Ja2)

The Watchers mentioned (N3)

Messiah's priesthood is eternal (Am-4Q547; Aa4)

Veil of the Temple Rent (B9)

Legend: **Ja**cob, **R**euben, **S**imeon, **L**evi, **Ju**dah, **I**ssachar, **Z**ebulun, **D**an, **N**aphtali, **G**ad, **As**her, **Jo**seph, **B**enjamin, **K**ohath, **Am**ram, **Aa**ron

The Messianic prophecies that occur numerous times throughout the testaments are given in the above chart. Now we want to focus our attention on the more complex prophecies.

Levi 4 seems to teach that the prophecy in Genesis 12:3 refers to the Messiah.

And I will bless them that bless thee, and curse him that curseth thee: and in thee will all families of the earth be blessed. (Genesis 12:3)

Levi instructs his sons to teach about the coming Messiah that those who "bless Him will be blessed, but those who curse Him will perish."

In Levi 8, Levi is given a prophecy in which he is told that there will be three different priesthoods. The last one is a priesthood that the Messiah brings. It states the Messiah will be a "King from Judah, and will establish a new priesthood, after the fashion of the Gentiles, to all the Gentiles."

This sounds like somewhere in the genealogy Jesus is not only a direct descendant of Judah through David but also a descendant of Levi. Elisabeth, the mother of John the Baptist, was a Levite and she was also a cousin of Mary, Jesus' mother.

Levi 18 teaches the Messiah's children (true believers) will have power over evil spirits.

Benjamin 9 states that the Messiah is the only begotten of God and He will be lifted up on a tree. The Essenes were to look for the sign of the veil in the temple being supernaturally rent, or torn in two. This was foretold to be a sign that the priesthood had rejected the Messiah and that God was then rejecting the priesthood. Once the Essenes saw the fulfillment of that particular sign, they no longer offered sacrifices in the Jerusalem temple. The Messiah was to be buried, resurrect, and ascend. Afterwards, the Spirit of God would be poured out on all believers (Gentiles included) in the form of fire.

Judah 24 says the Messiah is a root of Jacob (called a star, branch, and rod) and the ruler over the righteous Gentiles, saving everyone who calls on the Lord.

Simeon 7 teaches that the Messiah will be both king and priest; but says it in such a way that you cannot tell if it is two messiahs, or one messiah who holds both offices simultaneously. We know now that it was one messiah holding two offices. This might have been the reason that some first century BC rabbis thought there would be two messiahs: King Messiah, a son of David, and Priest Messiah, a son of Joseph.

Amram (4Q547) gives the impression that the names of the patriarchs are themselves a prophecy and starts to reveal what their names mean (including Moses and Aaron) and how they relate to the Messiah's priesthood. He then reveals that Enoch, the seventh from Adam, preserved the prophecies and history in his book and the books of his forefathers.

Naphtali 5 predicts that there will be seven kingdoms that will rule over Israel until the time of the Messiah. These are listed as the Assyrians, Medes, Persians, [Elamites, Gelachæans,] Chaldeans, and Syrians. The Elamites and Gelachæans are not listed in some manuscripts. We know that Israel was ruled over by Egypt, Assyria, Babylon, the Medes and Persians together, the Grecian Seludian kingdom headquartered in Syria, and then Rome. They will later be ruled over by the ten nations described in Daniel and Revelation.

According the Geoffrey Keating, one of the few surviving Gaelic historians, the Gaelic and Hebrew languages were very similar right after the fall of the tower of Babel. See Ancient Post-Flood History, chapter 13 for details. The word "Gelach" in Gaelic means the moon. So, in this vision, Gelachæans could mean "moon people." This is significant because a very similar prophecy is found in the Book of Gad the Seer, chapters 1-2. In those chapters the moon represents the Jewish kingdom, which is usurped by two anti-Semitic powers represented by a donkey and camel. These are defined as the end times religious powers of Islam and Roman Catholicism.

Could the ten nations of Daniel and Revelation be comprised of nations that are strictly Roman Catholic and Islamic?

8

THE JUBILEE PROPHECY

One of the most interesting prophecies is given in Levi 16–17. Levi 16 states that there is a seventy-weeks prophecy given in the book of Enoch, which we do not have. During this four hundred and ninety years, all of Israel will go astray. The priesthood will become profane, the sacrifices polluted, and the law corrupted. The four gospels show that the priesthood was indeed corrupt and the law was twisted into what the corrupt priesthood wanted it to mean. Many times Jesus rebuked the Sadducees and Pharisees over these kinds of issues. They did call the Messiah a deceiver. Jesus was crucified and the nation of Israel was desolated.

Levi 17 shows the specifics of how and when this would happen. The school of Elijah taught human time was divided into three sets of two-thousand-year periods known as ages. There was the age of Chaos, from Creation to the call of Abraham. The second age was called the age of Torah, extending from the call of Abraham to the dissolving of the sacrificial system. The third age was called the Messianic age. Christians call this the Church Age. After the Messianic age, there was to be a one-thousand-year period of a Messianic Kingdom. Christians call this the Millennial Reign. Each age is broken up into periods of five-hundred years called Onahs (see the Hebrew commentary on the Epistle of Elijah entitled the Tana Eliyahu for details). Levi described the events that occur in the last five-hundred-year period of the age of Torah. It is divided into ten jubilees of fifty years each. In the last jubilee of the previous five-hundred-year period, Nehemiah (Nehemiah 2:1-8) gained permission from Artaxerxes to rebuild Jerusalem. This was in 444 BC. Here is a timetable for the jubilees from Levi 17.

Jub.	Date	
	587 BC	1st Temple Destroyed
	517 BC	2nd Temple Dedicated
	444 BC	Artaxerxes' decree (70 weeks prophecy – Daniel 9)
1	425-375 BC	
2	375-325 BC	
3	325-275 BC	
4	275-225 BC	
5	225-175 BC	
6	175-125 BC	Antiochus Epiphanes 163 BC
7	125-75 BC	Week five, 96-89 BC – Civil War Week seven, 82-75 BC – Corrupt priests arise
8	75-25 BC	Herod the Great 37 BC
9	25 BC - 25 AD	

10	25-75 AD	Week one, AD 25-32
		    Messiah crucified AD 32
		Week seven, AD 68-75
		    Sacrifices abolished ~ Council of Yavneh AD 75

The important thing to note is that the priesthood was restored after the Babylonian captivity, but began to fall apart jubilee by jubilee. He predicts some form of war, dispersion, and a return to sanctify the temple in the fifth week of the seventh Jubilee. This fifth week is exactly the same time period as the civil war between the Sadducees and Pharisees.

We know we have the jubilees dated correctly, not only because it agrees with the timetable of the destruction of Solomon's temple being 3338AM and 587 BC, but because of another Dead Sea Scroll called the 11QMelchizedek (see *Conclusion: Related Dead Sea Scrolls* for the translation). In column 2 of this work, it states that the coming Messiah will fulfill several prophecies, including when Daniel 9 says He would come. It says, "This event will take place in the first week of the jubilee that occurs after the ninth jubilee." In AD 70 the Jerusalem temple was destroyed. In AD 73 Titus destroyed the Jewish temple in Alexandria, Egypt (see Josephus Wars 7). Two years later, in AD 75, we have the first council of Yavneh where the Sanhedrin ruled that there was no more need for a temple and sacrificial system. God put it into their hearts to end an age as He predicted! Now, AD 75 minus a fifty-year jubilee would bring the close of the ninth jubilee to AD 25. One Shemittah (week of years) later would be (25+7) AD 32, the year the Messiah was crucified!

It is most important that we focus on weeks five and seven of the seventh jubilee. After Judah Maccabee led the successful revolt against Antiochus Epiphanes in 165 BC, his successors started the Hasmonean Dynasty. When both the Seleucid and Roman Empires recognized Israel as an independent nation in 110 BC, John Hyrcanus started a campaign of conquest of neighboring nations. He ruled as king and high priest which was forbidden. The Jews who supported the high priest king and the idea of priestly rule became known as Sadducees. Their name was taken from Zadok the priest. Dissenters arose who believed the king did not have the right to force non-Jews to convert to Judaism and be circumcised. They were known as separatists, or Pharisees in Hebrew.

In 103 BC, Alexander Jannaeus became the next Hasmonean ruler. He not only continued the idea of priestly rule and forcing all Jews and Gentiles to be circumcised, but all Jews and Gentiles must follow the priestly code. This command led to the Pharisees' rebellion. The Pharisees believed that the law of priests was only meant for priests and not common Jews or Gentiles. They said the king had no right to force conversion or require non-priests to follow the priestly code. This plunged Israel in to an eight-year civil war, from 96-88 BC.

During the intense persecution of the Pharisees, Simeon ben Shetach, a Pharisee and Nasi (president of the Sanhedrin), fled to safety in Alexandria, Egypt, where he met two men Shmya and Abtalion, who were natives of Alexandria, but direct descendants of the king of Assyria. They were converted to Judaism. The persecution ended; and he returned to Jerusalem. When his sister, Queen Salome of Alexandria, became the next Hasmonean Ruler, Simeon and the Pharisees became very powerful. Simeon ben Shetach started mandatory Torah schools replacing the long-standing rule that the fathers teach their sons the Torah. All children were required to attend these schools for proper indoctrination. He then brought his two Assyrian converts to Jerusalem and they succeeded him as rulers in the Sanhedrin. They changed the standard way of interpreting Torah and replaced it with what would become known as Midrashic interpretation. They were the first "Darshan", or preachers. Their new method of Torah interpretation was called "Derush," or oral tradition. From this point forward, legal rulings of the Sanhedrin were binding on all, and were to be enforced for all future generations.

A new denomination emerged from this called the Essenes. They agreed with the Pharisees that forced conversion and forced observance of the priestly code by non-priests was wrong. However, they disagreed with the new doctrine that the tradition of "Oral Torah" was equal to the written Torah. They believed no one had the power to go against the written Torah and the written histories of the forefathers.

Levi 17 says in the seventh week priests would come that would bring great corruption. Dead Sea Scroll 4Q385a says that this would be three priests, and 4Q387 says that by the end of the tenth jubilee, "all of Israel would be walking in madness." I believe these priests were Simeon ben Shetach, Shmya, and Abtalion.

Conclusion: Related Dead Sea Scrolls

The following Dead Sea Scrolls provide a more in-depth look at Bible prophecy from the Essenes' point of view. Like Christians, Essenes believed these prophecies are fulfilled by the Messiah. Pharisees disagreed.

11QMelchizedek Column 2

"Moses said, 'In the year of the jubilee, each of you will be freed to return home [Lev. 25:13]' and he described how, saying, 'Now this is the manner of the release: Let every creditor remit what he has lent his neighbor. He shall not press his neighbor or his brother for repayment, for the LORD›s release has been proclaimed [Deut. 15:2].' Its interpretation pertains to the end of days. The captives Moses speaks of are those whom Isaiah says 'To proclaim freedom to the captives [Isa 61:1].' Its interpretation is that the LORD will assign those freed to the sons of heaven and the lot of Melchizedek. Even those, whose teachers had deliberately hidden and kept secret from them the truth about their inheritance through Melchizedek. The LORD will cast their lot amid the portions of Melchizedek, who will make them return [or repent] and will proclaim freedom to them, to free them from the debt of all their iniquities. This event will take place in the first week of the jubilee that occurs after the ninth jubilee.

"Now the Day of Atonement is the end of the tenth jubilee, when atonement (is made) for all the sons of heaven, for the men of the lot of Melchizedek... It is the time of Melchizedek's 'Day of Grace.' He will, by His strength, raise up the holy ones of God to execute judgment as it has been written concerning Him in the songs of David, as it says, 'Elohim stands in the divine assembly, in the midst of Elohim He judges [Ps 82:1].' He said, 'Above it, to the heights, return. El will judge the nations [Ps 7:8–9].' When he said, 'How long will you judge unjustly and show impartiality to the wicked? Selah [Ps 82:2].' Its interpretation concerns Belial and the spirits of his lot who turn away from the commandments of El in wickedness. Melchizedek will exact the vengeances of the judgments of El...

"This is the 'Day of Peace' about which God spoke through Isaiah the prophet [52:7] who said, 'How beautiful on the mountains are the feet of the Messenger who proclaims peace, the Messenger of good who proclaims salvation, saying to Zion, "Your God reigns!"' Its interpretation is that the mountains are prophets' predictions about the Messenger and the Messenger is the one anointed of the Spirit about whom Daniel said, 'Until Messiah, the Prince, (there will be) seven weeks [Dan 9:25].' He is the Messenger of good who proclaims salvation. He is the one about whom it is written, when it says, 'to comfort those who mourn... [Isa 61:2-3],' to 'instruct them in all the ages of the world in truth.'

"Zion is those who uphold the covenant, those who turn aside from walking in the ways of the people. But 'your God' is Melchizedek, who will save them from the hand of Belial. As for that which he has said, 'You will blow the signal-horn in the seventh month [Lev 23:24 or 25:9].' ...the divisions of the times...

4Q385a Fragment 5

"...three priests who will not walk in the ways of the former priests, who completely followed the God of Israel. In their days, pride will cause many to act wickedly against the covenant and become the slaves of foreign things. Israel will be rent asunder in that generation, each man fighting against his neighbor over the Torah and the Covenant. I will send hunger upon the land, but not for bread or water, but to hear the Word of the Lord."

4Q387

"...at the completion of ten jubilees, Israel will be walking in madness..."

4Q252 Col. 5

"'The scepter shall not depart from the tribe of Judah [Gen. 49:10].' The interpretation is while Israel has self-rule, there will not be anyone cut off who sits on the throne of David, for 'the staff' represents the covenant of kingship, and 'the standards' are the thousands of Israel. …until the Messiah of righteousness comes, the branch of David [Isa. 11:1-2; Zech. 3:8], for to Him and His children have been given the covenant of the kingship of His people for everlasting generations… it is the assembly of the men of…"

Florilegium

"Yahweh declares that He will build a house for David, and He shall set up his seed after him, and shall establish his royal throne forever. 'I shall be to him as a father, and he will be to Me as a son [2 Sam. 7:13-14].' He is 'the Shoot of David' who will arise with the Interpreter of the Law, who… in Zion in the last days; as it is written, 'And I shall raise up the tabernacle of David that is fallen [Amos 9:11; Acts 15:16].' That 'tabernacle of David that is fallen' is He who will arise to save Israel…

"'Why do the nations rage and the peoples imagine a vain thing? The kings of the earth set themselves, and the rulers take counsel together against the LORD and against His Messiah [Psalm 2:1-2].' The interpretation of the passage is that the nations and rulers will come against the Elect of Israel in the last days. This will be a 'time of trial' that is coming … as it is written in the book of Daniel the prophet, 'For the wicked to act wickedly [Dan. 11:32], the righteous shall make themselves white and purify themselves [Dan. 11:35],' and 'a people knowing God will seize [Dan. 11:32] …' The interpretation is after the… when he goes down from."

PART 3

ANCIENT ORDER
OF
MELCHIZEDEK

~

INTRODUCTION

M any people ask, "Who was Melchizedek mentioned in Genesis 14? And why did he bless Abraham?"

In this book we will discover that the original priests God created through Adam, were both kings and priests. When anointed with the Holy Spirit, they were also prophets. These king-priest-prophets were called Melchizedekian priests.

We will look at the history, theology, and prophecy of the Melchizedekian priests from many sources. These will include books of the Bible (Genesis and the Psalms), Jewish history books (the Ancient Book of Jasher and Josephus), Dead Sea Scroll Testaments (authored by Noah, Levi, Kohath, Amram, Aaron, and others), other Dead Sea Scrolls (Enoch, Jubilees, 4QMelchizedek, and others), and documents from Elijah's School of the Prophets. We will also look at what the early church fathers taught about the Melchizedekian priesthood.

We will learn how Jacob split up the Melchizedekian priesthood into three parts. The kings of Israel would come through his son Judah, the priests through his son Levi, and the birthright (prophetical line) would go to Joseph. This was to continue until the Messiah would come and reestablish the Melchizedekian priesthood. During the dispensation of Moses, God judged any king of Israel who tried to reestablish the Melchizedekian priesthood by adding the priesthood to his office. This amounted to saying that he was the promised Messiah.

When John the Baptist (who was of the priestly line of Zadok) baptized Jesus (who was a direct descendant of King David) into the priesthood, and the Holy Spirit came upon Him, this reestablished the long-lost Melchizedekian priesthood.

We will break this study up into three parts: Melchizedekian history, Melchizedekian theology, and Melchizedekian prophecy.

In the first section, we will pull together all the information we can gather about the history and practice of the ten Melchizedekian priests who have walked the earth.

In the second part, we will concentrate on the theology. What does all of this mean to Christians and Jews and what does it have to do with our salvation? We will do in-depth studies of Hebrews 5-8, Psalm 110, and the Epistles of Peter, Paul, and John.

In the last section, we will concentrate on the prophecies about the reestablishment of the Melchizedekian priesthood and the Messiah from the Dead Sea Scrolls themselves.

9

WHAT IS A MELCHIZEDEKIAN PRIEST?

The Apostle Paul gives the definition of the word "Melchizedek" in the book of Hebrews.

> To whom also Abraham gave a tenth part of all; first being by interpretation King of Righteousness, and after that also King of Salem, which is, King of peace. (Hebrews 7:2)

The Hebrew word "melek" means "king" and the Hebrew word "zedek" means "righteous." Melchizedek is properly translated as "King of Righteousness." The word Melchizedek can also be translated as "King of the Zadok priests."

The priests who lived in Qumran were direct descendants of the Jewish high priest Zadok. They were priests of righteousness. They were waiting for the Teacher of Righteousness to come. This righteous teacher, or Zadok teacher, was the Messiah.

First, we need to see that there was a real person named Levi. He was one of the twelve sons of Jacob and became the father of the tribe of Levi. Only his descendants can be Levitical priests. So, there is a priestly "Order of Levi." Levi's son was Kohath. Kohath's son was

Amram. Amram had two sons, Moses and Aaron. Aaron became the first high priest of the nation of Israel after the Egyptian Exodus. Only direct descendants of Aaron can be Aaronic priests. So, there is a priestly "Order of Aaron." There is also a priestly "Order of Melchizedek."

The Apostle Paul stated that Jesus was ordained after the Order of Melchizedek, not the Order of Aaron or the Order of Levi. Jesus is a Melchizedekian priest, not an Aaronic priest or Levitical priest. Some have tried to teach that the Melchizedekian priest who appeared to Abraham was a Christophany, a pre-incarnate appearance of Jesus Christ. But they fail to see that Jesus became a priest after the order of Melchizedek.

...even Jesus, having become a high priest forever after the order of Melchizedek. (Hebrews 6:20 MKJV)

What modern Rabbis teach about Melchizedek comes from the Talmud, which is also called the "oral law." Jesus called this the "tradition of the elders." This teaching says there was no "Order of Melchizedek." Melchizedek was the name of a man who happened to be a priest of the Most High God.

On the contrary, the Dead Sea Scrolls teach there never was a man named Melchizedek. Melchizedek was an order of priests.

The Levitical and Aaronic priests were just priests. The apostle Paul teaches that any kind of priest is a human picked to intercede with God on behalf of other people. The Melchizedekian priests were a combination of priest, king, and prophet.

The Dead Sea Scrolls give us many details about the history and practice of the ten Melchizedekian priests ranging from Adam to the Messiah, Jesus Christ.

10

MELCHIZEDEKIAN HISTORY

The Pre-Flood World

According to ancient sources, Adam was the first king-priest-prophet. In this chapter we will trace the history of the Melchizedekian priests from Adam down to Noah. Here is their history.

Adam

Scripture says that God created Adam and gave him dominion over all the earth. This makes him king over the entire earth.

> And God said, Let us make man in our image, after our likeness: and let them have dominion over the fish of the sea, and over the fowl of the air, and over the cattle, and over all the earth, and over every creeping thing that creepeth upon the earth. So God created man in His own image, in the image of God created He him; male and female created He them. And God blessed them, and God said unto them, Be fruitful, and multiply, and replenish the earth, and subdue it: and have dominion over the fish of the sea, and over the fowl of the air, and over every living thing that moveth upon the earth. (Genesis 1:26–28)

We know God talked with Adam and revealed to him that there was a need for a savior. God told him one of his descendants would be that savior.

> And I will put enmity between thee and the woman, and between thy seed and her seed; it shall bruise thy head, and thou shalt bruise His heel. (Genesis 3:15)

Jewish historian Josephus stated that God revealed to Adam there would be times of an apostasy followed by a destruction of the earth. Adam recorded this in his Testament. We do not have the Testament of Adam in its entirety from the Dead Sea Scrolls, but we have fragments of most of the testaments. Adam testified that destruction would happen once by a flood of water and once by fire, but apparently he was unsure which would occur first. Josephus records that Adam said:

> The world was to be destroyed at one time by the force of fire, and at another time by the violence and quantity of water. (Josephus' Antiquities 1.2.3)

Adam was the king and a prophet, but was he also a priest? Genesis gives us a clue to answer this question. Moses records that both Cain and Abel knew a blood sacrifice was required, performed in a certain manner, at a predetermined place and time.

> And in process of time it came to pass, that Cain brought of the fruit of the ground an offering unto the LORD. And Abel, he also brought of the firstlings of his flock and of the fat thereof. And the LORD had respect unto Abel and to his offering. (Genesis 4:3, 4)

The phrase "process of time" is thought to be an idiom. The Hebrew literally says, "after the end of the day." It is thought to indicate the year's end. The meaning is that at the appointed day (New Year's Day, Nisan 1), and place (the entrance to Eden), every male priest would return and give a blood sacrifice. The question here is: where did Abel and Cain learn to give a proper blood offering and a proper grain offering? This would either be from God Himself or from Adam. In either case, we see the priesthood here in the text.

Seth

After Cain murdered Abel and fled, it was obvious that neither of them would be the next Melchizedekian priest-king. When Adam was one hundred and thirty years old, he had a son whom he named Seth. This would be the Jewish year 130 AM. Seth was righteous, but there was no indication that Seth was to be the promised Messiah or the next King of Righteousness.

Enos

When Seth was one hundred and five years old, he had a son whom he named Enos. This would have been 235 AM. Enos was godly, but it is recorded that in his days there was an apostasy.

> And it was in the days of Enosh [Enos] that the sons of men continued to rebel and transgress against God, to increase the anger of the Lord against the sons of men. And the sons of men went and they served other gods, and they forgot the Lord who had created them in the earth: and in those days the sons of men made images of brass and iron, wood and stone, and they bowed down and served them. And every man made his god and they bowed down to them, and the sons of men forsook the Lord all the days of Enosh and his children; and the anger of the Lord was kindled on account of their works and abominations which they did in the earth. (Ancient Book of Jasher 2:3–5)

Cainan

When Enos was ninety years old, he had a son whom he named Cainan. This would have been 325 AM. When Cainan was forty years old, in 365 AM, he became wise in the things of God and prophecy. He understood that the water destruction would come first. He was just not sure when it would happen. Notice that Cainan wrote these things down in his testament.

> And Cainan grew up and he was forty years old, and he became wise and had knowledge and skill in all wisdom, and he reigned over all the sons of men, and he led the sons of men to wisdom and knowledge.... And Cainan knew by his wisdom that God would destroy the sons of men for having sinned upon earth, and that the Lord would in the latter days bring upon them the waters of the flood. And in those days Cainan wrote upon tablets of stone, what was to take place in time to come, and he put them in his treasures. (Ancient Book of Jasher 2:11–13)

God sent minor floods and pestilences to get the people's attention; and then God used Cainan to start a revival. Seeing God's hand on Cainan, Adam made him the second king of the earth, the second King of Righteousness.

> Cainan reigned over the whole earth, and he turned some of the sons of men to the service of God. (Ancient Book of Jasher 2:14)

The revival seems to be short lived. Cainan had a son whom he named Mahalaleel. Mahalaleel was born in 395 AM. Jasher says,

> For in those days the sons of men began to trespass against God, and to transgress the commandments which he had commanded to Adam. (Ancient Book of Jasher 2:19)

Enoch

While things were getting worse and worse with most of the people on earth, Mahalaleel had a son whom he named Jared and Jared had a son whom he named Enoch. Enoch was born in 622 AM. When Enoch grew up, he wholly followed the ways of the Lord and led another revival. Enoch's revival was much more successful than that of Cainan. Seeing God's hand move so mightily through Enoch, he was made the third King of Righteousness in 687 AM.

> Enoch reigned over the sons of men two hundred and forty-three years, and he did justice and righteousness with all his people, and he led them in the ways of the Lord. (Ancient Book of Jasher 3:12)

Notice how a true man of God will gladly step down if it fulfills prophecy. We should all be glad to be a part of God's plan, but be mindful to never be in a position of standing in His way.

God gave Enoch a prophecy that the Messiah would come seventy generations from his time. See Ancient Book of Enoch 10. Luke 3:23–38 verifies that Jesus Christ is the seventieth generation from Enoch.

Most followed Enoch, but not completely. Slowly he began to withdraw from political life and spend more and more time alone with God. In 987 AM, God raptured Enoch as the Scripture says:

> And Enoch walked with God: and he was not; for God took him. (Genesis 5:24)

Enoch was an amazing prophet. He named his son Methuselah. That name is made up of two Hebrew words: "meth" meaning "death" and "selah" meaning "to send." These two words put together form a Hebrew sentence. Methuselah's name means "when he is dead, it shall be sent." If you look carefully at the genealogical records given in Genesis

5, Jasher 5–6, and the Seder Olam 1, it is clear that Methuselah died in the year of the flood.

Methuselah

After Enoch's rapture, his son Methuselah was made the next King of Righteousness.

> All the days that Enoch lived upon earth, were three hundred and sixty-five years. And when Enoch had ascended into heaven, all the kings of the earth rose and took Methuselah his son and anointed him, and they caused him to reign over them in the place of his father. And Methuselah acted uprightly in the sight of God, as his father Enoch had taught him, and he likewise during the whole of his life taught the sons of men wisdom, knowledge and the fear of God, and he did not turn from the good way either to the right or to the left. (Ancient Book of Jasher 4:1–3)

But it was not long until another apostasy came, and the people turned away from God and His ways.

> But in the latter days of Methuselah, the sons of men turned from the Lord, they corrupted the earth, they robbed and plundered each other, and they rebelled against God and they transgressed, and they corrupted their ways, and would not hearken to the voice of Methuselah, but rebelled against him. (Ancient Book of Jasher 4:4)

Methuselah had a son whom he called Lamech. Lamech then had a son whom he named Noah. Noah was born in 1056 AM. We are not told much of Lamech, but Jewish legends state he was not very godly. Methuselah knew by inspiration of the Holy Spirit that his grandson,

Noah, would be the one. Not the Messiah who would be seventy generations from his father Enoch, but that Noah would be the next King of Righteousness.

Noah

Noah grew up and followed the ways of God as taught by his grandfather Methuselah. Noah was given all the patriarchal writings from Adam to his time. During this time even the descendants of Seth became corrupt.

> Now this posterity of Seth continued to esteem God as the Lord of the universe, and to have an entire regard to virtue, for seven generations; but in process of time they were perverted, and forsook the practices of their forefathers; and did neither pay those honors to God which were appointed them, nor had they any concern to do justice towards men. But for what degree of zeal they had formerly shown for virtue, they now showed by their actions a double degree of wickedness, whereby they made God to be their enemy. (Josephus' Antiquities 1.3.1)

In 1536 AM, God gave Noah a prophecy that man had one hundred and twenty years to repent or the flood judgment would occur. Methuselah and Noah preached repentance for the entire one-hundred-and-twenty-year period.

As a side note, you know neither of these two godly men was stupid. After only a few years I think they realized there would be no revival this time. But they did not stop because it was useless. Instead they continued, at least, to be an example of righteousness and a witness for future generations. If you are a minister and see no fruit yet, realize it is not your job to save people. It is your job to be a witness for Him. Do not stop doing what God has called you to do because you do not understand what is going on. Just be a witness.

Noah records in his Testament that he was told he would be the next King of Righteousness after the flood.

> You will govern the entire earth; all that is upon it, including the mountains and the seas. (Testament of Noah, Col. 7)

In column 10 of the Testament of Noah, Noah describes the offering he did as a priest. The atonement offering was a goat. The thank offering was an ox, ram, sheep, and turtledoves with salt. The meal offering was with wheat, oil and incense. This incense was most likely frankincense. So again, we see king, priest, and prophet in one person. This is a Melchizedekian priest.

> I atoned for the whole earth. First, I offered a male goat... afterward I burned the fat upon the fire. Second, I offered a thank offering consisting of ox, ram, and sheep. Then I poured out all of their blood on the base of the altar, and burned all of their flesh on the altar. Third, I offered the young turtledoves (flesh and blood) with them upon the altar. Then I offered fine wheat flour, mixed together with oil containing incense, for their meal offerings. I said a blessing, and was putting salt on all of them, and the scent of my offering rose up to the heavens. (Testament of Noah, Col. 10)

The Flood occurred in 1656 AM. The fragments of the Testament of Noah that were found in the Dead Sea Scrolls reveal some interesting details for our study.

In column 8 it is written that Noah had the "written accounts" of the patriarchs with him aboard the ark.

At this point we have the preflood list of Melchizedekian priests, or king-priest-prophets. These include:

Adam,

Cainan,

Enoch,
Methuselah, and
Noah.

Conclusion

At the time of the Flood we have Noah, the fifth King of Righteousness (priest, king, and prophet) taking with him aboard the Ark all the
patriarchal testaments. He knew the Messiah would come seventy generations after Enoch, which would be sixty-six generations after one of
his three children. Which one of his children would the Messiah come
from? He did not know. But he knew that through one of them a
descendant would come to create a great nation that would usher in the
reign of the Messiah.

The Flood to Abraham

After spending an entire year in the Ark, Noah and his family went out
from the Ark in Nisan of the Jewish year 1657 AM.

> And it came to pass in the six hundredth and first year, in the
> first month, the first day of the month, the waters were dried
> up from off the earth: and Noah removed the covering of the
> ark, and looked, and, behold, the face of the ground was dry.
> (Genesis 8:13)

After they left the Ark, Noah did sacrifice to God as we detailed in
the last chapter.

> And on the new moon of the third month he went forth from
> the ark, and built an altar on that mountain [Lubar]. And
> he made atonement for the earth, and took a kid and made

atonement by its blood for all the guilt of the earth. (Ancient Book of Jubilees 6:1, 2)

And Noah builded an altar unto the LORD; and took of every clean beast, and of every clean fowl, and offered burnt offerings on the altar. (Genesis 8:20)

After Noah's sacrifice, God made a covenant with him and his sons. This is recorded in Genesis 9. It is referred to as the Rainbow Covenant, but it is properly called the Noahide Covenant. God promised not to destroy the earth again with water and set the rainbow in the sky as a sign of the covenant between God and all of the Gentile nations (His creatures). God then instructed Noah to teach his sons to observe what became known as the Seven Noahide Laws.

They were commanded to spread out over the earth and create nations. Each Gentile nation was to create courts of justice, and to punish murder, theft, fornication, idolatry, and blasphemy. They were to add other laws as they saw fit for their individual countries, but never abolish the seven fundamental laws. Blasphemy was defined as not believing everything the prophets said about sin, salvation, and the coming Messiah. Most Gentile nations quickly became idolatrous and forgot the teachings of the prophets.

The Testament of Noah reveals that Noah had a prophetic dream about the end of his age. There would be an apostasy, an Antichrist figure, and one who would begin the holy nation who would usher in the prophesied Messiah.

Columns 13 through 15 of the Testament of Noah contain the dream. It is heavily fragmented, but we will recreate the clear parts here.

Noah saw a small cedar tree that grew into a large tree and filled the earth. He was told in the dream that he, as king of the earth, was that tree. Other Dead Sea Scrolls teach that cedar trees represent Gentile nations. This mighty tree had three large branches that blossomed out. These represented Noah's three sons: Shem, Ham, and Japheth.

The third branch had two small shoots that broke off and left the large branch. They went up to one of the other branches and started attacking it. They almost destroyed the upper branch, but a small twig from the upper branch separated itself and became an olive vine. The olive vine always represents the nation of believing Israel. This olive vine destroyed the attacking branches.

> With one branch separating from it and becoming an olive tree means the first son will not separate from you for all his days, and among his seed your name will be called. (Ancient Testament of Noah, Col. 14)

Shem was to be the next King of Righteousness and guard against the coming invasion and apostasy. Shem would not be able to stop it, just slow it down and save those whom he could. Before the apostasy would be complete, one would arise from his seed and destroy the apostate kingdom.

There are other parts to the dream, but this will suffice for our study. The obvious interpretation is that the two evil twigs were Nimrod and Canaan. They invaded Shem's portion and came together to form a one-world empire and a one-world religion. Then God used Abraham to form the nation of Israel and through them the Messiah would eventually come.

> Then I, Noah, awoke. It was morning and I blessed the everlasting God. I quickly went to Shem, my son, and told him everything, that through him the Righteous One would come, and that he had to preserve the knowledge and become the next priest of the Most High God. (Ancient Testament of Noah, Col. 15)

Noah ordained Shem to be the sixth Melchizedekian priest of the Most High God. Shem's son was Arphaxad, his grandson was Salah, and his great-grandson was Eber. Eber was born in 1723 AM, sixty-seven years after the Flood. His heart was perfect before the Lord his God. Was he to be the next King of Righteousness? Shem should wait until he could be sure. If God told Shem directly to anoint Eber as the next King of Righteousness he would, or if he witnessed Eber fulfilling the prophecy by destroying the apostasy, then he could be sure. But the growing apostasy was not yet full.

Shem and Eber kept the ancient records of their fathers that Noah had brought aboard the Ark and they wrote the historical records of their time. In time Eber was given a vision that a series of earthquakes would occur to further separate the nations. When Eber had his son, he named him Peleg which means "earthquake" in Hebrew.

Peleg's son was Reu, his grandson was Serug, his great-grandson was Nahor, and his great-great-grandson was Terah. Terah was born in 1878 AM. By now it was looking like the apostasy would not be fully developed and destroyed by a descendant of Shem until the end of the age (the year 2000 AM). But Shem had to live long enough to ordain the next King of Righteousness. Nimrod was born in 1908 AM. Nimrod was the son of Cush, and the grandson of Ham. By 1920 AM, Canaan already had a stronghold in Shem's land and Nimrod started attacking some of the Japhethites who lived at the most eastern parts of Shem's kingdom. By 1940 AM he had seized the throne of what would later be called Babylon, and welcomed the Canaanites under his rule.

> Now it was Nimrod who excited them to such an affront and contempt of God. He was the grandson of Ham, the son of Noah, a bold man, and of great strength of hand. He persuaded them not to ascribe it to God, as if it was through his means they were happy, but to believe that it was their own courage which procured that happiness. He also gradually changed the government into tyranny, seeing no other way of turning men from the fear of God, but to bring them into a constant depen-

dence on his power. He also said he would be revenged on God, if he should have a mind to drown the world again; for that he would build a tower too high for the waters to be able to reach! and that he would avenge himself on God for destroying their forefathers! (Josephus' Antiquities 1.4.2)

Nimrod not only changed the government into a tyranny but instituted a pagan religious system involving ancestor worship and religious rites connected with certain star patterns in the Zodiac.

Nimrod became an undisputed ruler and he made Terah a general in his army. When Terah was seventy years old, in 1948 AM, he had a son whom he called Abram. A prophecy was given at Abram's birth that he and his descendants would destroy Nimrod's kingdom.

Nimrod ordered the boy's death, but Terah secretly hid Abram until he was able to send him to the house of Noah which was still outside of Nimrod's reach.

And Abram was in Noah's house thirty-nine years, and Abram knew the Lord from three years old, and he went in the ways of the Lord until the day of his death, as Noah and his son Shem had taught him; and all the sons of the earth in those days greatly transgressed against the Lord, and they rebelled against him and they served other gods, and they forgot the Lord who had created them in the earth; and the inhabitants of the earth made unto themselves, at that time, every man his god; gods of wood and stone which could neither speak, hear, nor deliver, and the sons of men served them and they became their gods. (Ancient Book of Jasher 9:6)

When Abram was forty-nine years old, he went back to the house of his father. Abram convinced Terah to leave the idols and follow the Most Hight God. This angered Nimrod who sought to kill Abram. Abram and his family, along with Terah and many people, fled from Nimrod and went to dwell in the city of Haran.

Nimrod would have pursued him to kill the entire group, but in 1997 AM, the providence of Elam led by Chedorlaomer rebelled against Nimrod. With Nimrod's full attention to this war, Abram and his people were left alone. At the end of the first age, 2000 AM, Nimrod had this dream.

> The king fell asleep and dreamed that he was standing with his troops and hosts in a valley opposite the king's furnace. And he lifted up his eyes and saw a man in the likeness of Abram coming forth from the furnace, and that he came and stood before the king with his drawn sword, and then sprang to the king with his sword. When the king fled from the man, for he was afraid and while he was running, the man threw an egg upon the king's head, and the egg became a great river. And the king dreamed that all his troops sank in that river and died. And the king took flight with three men who were before him and he escaped. And the king looked at these men and they were clothed in princely dresses as the garments of kings, and had the appearance and majesty of kings. And while they were running, the river again turned to an egg before the king, and there came forth from the egg a young bird which came before the king, and flew at his head and plucked out the king's eye. And the king was grieved at the sight, and he awoke out of his sleep and his spirit was agitated; and he felt a great terror. (Ancient Book of Jasher 12:45–50)

The interpretation was given that Abram would cause the downfall of Nimrod's kingdom and a descendant of Abraham would kill Nimrod. This was God's last act toward Nimrod to cause him to repent.

The end of the age had come and gone and Shem did see Abram

leading a small revival within his family and he did see the breakup of the empire but God had not directly spoken to Abram or Shem about the prophecy. Nimrod's empire was still partly present. So, Shem waited to see what God would do.

Eventually God did speak to Abram. God changed his name to Abraham and made the covenant with him. He was to be the next King of Righteousness and father the nation through whom the Messiah would come.

> Now the LORD had said unto Abram, Get thee out of thy country, and from thy kindred, and from thy father's house, unto a land that I will shew thee: And I will make of thee a great nation, and I will bless thee, and make thy name great; and thou shalt be a blessing: And I will bless them that bless thee, and curse him that curseth thee: and in thee shall all families of the earth be blessed. (Genesis 12:1–3)

Abraham was the fourteenth generation from Enoch; so the Messiah's coming was still quite a long way off.

As Chedorlaomer captured more territory, he took control of Sodom and Gomorrah and the cities of the plains. He slew all of the giant clans. He left a wake of complete destruction everywhere he went. In time, Sodom and the other cities of the plains rebelled against Elam. Chedorlaomer squelched the rebellion by slaughtering many and taking prisoners, among whom was Lot, Abraham's nephew. This was it! Surely the fulfillment of the prophecy was just around the corner. With Nimrod's kingdom diminished and Chedorlaomer on a rampage, could Abraham defeat Chedorlaomer and take control as prophesied? Abraham rose up, killed Chedorlaomer, slaughtered his forces, rescued his nephew Lot, and returned the captives to the cities.

Shem wasted no time coming down to Abraham to anoint him as the next Melchizedekian priest. Moses said this about the event.

And the king of Sodom went out to meet him after his return from the slaughter of Chedorlaomer, and of the kings that were with him, at the valley of Shaveh, which is the king's dale. And Melchizedek king of Salem brought forth bread and wine: and he was the priest of the most high God. And he blessed him, and said, Blessed be Abram of the most high God, possessor of heaven and earth: And blessed be the most high God, which hath delivered thine enemies into thy hand. And he gave him tithes of all. (Genesis 14:17–20)

Jasher says this about the event.

And Bera king of Sodom, and the rest of his men that were with him, went out from the lime pits into which they had fallen, to meet Abram and his men. And Adonizedek king of Jerusalem, the same was Shem, went out with his men to meet Abram and his people, with bread and wine, and they remained together in the valley of Melech. And Adonizedek blessed Abram, and Abram gave him a tenth from all that he had brought from the spoil of his enemies, for Adonizedek was a priest before God. (Ancient Book of Jasher 16:10–12)

The date given for this event was 2021 AM, which would make Abraham seventy-three years old.

Shem passed away at the age of six hundred, in 2158 AM. Eber then took full control of the School of the Prophets and continued their work teaching the whole council of God and recording history.

Conclusion

This makes Shem the sixth, and Abraham the seventh, Melchizedekian priest.

Abraham to Levi

Abraham was one hundred years old when he had a son whom he named Isaac. Moses taught that God swore in an oath that He would enter the next covenant with Isaac.

> And there was a famine in the land, beside the first famine that was in the days of Abraham. And Isaac went unto Abimelech king of the Philistines unto Gerar. And the LORD appeared unto him, and said, Go not down into Egypt; dwell in the land which I shall tell thee of: Sojourn in this land, and I will be with thee, and will bless thee; for unto thee, and unto thy seed, I will give all these countries, and I will perform the oath which I sware unto Abraham thy father; And I will make thy seed to multiply as the stars of heaven, and will give unto thy seed all these countries; and in thy seed shall all the nations of the earth be blessed; Because that Abraham obeyed my voice, and kept my charge, my commandments, my statutes, and my laws. (Genesis 26:1–5)

After the death of Sarah, Abraham buried her at the interment of kings. Many kings of the land attended her funeral, including Shem, Noah's son. Shem's sons Eber and Abimelech, together with Aner, Eshcol and Mamre were also there. Abraham recognized Isaac was ordained by God, so he sent him to learn the ways of God and how to be a priest of the Most High God.

> And when the days of their mourning passed by Abraham sent away his son Isaac, and he went to the house of Shem and Eber, to learn the ways of the Lord and his instructions, and Abraham remained there three years. (Ancient Book of Jasher 24:17)

Isaac always thought that Esau, his firstborn, would be the next priest, even though Isaac's father, Abraham, knew God had selected Jacob over Esau. This was actually easy for all to see. Jacob was a "man of the tents," meaning he loved to study the prophecies. It was well known that Esau could not care less for the things of God. But Isaac's mind was made up. Jacob should not have deceived his father Isaac. God would have made Jacob the next heir to the blessing no matter what.

> And his father Isaac said unto him, Come near now, and kiss me, my son. And he came near, and kissed him: and he smelled the smell of his raiment, and blessed him, and said, See, the smell of my son is as the smell of a field which the Lord hath blessed: Therefore God give thee of the dew of heaven, and the fatness of the earth, and plenty of corn and wine: Let people serve thee, and nations bow down to thee: be lord over thy brethren, and let thy mother's sons bow down to thee: cursed be every one that curseth thee, and blessed be he that blesseth thee. And it came to pass, as soon as Isaac had made an end of blessing Jacob, and Jacob was yet scarce gone out from the presence of Isaac his father, that Esau his brother came in from his hunting. (Genesis 27:26–30)

What is interesting about the details of Genesis 27 is that even though Isaac's mind was set, he recognized God's hand on Jacob. As Americans we would say "he deceived me" and, therefore, my oath is null and void. But Jacob knew that if God wanted Esau to have the inheritance, God would have made it happen. God is in control. We should all learn that lesson from Jacob.

> And it was after the death of Abraham that God blessed his son Isaac and his children, and the Lord was with Isaac as he had been with his father Abraham, for Isaac kept all the command- ments of the Lord as Abraham his father had commanded him;

he did not turn to the right or to the left from the right path which his father had commanded him. (Ancient Book of Jasher 26:39)

Esau would not repent and become a godly man. God had made it clear that His hand was on Jacob, so Isaac sent Jacob to study for the priesthood.

At that time Isaac sent his younger son Jacob to the house of Shem and Eber, and he learned the instructions of the Lord, and Jacob remained in the house of Shem and Eber for thirty-two years, and Esau his brother did not go, for he was not willing to go, and he remained in his father's house in the land of Canaan. (Ancient Book of Jasher 28:18)

God spoke to Jacob and renewed the covenant with him as He did with Isaac his father. This happened in a dream Jacob had while in Bethel.

And he dreamed, and behold a ladder set up on the earth, and the top of it reached to heaven: and behold the angels of God ascending and descending on it. And, behold, the LORD stood above it, and said, I am the LORD God of Abraham thy father, and the God of Isaac: the land whereon thou liest, to thee will I give it, and to thy seed; And thy seed shall be as the dust of the earth, and thou shalt spread abroad to the west, and to the east, and to the north, and to the south: and in thee and in thy seed shall all the families of the earth be blessed. And, behold, I am with thee, and will keep thee in all places whither thou goest, and will bring thee again into this land; for I will not leave thee, until I have done that which I have spoken to thee of. And Jacob awaked out of his sleep, and he said, Surely the LORD is in this place; and I knew it not. (Genesis 28:12–16)

Jacob studied with Shem and Eber at the School of the Prophets until the death of Shem in 2158 AM. Eber continued the school, but copies of all of the records were given to Levi for safe keeping. Eber died in 2187 AM, just twenty-nine years after his father, Shem, died. Shortly thereafter the area was overrun by the Amorites. They seized control of the area, took the records as their own, and even took the title of Adonizedek (the Lord of Righteousness) as their own. They took the records seriously because by the time Joshua was making the conquest of the land of Canaan, the Amorites had reproduced clans of giants.

> And it came to pass in those days, in the hundred and tenth year of the life of Isaac, that is in the fiftieth year of the life of Jacob, in that year died Shem the son of Noah; Shem was six hundred years old at his death. And when Shem died Jacob returned to his father to Hebron which is in the land of Canaan. (Ancient Book of Jasher 28:24–25)

In time Jacob had twelve sons. The eldest was Reuben, who should have inherited the promise, but he discredited himself through fornication. Jacob knew better than to do anything out of presumption, so he waited for the Lord to reveal to him what was to be done. At this time Levi, another son of Jacob, started having prophetic dreams and realized he needed to be saved!

> I, Levi, was born in Haran. When I was young, my father moved us to Shechem. When I was about twenty, Simeon and I took vengeance on Hamor for our sister Dinah. One day we were feeding our flocks in Abel-Maul, and the spirit of understanding of the Lord came upon me, and I understood that all men corrupt their way, and that righteousness had retreated behind walls and iniquity ruled. I grieved for mankind, and I prayed to the Lord that I might be saved. (Testament of Levi 2)

This is a very important point. Every human being is born with a sin nature and corrupts his or her ways. Every single person needs to be saved by believing in the revealed words of God through the prophets, and repenting of their sins. Once Levi understood this, he repented of his sins and God spoke to him in another dream.

> The Most High has heard your prayer. Your sins are forgiven, and you will become a son to Him, a servant and minister of His presence. You will shine the light of knowledge to Jacob, a sun to the seed of Israel. You and all your seed will be blessed until the Lord visits all the heathen in the tender mercies of His Son, even forever. (Testament of Levi 4)

Notice also that those saved did not reveal everything they knew about God to unbelievers. They waited until God started a relationship with the unbelievers and revealed things to them. Only when this happens do we truly know what God is doing, and that makes it unlikely that we will be conned by any unbeliever. When Levi told Jacob about the dreams, Jacob knew Levi was chosen. God then revealed to Jacob what was to be done.

> After two days Judah and I went up to Isaac after our father; and my grandfather blessed me according to all the words of the visions which I had seen. He would not come with us to Bethel. When we came to Bethel, my father Jacob had a vision concerning me, that I should become a priest unto the Lord; and he rose up early in the morning, and paid tithes of all to the Lord through me. We came to Hebron to dwell there, and Isaac continually taught me the law of the Lord, even as the angel of God showed to me. He taught me the law of the priesthood, of sacrifices, whole burnt offerings, first-fruits, free will offerings, and thank offerings. Every day he instructed me, and prayed for me before the Lord. (Testament of Levi 9)

Jacob sent Levi to learn the priesthood from Isaac his father. God had revealed to Jacob that the Melchizedekian priesthood was to be broken up until the coming of the Messiah.

> At that time the portion of birthright, together with the kingly and priestly offices, was removed from the sons of Reuben, for he had profaned his father's bed, and the birthright was given unto Joseph, the kingly office to Judah, and the priesthood unto Levi, because Reuben had defiled his father's bed. (Ancient Book of Jasher 36:15)

The prophecies stated that the Messiah would be born a direct descendant of Judah. He would be born as King. Afterwards, Messiah would have to be ordained into the priesthood by a priest of that order. This was the only way for Him to become a real priest. He would also have to be filled with the Holy Spirit to become a prophet. Only with these three offices uniting into one man could the Melchizedekian priesthood be recreated.

In the books of Kings and Chronicles, we read about some kings of Israel and Judah who tried to usurp the office of priest and were cursed of God for doing so. In effect, they were trying to make people believe they were the Messiah by restoring the ancient priesthood. But with Jesus, instead of being cursed, He was blessed with the Holy Spirit descending on Him in the form of a dove, proving God's blessing was on Him and testifying that He truly was the Messiah.

The Order of Levi

The priesthood part of the Order of Melchizedek was virtually the same as that of the newly created Order of Levi. Abraham had added the practice of circumcision to their laws. Jacob added some other stipulations. Moses would later add many more. The additions that Moses added would only be in effect until the coming of the Messiah.

Levi handed down the office of high priest to his son Kohath. Kohath instructed his children to observe all the laws of the priesthood and guard all of the testaments of their fathers which he had received from his father, Levi.

> You must keep the priesthood in every way that I have com-
> manded you... Amram, my son, I command you and your
> descendants...given to Levi my father, which he in turn gave
> to me along with all my writings as witness. You must take care
> of them. They are for you and your descendants and in them is
> great worth. It is important that they be carried on with you.
> (Testament of Kohath)

Kohath turned the priesthood over to his son Amram, with the instructions and records. According to the Testament of Amram, he left his wife and family in Egypt to go built the sepulchers of his fathers in the cave of Machpelah in Canaan. While there, a war broke out and because of it, he was trapped and could not get back to his family for forty-one years! When Amram was finally able to be reunited with his family, Moses had already been banished from Egypt. Amram turned over the priesthood and records to Aaron his firstborn, Moses' brother. They waited for the fulfillment of the prophecy God gave to Abraham. They waited for the end of the 430 years when God would deliver them from Egypt.

God sent Aaron visions about their deliverance and the coming of the Messiah. See the section in Melchizedekian Prophecy for a full study in these prophecies.

The year of the Exodus, 2448 AM, God commanded that high priests of Israel were to come only from the line of Aaron.

The high priests from the Exodus to the time of King Solomon were Aaron, Eleazar, Phinehas, Abishua, Bukki, Uzzi, Eli, Ahitub, Ahijah, Ahimelech, and Abiathar. In the days of King Solomon, a conspiracy formed against Solomon. The high priest, Abiathar, sided against

Solomon. Around 900 BC, Solomon deposed Abiathar and replaced him with a godly Levite descendant of Aaron named Zadok.

From this time on, only descendants of Zadok were allowed to be high priests. Legitimate Israeli kings could only come through the line of Judah, but later this lineage was narrowed to the line of David, a descendant of Judah. In the same way, a high priest had to be of the lineage of Levi, but in time it was narrowed to the lineage of Aaron, a descendant of Levi, and finally narrowed again to a descendant of Aaron, namely Zadok. The book of Ezekiel says in the millennial reign there will be priests in the Temple that are only from the line of Zadok.

> It shall be for the priests that are sanctified of the sons of Zadok; which have kept My charge, which went not astray when the children of Israel went astray, as the Levites went astray. (Ezekiel 48:11)

The Zadok line of high priests that extended from Zadok to the Babylonian captivity were: Ahimaaz, Azariah, Johnan, Azatiah, Amaria, Ahitub II, Zadok II, Shallum, Hilkiah, Azariah IV, Seraiah, and Jehozadak. After returning from the Babylonian captivity, the Zadok line started with Joshua the son of Jehozadak. Around 175 BC a rebellion occurred that deposed the godly line of Zadok. The priests after the return from Babylon were: Joshua, Joiakim, Eliashib, Joiada, Johanan, Jaddua, Onias I, Simon I, Eleazar, Manasseh, Onias II, Simon II, Onias III, Onaias IV, and Jason.

Most of us remember Antiochus Epiphanes, who persecuted the Jews. He killed all those who refused to live a Grecian lifestyle. They could not study the Bible, practice circumcision, or do Jewish sacrifices. The Jerusalem temple was desolated with idols and Jews were forced to sacrifice to pagan gods or be put to death. The Zadok priests refused to obey, and the assassination of Zadok priests began.

The Zadok priests knew of the apostasy that was to come, and under inspiration of the Holy Spirit, took the temple library to Qumran. There the Lord protected them, and they prepared the hearts of the people for the coming of the Messiah. They did this as best as they could in the midst of a growing apostasy in the Sanhedrin, and in the Pharisee and Sadducee parties.

The Dead Sea Scrolls found in Qumran and its surrounding caves are the legacy of the Zadok priests with a complete history from their point of view.

The community in Qumran called themselves "Yahad." This is a contraction of two Hebrew words. "Yah" is the name of God and "ehad" means "one" in the sense of one group of brothers. So, the name "Yahad" literally means unity in the Spirit of God. They believed they were led directly by the Holy Spirit, so they truly were "one in the Spirit."

Their major center of ritual that we call Qumran, they called New Damascus. We learn this in the Damascus documents. Their name "Damascus" is made up of two Hebrew words; "dam" meaning blood and "Masheq" meaning "heir" or "stronghold." Look this up in Strong's concordance. "Dam" is H1818 and "mashaq" is H4944. New Damascus was the stronghold of the ancient ways and those loyal to the true blood heir, the coming Messiah.

Incidentally, the term "Melchizedek" translates out to mean King (Melech) of Righteousness (Zedeq) but it could also be translated as the "King of the Zadok priests!"

Jesus and John the Baptist

We have seen from various ancient records the progression of the Melchizedekian priests and the School of the Prophets from Adam down to Jacob, who, under inspiration of the Holy Spirit, broke up the Melchizedekian priesthood into three separate offices. These were king, prophet, and priest. The Gospel of Matthew reveals the genealogical record of Jesus Christ. Matthew begins with Abraham, Isaac, and Jacob. We know Jacob split up the Melchizedekian priesthood and thereby creating the line of kings from Judah and the priestly line from Levi. Matthew clearly shows Jesus as a direct biological descendant of Judah and therefore heir to the throne of David and destined to be king of Israel.

> The book of the generation of Jesus Christ, the son of David, the son of Abraham. Abraham begat Isaac; and Isaac begat Jacob; and Jacob begat Judas and his brethren; And Judas begat Phares and Zara of Thamar; and Phares begat Esrom; and Esrom begat Aram; And Aram begat Aminadab; and Aminadab begat Naasson; and Naasson begat Salmon; And Salmon begat Booz of Rachab; and Booz begat Obed of Ruth; and Obed begat Jesse; And Jesse begat David the king; and David the king begat Solomon of her that had been the wife of Urias; And Solomon begat Roboam; and Roboam begat Abia; and Abia begat Asa; And Asa begat Josaphat; and Josaphat begat Joram; and Joram begat Ozias; And Ozias begat Joatham; and Joatham begat Achaz; and Achaz begat Ezekias; And Ezekias begat Manasses; and Manasses begat Amon; and Amon begat Josias; And Josias begat Jechonias and his brethren, about the time they were carried away to Babylon: And after they were brought to Babylon, Jechonias begat Salathiel; and Salathiel begat Zorobabel; And Zorobabel begat Abiud; and Abiud begat Eliakim; and Eliakim begat Azor; And Azor begat Sadoc; and Sadoc begat Achim; and Achim begat Eliud; And Eliud begat Eleazar; and Eleazar begat Matthan; and Matthan begat Jacob; And Jacob begat Joseph the husband of Mary, of whom was born Jesus, who is called Christ. (Matthew 1:1–16)

But what about the priestly lines and the School of the Prophets? God has graciously preserved that record too. The Ante-Nicene Fathers is a ten-volume work comprising what was written about the church and its history from AD 32 to AD 325. In this set there exists a record entitled "Hippolytus' Fragments on the Pentateuch." No one really realized what this document was, until after some of the Dead Sea Scrolls told of the ancient histories and apostasies. It is a complete record of the priestly prophetic line from the time of Moses down to the Church Age. To bridge the gap, remember that Jacob made Levi the priest. Levi handed that down to his son Kohath, who handed it to his son Amram. Amram was the father of Moses and Aaron. Hippolytus does not give the history of the kings of Israel nor high priests of Israel, but rather the prophetic line that ran the School of the Prophets, from Moses to John the Baptist. Here is that record:

> These following are the names of the teachers who handed down the Law in continuous succession after Moses the prophet, until the advent of Messiah: God delivered the most excellent Law into the hands of Moses the prophet, the son of Amram. (Hippolytus' Fragments on the Pentateuch)

He then gives a long line of their names:

1. Moses
2. Joshua
3. Othniel
4. Jehud
5. Shamgar
6. Baruk
7. Gideon
8. Abimelech
9. Taleg
10. Babin
11. Jephthah
12. Ephran
13. Elul
14. Abdon

15. Samson
16. Elkanah (father of Samuel the prophet)
17. Eli the priest
18. Samuel the prophet
19. Nathan the prophet
20. Gad the prophet,
21. Shemaiah the teacher
22. Iddo the teacher
23. Ahijah the Shilonite
24. Abihu
25. Elijah the prophet
26. Elisha the prophet
27. Micah the prophet
28. Abdiahu
29. Jehuda
30. Zacharias the teacher
31. Esaia the prophet (the son of Amos)
32. Jeremiah the prophet
33. Ezekiel
34. Hosea the prophet (the son of Bazi)
35. Joel the prophet
36. Amos the prophet
37. Obadiah
38. Jonan the prophet (son of Mathi, the son of Armelah, who was the brother of Elias the prophet)
39. Micha the Morasthite
40. Nachum the Alcusite
41. Habakkuk the prophet
42. Zephaniah the prophet
43. Haggai the prophet
44. Zechariah the prophet (the son of Bershia)
45. Malachi
46. Ezra the teacher

47. Shamai the chief priest
48. Jaduah
49. Samean
50. Antigonus
51. Joseph (son of Johezer) and Joseph (the son of Gjuchanan)
52. Jehosua (son of Barachia)
53. Nathan the Arbelite
54. Simeon (elder son of Shebach. This is the Simeon who held the Messiah in his arms.)
55. Jehuda
56. Zechariah the priest (father of John the Baptist)
57. Joseph (a teacher of the tribe of Levi)
58. Annas and Caiaphas

Hippolytus goes on to say:

Joseph delivered it to Annas and Caiaphas. Moreover, from them were taken away the priestly, and kingly, and prophetic offices. These were teachers at the advent of Messiah; and they were both priests of the children of Israel. Therefore, the whole number of venerable and honorable priests put in trust of this most excellent law was fifty-six, Annas and Caiaphas being excepted. And those are they who delivered it in the last days to the state of the children of Israel; nor did there arise any priests after them. This is the account of what took place with regard to the most excellent Law. (Hippolytus' Fragments on the Pentateuch)

What is the most interesting thing to note about this text is that Annas and Caiaphas were evil, but had the title of chief priest and leader of the School of the Prophets. In reality, if they became apostate, then by Mosaic Law, the true leader would be the last in succession. So, the head of the School of the Prophets in Qumran would fall back to this Joseph the Levite. If he died without having any children, it would revert back to the previous leader who would be Zechariah the priest, and his firstborn son was John the Baptist.

In the writings of Church Father Clement, a disciple of the Apostle Peter, there exists a historical record of how Simon Magus, of Acts 8:9–25, became the father of the Gnostic heretics. This is recorded in the Clement's Homilies 2.23–24 and the Recognitions of Clement 1.54; 2.8,11. At the beginning of this narrative, Clement explains that Simon was originally a disciple of John the Baptist in his school. Clement says,

> There was one John, a day-baptist, who was the forerunner of our Lord Jesus; and as the Lord had twelve apostles, bearing the number of the twelve months of the sun, so also he, John, had thirty chief men, fulfilling the number of days in a month, in which number was a certain woman called Helena, that not even this might be without a dispensational significance. (Clement's Homilies 2.23)

In keeping with the solar Dead Sea Scroll calendar, the higher teaching groups / Sanhedrin consisted of twelve and the lower teaching groups / Sanhedrin consisted of thirty. In this way the Essenes demonstrated the God-ordained use of the solar calendar and not the corrupted Pharisee / Sadducee lunar calendar. See Ancient Dead Sea Scroll Calendar by this author. In the Essene pattern, Jesus the Messiah had twelve disciples and John the Baptist, the lower teacher, had thirty disciples. This alone shows a strong Essene connection to Jesus Christ and John the Baptist, but there is more.

Josephus records that there were two groups of Essenes, the Qumran Essenes (godly Jews who kept the scrolls and studied the prophecies) and the Egyptian Essenes (who despised prophecy, and instead practiced a system of magic which was forbidden to Jews in Israel). Much like today, Christian denominations and cults both claim the name of "Christian."

Clement further says that Simon fell away from the study of the

Messianic prophecies and, not wanting to wait on the Lord, left John's school to travel to Egypt to study magic with the Egyptian Essenes. Upon Simon's return from Egypt, he found John was dead, the Messiah had come, and many of the old students were now following Jesus as the true Messiah. Some of John's school did not accept Jesus as Messiah and those were led by an old disciple of John named Dositheus.

> But of these thirty, the first and the most esteemed by John was Simon; and the reason of his not being chief after the death of John was as follows: He [Simon Magus] being absent in Egypt for the practice of magic, and John being killed, Dositheus desiring the leadership, falsely gave out that Simon was dead, and succeeded to the seat. But Simon, returning not long after, and strenuously holding by the place as his own, when he met with Dositheus did not demand the place, knowing that a man who has attained power beyond his expectations cannot be removed from it. Wherefore with pretended friendship he gives himself for a while to the second place, under Dositheus. But taking his place after a few days among the thirty fellow-disciples, he began to malign Dositheus as not delivering the instructions correctly. (Clement's Homilies 2.24)

Just like the cults of today, they come into a church claiming they believe the same doctrine and just want to be friends and study under the current pastor, all the while they intend to underhandedly cause division in the church. Simon caused doubt and division and then used his magic tricks to deceive. Eventually all the group and Dositheus himself fell for Simon's lies. Clement finished the narrative by saying,

> He raised Simon to his own place of repute; and thus, not many days after, Dositheus himself, while he (Simon) stood, fell down and died. (Clement's Homilies 2.24)

Some even of the disciples of John, who seemed to be great ones, have separated themselves from the people, and proclaimed their own master as the Christ. (Recognitions of Clement 1.54)

John the Baptist was baptizing in the Jordan river just eight miles from where Qumran was at that time. There is a Dead Sea Scroll called the Community Rule which records not only how to become an Essene, but how they started. The Community Rule says when the apostasy hit, the Holy Spirit spoke to their leaders, the Zadok priests, instructing them to move out of Jerusalem into the wilderness taking the temple library with them. They said that the Holy Spirit told them one of their order would fulfill the prophecy of Isaiah which says,

The voice of him that crieth in the wilderness, Prepare ye the way of the LORD, make straight in the desert a highway for our God. Every valley shall be exalted, and every mountain and hill shall be made low: and the crooked shall be made straight, and the rough places plain: And the glory of the LORD shall be revealed, and all flesh shall see it together: for the mouth of the LORD hath spoken it." (Isaiah 40:3–5)

In their mind the Essene order would keep proper doctrine and wait for the coming of the Messiah. When He came, He would destroy the Pharisees and Sadducees and end the corrupt Levitical priesthood by establishing a new Melchizedekian order and usher in a new age called the Age of Grace. I have more on this in the section, Melchizedekian Prophecy. The Community Rule says,

When these join the [Essene] community in Israel and comply with the community rules, they are to separate themselves from the men of sin and dwell in the desert in order to open His path. "As it is written The voice crying in the wilderness, Prepare the

way of the LORD, make a straight highway in the desert for our
God. [Isaiah 40:3]." (Community Rule, col. 8)

The Gospel of John records John the Baptist's answer to the Pharisee's question of who he was,

Then they said to him, "Who are you so that we may give an answer
to those who sent us? What do you say of yourself?" He said, "I am 'the
voice of one crying in the wilderness: Make straight the way of the Lord,'
as the prophet Isaiah said." (John 1:22–23 MKJV)

We know Jesus the Messiah never committed any sin. So why did
John baptize Jesus? John was baptizing Him into the priesthood. If Jesus
was the Messiah born of the kingly lineage of David, and John baptized
Him into the Priesthood, and God blessed it by sending the Holy Spirit
to make Him a prophet, it would mean the reestablishing of the ancient
Melchizedekian priesthood. Scripture records,

> Then cometh Jesus from Galilee to Jordan unto John, to be bap-
> tized of him. But John forbad Him, saying, I have need to be
> baptized of Thee, and comest Thou to me? And Jesus answering
> said unto him, Suffer it to be so now: for thus it becometh us to
> fulfil all righteousness. Then he suffered Him. And Jesus, when
> He was baptized, went up straightway out of the water: and, lo,
> the heavens were opened unto Him, and He saw the Spirit of
> God descending like a dove, and lighting upon Him: And lo a
> voice from heaven, saying, This is My beloved Son, in whom I
> am well pleased. (Matthew 3:13–17)

John knew that Jesus was sinless, which is why he said, "I have
need to be baptized of Thee, and comest Thou to me?" Jesus needed
John to baptize Him into the priesthood to reestablish the Melchizedekian priesthood, which would make it possible for Jesus to "fulfill all
righteousness."

We do not see the School of the Prophets again until the book of Acts when the school's leader came down from Antioch with some of his students to give a prophecy to the apostle Paul.

> And in these days came prophets from Jerusalem unto Antioch. And there stood up one of them named Agabus, and signified by the Spirit that there should be great dearth throughout all the world: which came to pass in the days of Claudius Caesar. (Acts 11:27–28)

> And as we tarried there many days, there came down from Judaea a certain prophet, named Agabus. And when he was come unto us, he took Paul's girdle, and bound his own hands and feet, and said, Thus saith the Holy Ghost, So shall the Jews at Jerusalem bind the man that owneth this girdle, and shall deliver him into the hands of the Gentiles. (Acts 21:10–11)

This makes John the Baptist the leader of the School of the Prophets and an Essene. This means he was the only one with the authority to baptize Jesus into the priesthood! The ancient church fathers record the successors to Agabus and the School, but this will suffice for now.

Church Father Hippolytus concludes his narrative by describing that Titus destroyed the Jerusalem temple and the nation of Israel was dissolved, all because of the apostasy of the Sadducees and Pharisees.

> And after the ascension of Christ into heaven, came King Titus, son of Vespasian king of Rome, to Jerusalem, and besieged and took it. And he destroyed the edifice of the second house, which the children of Israel had built. Titus the king destroyed the house of the sanctuary, and slew all the Jews who were in it, and bathed Zion in their blood. And after that deportation the Jews were scattered abroad in slavery. Nor did they assemble any more in the city of Jerusalem, nor is there hope anywhere of

their returning. Jerusalem was laid waste because Shemaia and Antalia (Abtalion) perverted the law. Hippolytus' Fragments on the Pentateuch)

Conclusion

Church Father Hippolytus gives the lineage of the leader of the School of the Prophets from the time of Moses down to John the Baptist. We have seen the biblical record of Jesus being born of the lineage of King David, being baptized into the priesthood by John the Baptist, the leader in the Zadok / Essene movement, and the Holy Spirit descending on Jesus like a dove adding the spirit of prophecy to the event. Thus, Jesus was then made priest, king, and prophet. The Melchizedekian priesthood that was divided by Jacob was now restored in Jesus Christ.

11

MELCHIZEDEKIAN THEOLOGY

Melchizedek in the Bible

In this section on Melchizedekian theology, we turn to Jesus, Moses, King David, and the apostles Paul and Peter, to carefully learn what they taught about the Messiah's priesthood and covenant, and how that relates to the Melchizedekian priesthood.

First, we will look at how Paul and Jesus used Psalm 110 to teach about the Messiah's new priesthood.

Second, we will look at the theology of the apostle Paul about the Melchizedekian priesthood in Hebrews 5 through Hebrews 8.

Lastly, we will tie all of this together by looking at teachings from the apostles Peter, John, and Paul.

Psalm 110

King David wrote Psalm 110 about 1000 BC. It is about the coming Messiah.

Modern Judaism teaches that Psalm 110 refers to Genesis 14:17–24, where a man named Melchizedek blessed Abraham and prophetically transferred the office of priest to Abraham's descendant Aaron. So, in their mind there is no difference between a Melchizedekian priest and an Aaronic priest. They are one and the same. They also believe that Psalm 110 teaches that the priesthood of Aaron is eternal. All of this is a modern-day error and stems from a teaching in The Zohar, a Kabalistic book written in the middle ages.

In the first century AD, all three sects of Jews, the Sadducees, the Pharisees, and the Essenes, believed that this text referred to the promised Messiah. One of the titles for the Messiah was "Son of David." There are many places throughout the Gospels where the people called Jesus the "Son of David." That was the people's way of acknowledging that they believed that Jesus was indeed the promised Messiah. A few references where people ask for mercy and healing from Jesus by calling Him the "Son of David" are: Matthew 9:27; 15:22; 20:30; 21:9; 21:15; 22:42; Mark 10:47-48; 12:35; Luke 18:38-39.

The Essenes still believed that the Messiah would be God incarnate, but the Pharisees and Sadducees had started teaching that the Messiah would be just a man sent by God to win a war. When the Pharisees were giving Jesus trouble, He decided to ask them a question from Psalm 110 that would silence them.

> While the Pharisees were gathered together, Jesus asked them, saying, What think ye of Christ? whose son is He? They say unto Him, The Son of David. He saith unto them, How then doth David in spirit call Him Lord, saying, The LORD said unto my Lord, Sit Thou on My right hand, till I make Thine enemies Thy footstool? If David then call Him Lord, how is He his son? And no man was able to answer Him a word, neither durst any man from that day forth ask Him any more questions. (Matthew 22:41–46)

The Gospel of Mark gives the same record but reveals that the "scribes," or Essenes, were known to teach that the Messiah was God incarnate. The term "scribe" is used for Essenes when referring to those who kept the written records of the temple library. Sometimes it also refers to those who copied court documents regardless of affiliation. Mark is referring to those who kept the temple scrolls; therefore, these scribes were Essenes.

> And Jesus answered and said, while He taught in the temple, How say the scribes that Christ is the Son of David? For David himself said by the Holy Ghost, The LORD said to my Lord, Sit Thou on My right hand, till I make Thine enemies Thy footstool. David therefore himself calleth Him Lord; and whence is He then his son? And the common people heard Him gladly. (Mark 12:35–37)

An Essene would have answered correctly by saying the Christ, or Messiah, is a direct descendant of King David and therefore would be subject to His father King David, but since the Messiah is God incarnate, David would call Him "Lord," instead of the other way around. The Pharisees, who wanted to make the Christ a mere man, couldn't answer this question without causing themselves even more disgrace in the eyes of the people. They refused to answer the question.

This proves that all three sects knew this Psalm of David refers to the coming Messiah and not Aaron. They also knew that there is a difference between the two orders of priests. The two priesthoods were not the same. With this in mind let us look at Psalm 110 closely,

> A Psalm of David. The LORD said unto my Lord, Sit Thou at My right hand, until I make Thine enemies Thy footstool. The LORD shall send the rod of Thy strength out of Zion: rule Thou in the midst of Thine enemies. Thy people shall be willing in the day of Thy power, in the beauties of holiness from the womb of the morning: Thou hast the dew of Thy youth. The LORD hath sworn, and will not repent, Thou art a priest for ever after the order of Melchizedek. The Lord at Thy right hand shall strike

through kings in the day of His wrath. He shall judge among the heathen, He shall fill the places with the dead bodies; He shall wound the heads over many countries. He shall drink of the brook in the way: therefore shall He lift up the head. (Psalms 110:1–7)

So, the Messiah is the "Son of David." David knows "the LORD" is God the Father, and that the Messiah is his "Lord," or God incarnate. So how does this God-man, born king of the lineage of David save us by a priestly action? The Law of Moses forbids anyone not of the lineage of Levi to be made a Levitical priest. God the Father swears an oath that cannot be broken, the Messiah will be a priest of the Order of Melchizedek, not of the Order of Levi.

The Apostle Paul used Psalm 110 several times in his teaching about Jesus and the Melchizedekian order in the book of Hebrews.

The Book of Hebrews

The Apostle Paul teaches on the Melchizedekian order in several chapters in the book of Hebrews. First let us outline the book of Hebrews to see why Paul talks about the order so much.

Paul was writing to the Hebrew priests who were serving in the temple. Some were thinking about accepting Jesus as Messiah and others basically believed, but did not want to stop being priests. The temple would be destroyed within the next twenty years.

The book of Hebrews is divided into two sections. Chapters one through ten deal with the theology of Jesus Christ. Chapters eleven through thirteen deal with practical matters of the Christian walk.

In each chapter of the first section of the book of Hebrews, Paul describes how Jesus is superior to everything held dear to the Jews. Jesus is the Messiah, and all rituals and Mosaic Laws were types and shadows to point to Him. He fulfilled everything they pointed to. All the temple priests needed to do would be to accept the Messiah now before it was too late.

Here is an outline of the chapters of the first section.

1. Jesus is superior to all the prophets and angels.
2. Jesus is superior to all men.
3. Jesus is superior to Moses.
4. Jesus brings a rest superior to the Sabbath.
5. Jesus is superior to the Levitical priesthood.
6. Paul warns not to reject the Messiah.
7. Jesus is of the Order of Melchizedekian priests.
8. Jesus brings a superior new covenant.
9. The superiority of the heavenly tabernacle and new covenant is compared to the earthly Mosaic tabernacle and the old Mosaic covenant.
10. Jesus' one-time sacrifice is superior to the sacrifices of all the bulls and goats.

Hebrews 5

In this first part of Hebrews 5, Paul begins teaching about the priesthood of Jesus Christ. Paul's first point is that all priests are taken from men to intercede between men and God. There are no angel priests, just human priests. Human priests must offer sacrifice for themselves first, in order to be able to offer sacrifice on the behalf of others.

> For every high priest taken from among men is ordained for men in things pertaining to God, that he may offer both gifts and sacrifices for sins: Who can have compassion on the ignorant, and on them that are out of the way; for that he himself also is compassed with infirmity. And by reason hereof he ought, as for the people, so also for himself, to offer for sins. (Hebrews 5:1–3)

Paul's second point is that only God can ordain a priest. God spoke and ordained Aaron to be the first high priest of the Aaronic priesthood.

> And no man taketh this honour unto himself, but he that is called of God, as was Aaron. (Hebrews 5:4)

In the same way, God spoke and ordained Jesus to be a high priest. To prove Jesus is a priest ordained by God and not by men, Paul quotes two biblical passages. The first is from Psalm 2.

Paul quotes part of Psalm 2 to remind them that the prophecy shows their rulers would be enraged against Him and seek to kill Him. This is exactly what happened to Jesus.

> Why do the heathen rage, and the people imagine a vain thing? The kings of the earth set themselves, and the rulers take counsel together, against the LORD, and against His anointed [Messiah]… I will declare the decree: the LORD hath said unto Me, Thou art My Son; this day have I begotten Thee. (Psalms 2:1–2, 7)

The Apostle Paul is quoting this not only to prove Jesus was to be persecuted, but also to show when He was to be ordained as a priest. It was when the Father would say "Thou art My Son, today have I begotten Thee."

> So also Christ glorified not Himself to be made an high priest; but He that said unto Him, Thou art My Son, today have I begotten Thee. (Hebrews 5:5)

Jesus was from the tribe of Judah, not Levi, so it was illegal for Him to be ordained as a Levitical priest. So, Paul immediately reminds them that the prophecy in Psalm 110 dictated that the Messiah was to be a priest of a different order. He was to be a Melchizedekian priest.

As He saith also in another place, Thou art a priest for ever after the order of Melchisedec. (Hebrews 5:6)

The second passage quoted is from Psalm 110.

The LORD hath sworn, and will not repent, Thou art a priest for ever after the order of Melchizedek. (Psalms 110:4)

Jesus was perfect so He did not have to offer anything for Himself. Paul then explains that the Messiah, the new Melchizedekian priest, was to offer Himself for the sins of His people. This would once and for all time bring an "eternal salvation."

Who in the days of His flesh, when He had offered up prayers and supplications with strong crying and tears unto Him that was able to save Him from death, and was heard in that He feared; Though He were a Son, yet learned He obedience by the things which He suffered; And being made perfect, He became the author of eternal salvation unto all them that obey Him; Called of God an high priest after the order of Melchisedec. (Hebrews 5:7–10)

When did God ordain Jesus as high priest? When He said, "Thou art My Son; this day have I begotten Thee." We see in Matthew 3 and Mark 1, that this happened when John the Baptist baptized Jesus into the priesthood.

Then cometh Jesus from Galilee to Jordan unto John, to be baptized of him. But John forbad Him, saying, I have need to be baptized of Thee, and comest Thou to me? And Jesus answering said unto him, Suffer it to be so now: for thus it becometh us to fulfil all righteousness. Then he suffered Him. And Jesus, when

He was baptized, went up straightway out of the water: and, lo, the heavens were opened unto Him, and He saw the Spirit of God descending like a dove, and lighting upon Him: And lo a voice from heaven, saying, This is My beloved Son, in whom I am well pleased. (Matthew 3:13–17)

The Apostle Paul ends the fifth chapter of Hebrews by saying,

Of whom we have many things to say, and hard to be uttered, seeing ye are dull of hearing. For when for the time ye ought to be teachers, ye have need that one teach you again which be the first principles of the oracles of God; and are become such as have need of milk, and not of strong meat. For every one that useth milk is unskilful in the word of righteousness: for he is a babe. But strong meat belongeth to them that are of full age, even those who by reason of use have their senses exercised to discern both good and evil. (Hebrews 5:11–14)

Notice that there are many things Paul could teach them about Jesus and the Melchizedekian priesthood, but the Pharisaical priests were "dull of hearing." The Hebrew idiom "dull of hearing" does not mean they were stupid, that they could not understand plain speech. It means obstinate. If Paul would have just spelled it out clearly, they would have rejected his teaching as "that old Essene garbage." So, Paul had to take it slowly and prove point by point from the only writing both he and the Pharisees accepted, the Torah.

Conclusion

In Hebrews 5 the Apostle Paul states that Jesus is the Messiah, and that He was ordained into the priesthood by God the Father. Jesus is not a Levitical priest, but a priest of the Order of Melchizedek. Jesus was ordained into this priesthood when John the Baptist baptized Him. Paul said there was a lot more he could tell us about the Melchizedekian order, but the Pharisees would refuse to listen to him if he was too direct with them. Thanks to the Dead Sea Scrolls, we now know a lot more of what Paul could have recorded in the book of Hebrews.

Hebrews 6

In chapter 6 of the book of Hebrews, Paul continues his thought of not obsessing about small points of the Mosaic Law, but rather to go on to a perfect understanding of the Messiah and His new priesthood.

> Therefore leaving the principles of the doctrine of Christ, let us go on unto perfection; not laying again the foundation of repentance from dead works, and of faith toward God, Of the doctrine of baptisms, and of laying on of hands, and of resurrection of the dead, and of eternal judgment. And this will we do, if God permit. (Hebrews 6:1–3)

Paul then gives a warning not to reject the Messiah and His Melchizedekian priesthood.

> For it is impossible for those who were once enlightened, and have tasted of the heavenly gift, and were made partakers of the Holy Ghost, And have tasted the good word of God, and the powers of the world to come, If they shall fall away, to renew them again unto repentance; seeing they crucify to themselves the Son of God afresh, and put Him to an open shame. For the earth which drinketh in the rain that cometh oft upon it, and bringeth forth herbs meet for them by whom it is dressed, receiveth blessing from God: But that which beareth thorns and briers is rejected, and is nigh unto cursing; whose end is to be burned. (Hebrews 6:4–8)

These temple priests were there. They saw how the Messiah fulfilled these prophecies. They should not, they could not, in good conscience, forget those things and just go back to doing the daily temple sacrifices. Paul warned that the end of those who reject Messiah is to be burned. When Paul wrote the Book of Hebrews, there were only about fifteen years left before the great temple in Jerusalem would be burned. Those who rejected the Messiah and held to the old ways and fought the Romans were either killed or taken into captivity. Paul is warning them they only have a few years to make a decision or it will be made for them. Today we should take to heart that same warning. We only have a few years before the tribulation starts. We all must make a decision to accept the Messiah's free gift of salvation while we are still able to do so.

Paul then pleaded with them to not allow Satan to cloud their minds. They should not forget their commitment to the Messiah. Their lives depended on it.

> But, beloved, we are persuaded better things of you, and things that accompany salvation, though we thus speak. For God is not unrighteous to forget your work and labour of love, which ye have shewed toward His name, in that ye have ministered to the saints, and do minister. And we desire that every one of you do shew the same diligence to the full assurance of hope unto the end: That ye be not slothful, but followers of them who through faith and patience inherit the promises. (Hebrews 6:9–12)

Paul then reminded them God swore an oath that the nation of Israel would exist. Likewise, He swore an oath that the Messiah would be a Melchizedekian priest. Neither of these oaths of God can be changed.

> For when God made promise to Abraham, because He could swear by no greater, He sware by Himself, Saying, Surely bless-

ing I will bless thee, and multiplying I will multiply thee. And so, after he had patiently endured, he obtained the promise. For men verily swear by the greater: and an oath for confirmation is to them an end of all strife. Wherein God, willing more abundantly to shew unto the heirs of promise the immutability of His counsel, confirmed it by an oath: That by two immutable things, in which it was impossible for God to lie, we might have a strong consolation, who have fled for refuge to lay hold upon the hope set before us: Which hope we have as an anchor of the soul, both sure and steadfast, and which entereth into that within the veil; Whither the forerunner is for us entered, even Jesus, made an high priest for ever after the order of Melchisedec. (Hebrews 6:13–20)

When God wants you to know He is going to do something, that it is certain, and there is absolutely no way that God's decree will be stopped, He swears an oath. Paul gives the example that God swore an oath to Abraham that the nation of Israel would exist. The priests reading this New Testament epistle are living proof that that promise was fulfilled. In the same way, if God swore an oath that Jesus would be made a high priest after the Order of Melchizedek, it must be so, or God would be a liar. If this is true, His new priesthood has replaced the Aaronic priesthood in the same way that the Zadok priests said it would happen.

Conclusion

In chapter 6 of Hebrews, Paul teaches us that we should not be caught up in points of the Mosaic Law, but be focused on more important things, like the prophecies about the Messiah, His new covenant and priesthood. Never let some point of the Law keep you away from the Messiah.

Hebrews 7

Hebrews 7 is the chapter we want to take very slowly. First Paul says,

> For this Melchisedec, king of Salem, priest of the most high God, who met Abraham returning from the slaughter of the kings, and blessed him; To whom also Abraham gave a tenth part of all; first being by interpretation King of righteousness, and after that also King of Salem, which is, King of peace. (Hebrews 7:1–2)

If Paul would have been speaking of the man "Levi" it would be spelled l-e-v-i. If he would have been speaking of a Levite priest, the Hebrew would still be spelled l-e-v-i. In Hebrew, a "y" sound is added to the end of the name of a nation like "Israel" to make it "Israeli." So, the addition to the word changes it from the name of the man, Israel, to the name of the people, Israeli. This chapter is going to be concentrating on the office of Melchizedek not any one person who held that office.

With this in mind, verse 1 is usually interpreted as "this man who was named Melchizedek was…" instead of the way the context suggests, which is "this Melchizedekian priest was…" Either way it is referring to the one who blessed Abraham in Genesis 14:17–24. But we will see why this has to be interpreted as "this Melchizedekian priest."

Paul gives the definition of what the word "Melchizedek" means. It is two Hebrew words added together to create the title of a priesthood. The word "Melech" means king and the word "Zedek" means righteous or righteousness. So, Melchizedek means "King of Righteousness." Alternatively, it could be translated as King of the Zadok priests.

The priest who blessed Abraham was the king of Salem. The word "Salem" is a derivative of "shalom" which means "peace" in Hebrew. Salem was a small area like a suburb in Jerusalem, where Shem and Eber had their School of the Prophets. The name later came to mean the whole area. Later still, when King David took over the city, it was renamed Jerusalem.

There is much confusion about verse 3. Most read it as "the man Melchizedek was without father or mother..." which would mean he was not human. This is why many have taught that this refers to a Christophany, a pre-incarnate appearance of Jesus Christ. Christophanies are recorded as happening in other places in the Old Testament. But this is not one of them. Let us read it very carefully.

> Without father, without mother, without descent, having neither beginning of days, nor end of life; but made like unto the Son of God; abideth a priest continually. (Hebrews 7:3)

If we understand that Paul is speaking about the order of Melchizedek contrasted with the order of Levi, it suddenly makes sense.

To be a Levitical priest one had to be not only a Jew (no Gentiles allowed), but one had to be a direct descendant of Levi (no other tribes allowed). This applies to both the mother and the father.

> Bring the tribe of Levi near, and present them before Aaron the priest, that they may minister unto him. And they shall keep his charge, and the charge of the whole congregation before the tabernacle of the congregation, to do the service of the tabernacle. (Numbers 3:6–7)

The Levite must start apprenticing at the age of twenty, start actually performing his duties as priest by the age of twenty-five, and there was a mandatory retirement at the age of fifty.

> This is it that belongeth unto the Levites: from twenty and five years old and upward they shall go in to wait upon the service of the tabernacle of the congregation: And from the age of fifty years they shall cease waiting upon the service thereof, and shall serve no more. (Numbers 8:24–25)

In contrast, the superior Melchizedekian priesthood does not have any requirement of being from a certain tribe of Israel. A Melchizedekian priest starts performing his duties as a priest whenever the last high priest, or God, ordains him. Unlike the Levitical priesthood, the Melchizedekian priesthood is only stopped by death. There is no mandatory retirement. So, let's put these verses together with the added information from the book of Numbers.

> For this Melchisedekian priest, king of Salem, priest of the most high God, who met Abraham returning from the slaughter of the kings, and blessed and ordained him; To whom also Abraham gave a tenth part of all; the priesthood's name is first being by interpretation King of righteousness, and after that also King of Salem, which is, King of peace; this superior priesthood is without father, without mother, without descent, having neither beginning of days, nor end of life; so unlike the order of Levi, the order of Melchizedek is made like unto the Son of God; the Melchizedekian order and the Messiah can both abide as a priest continually, the order of Levi cannot. (Hebrews 7:1–3 paraphrased)

The Apostle Paul then turns to another point proving the superiority of the priesthood of Jesus. Only the Levitical priesthood can collect tithes from the children of Israel. But Abraham paid tithes to his teacher / Melchizedekian priest when Levi had not yet been born. So, in a sense, Levi was paying tithes to the Melchizedekian priest. That should fully show its superiority.

> Now consider how great this man was, unto whom even the patriarch Abraham gave the tenth of the spoils. And verily they that are of the sons of Levi, who receive the office of the priesthood, have a commandment to take tithes of the people according to the law, that is, of their brethren, though they come out

of the loins of Abraham: But he whose descent is not counted from them received tithes of Abraham, and blessed him that had the promises. And without all contradiction the less is blessed of the better. And here men that die receive tithes; but there he receiveth them, of whom it is witnessed that he liveth. And as I may so say, Levi also, who receiveth tithes, payed tithes in Abraham. For he was yet in the loins of his father, when Melchisedec met him. (Hebrews 7:4–10)

Notice also that verse 6 [below] says that the person who was the Melchizedekian priest who blessed Abraham did, indeed, have a genealogical descent. His descent was not after Levi, but was much older. So, we know Paul's point was to contrast the two different orders of priests.

But he whose descent is not counted from them received tithes of Abraham, and blessed him that had the promises. (Hebrews 7:6)

Paul then asks the question (verse 11) why would God send the Messiah to be a priest but not of the Order of Aaron? The only answer could be that the Order of Aaron was not good enough. That order of priests, with its laws, cannot save. But the Messiah can.

If therefore perfection were by the Levitical priesthood, (for under it the people received the law,) what further need was there that another priest should rise after the order of Melchisedec, and not be called after the order of Aaron? (Hebrews 7:11)

Paul now gives a startling announcement, one that we need to grasp today. If there is a change in the priesthood, then there must also be a change in the priestly laws. Levitical priests must retire at fifty. The Melchizedekian priest does not have a mandatory retirement, and since the Messiah will never die, His priesthood is now eternal!

For the priesthood being changed, there is made of necessity a change also of the law. For he of whom these things are spoken pertaineth to another tribe, of which no man gave attendance at the altar. For it is evident that our Lord sprang out of Juda; of which tribe Moses spake nothing concerning priesthood. And it is yet far more evident: for that after the similitude of Melchisedec there ariseth another priest, Who is made, not after the law of a carnal commandment, but after the power of an endless life. For he testifieth, Thou art a priest for ever after the order of Melchisedec. (Hebrews 7:12–17)

Many of our Hebrew Roots brothers want to be under the Mosaic Law, here referred to as the Levitical law. They believe Jesus just changed a few things here and there, but Paul makes it clear that we are in a whole different priesthood, with completely different laws and a completely different covenant. When God swore the oath to make Jesus the Melchizedekian priest, He made it eternal. God swore it would be forever!

For there is verily a disannulling of the commandment going before for the weakness and unprofitableness thereof. For the law made nothing perfect, but the bringing in of a better hope did; by the which we draw nigh unto God. And inasmuch as not without an oath He was made priest: (For those priests were made without an oath; but this with an oath by Him that said unto Him, The Lord sware and will not repent, Thou art a priest for ever after the order of Melchisedec). (Hebrews 7:18–21)

Now we know how the priesthood of Jesus Christ is different from both the Melchizedekian and Aaronic priesthoods. Both had to hand the priesthood over to others, either because of mandatory retirement or because of death. Jesus is eternal and will never hand the priesthood over to another. It is our Lord and Savior, Jesus Christ, who truly makes the Melchizedekian priesthood superior to any other!

By so much was Jesus made a surety of a better testament. And they truly were many priests, because they were not suffered to continue by reason of death: But this man, because He continueth ever, hath an unchangeable priesthood. Wherefore He is able also to save them to the uttermost that come unto God by Him, seeing He ever liveth to make intercession for them. For such an high priest became us, who is holy, harmless, undefiled, separate from sinners, and made higher than the heavens; Who needeth not daily, as those high priests, to offer up sacrifice, first for his own sins, and then for the people's: for this He did once, when He offered up Himself. For the law maketh men high priests which have infirmity; but the word of the oath, which was since the law, maketh the Son, who is consecrated for evermore. (Hebrews 7:22–28)

Conclusion

In this chapter we learned that Melchizedek was an order, not a person. Verse six says that the Melchizedekian priest that blessed Abraham did have a genealogical family tree (descent, father, and mother); he was just not a descendant of Levi. The priesthood of Levi was abolished and replaced by the Melchizedekian priesthood. This also makes a change in the law system and a change in the covenants.

Hebrews 8

Paul starts Hebrews 8 by summarizing his theology about the Messiah. From this point on Jesus is the only high priest. He will be the only high priest throughout eternity. Jesus serves His priestly duty in the real sanctuary in heaven. The earthly Mosaic tabernacle was just a copy or a type that symbolized the real one.

Now of the things which we have spoken this is the sum: We have such an high priest, who is set on the right hand of the throne of the Majesty in the heavens; A minister of the sanctuary, and of the true tabernacle, which the Lord pitched, and not man. (Hebrews 8:1–2)

Jesus offered Himself, not animals, for a sacrifice. All the temple ceremonies were simply rituals that pointed to what the Messiah would do to bring eternal salvation for all mankind.

For every high priest is ordained to offer gifts and sacrifices: wherefore it is of necessity that this man have somewhat also to offer. For if He were on earth, He should not be a priest, seeing that there are priests that offer gifts according to the law: Who serve unto the example and shadow of heavenly things, as Moses was admonished of God when he was about to make the tabernacle: for, See, saith He, that thou make all things according to the pattern shewed to thee in the mount. (Hebrews 8:3–5)

Not only was the Messiah's sacrifice superior to the earthly sacrifices done in the temple in Jerusalem, but His covenant is superior to the covenant of Moses as well. His new covenant replaces the old covenant because there were problems with that old covenant. Namely, that it could condemn you for sinning, but it could not provide any means of reconciliation toward God for mankind.

But now hath He obtained a more excellent ministry, by how much also He is the mediator of a better covenant, which was established upon better promises. For if that first covenant had been faultless, then should no place have been sought for the second. (Hebrews 8:6–7)

That new covenant needs to replace the old to bring a way of reconciliation. This Melchizedekian covenant was prophesied by the prophet Jeremiah.

Behold, the days come, saith the LORD, that I will make a new
covenant with the house of Israel, and with the house of Judah:
Not according to the covenant that I made with their fathers in
the day that I took them by the hand to bring them out of the
land of Egypt; which My covenant they brake, although I was
an husband unto them, saith the LORD: But this shall be the covenant that I will make with the house of Israel; After those days,
saith the LORD, I will put My law in their inward parts, and write
it in their hearts; and will be their God, and they shall be My
people. And they shall teach no more every man his neighbour,
and every man his brother, saying, Know the LORD: for they
shall all know Me, from the least of them unto the greatest of
them, saith the LORD: for I will forgive their iniquity, and I will
remember their sin no more. (Jeremiah 31:31–34)

Paul quotes this passage from Jeremiah explaining it this way.
There is a fault in them and the Law. God will bring a new covenant
that is completely different from the one that was given on Mount
Sinai.

For finding fault with them, He saith, Behold, the days come,
saith the Lord, when I will make a new covenant with the house
of Israel and with the house of Judah: Not according to the covenant that I made with their fathers in the day when I took them
by the hand to lead them out of the land of Egypt; because they
continued not in My covenant, and I regarded them not, saith
the Lord. (Hebrews 8:8–9)

This covenant will be placed in their hearts. The apostle Paul calls
this the "new man," in Ephesians 4. The new man is a new nature that
all Christians have. That does not mean we cannot fall into sin, but that
our new nature wants to follow God's ways instead of sinning. Our old
man is still present and wants to sin.

> For this is the covenant that I will make with the house of Israel
> after those days, saith the Lord; I will put my laws into their
> mind, and write them in their hearts: and I will be to them a
> God, and they shall be to Me a people. (Hebrews 8:10)

There is a Dead Sea Scroll called the Damascus Document. In this scroll, the Essenes of Qumran call the new covenant the Covenant of Damascus. Many have wondered why. It has nothing to do with Damascus, Syria. Damascus is the Essene name for their city that we today call Qumran. The word "Damascus" is made up of two Hebrew words; "dam," meaning blood, and "mashaq" meaning "heir" or "stronghold." The new covenant of Damascus is the new covenant of the blood heir. It is the new covenant of the Messiah!

This new covenant was given at Pentecost with the Holy Spirit for all who would accept it. Many rejected it and became apostate. In the millennial kingdom the nation of Israel will corporately accept Jesus as the promised Messiah and enter into the new covenant. This is why we have Christians today who are in the new covenant and orthodox Jews who are not yet in the new covenant.

> And they shall not teach every man his neighbour, and every
> man his brother, saying, Know the Lord: for all shall know Me,
> from the least to the greatest. For I will be merciful to their
> unrighteousness, and their sins and their iniquities will I remem-
> ber no more. (Hebrews 8:11–12)

Paul ends the chapter by stating that the fact that there is a new covenant means that there was an old covenant. The old covenant was for the Age of Torah according to the scrolls, and the new covenant is for the Age of Grace. If the Age of Torah ended in AD 75 as predicted by the school of Elijah, and the epistle to the Hebrews was written in the 50s AD, then the old covenant vanished away within fifteen years of the writing of this epistle. This is exactly what the Apostle Paul says.

In that He saith, A new covenant, He hath made the first old. Now that which decayeth and waxeth old is ready to vanish away. (Hebrews 8:13)

Conclusion

In this chapter we learned that Jesus is our eternal High Priest. He is of the Order of Melchizedek and not of the Order of Levi (also called the Order of Aaron). The old Order of Levi was done away with in AD 75 at the end of the Age of Torah. The old priesthood with its old covenant could point out sin and condemn the guilty but could do nothing to fix the problem. The new covenant fixed the problem and reconciled us to God. Now all believers, both Jew and Gentile, have the Holy Spirit dwelling in them which gives them a new nature. Our new nature wants to serve God, but our old nature is still present in us and can lead us back into sin.

King-Priests

Christians are people who follow Jesus Christ and His teachings. Jesus, the Messiah, is our great high priest and He is our King. The apostle Paul teaches us that Jesus is our eternal Melchizedekian priest. Christians are not one ethnic group, but are groups of people from every walk of life. We have come together to form a new nation, a people united by Jesus Christ Himself. Originally this was supposed to start with the nation of Israel.

Now therefore, if ye will obey My voice indeed, and keep My covenant, then ye shall be a peculiar treasure unto Me above all people: for all the earth is Mine: And ye shall be unto Me a kingdom of priests, and an holy nation. These are the words which thou shalt speak unto the children of Israel. (Exodus 19:5–6)

The Gentiles would have been added to them, but they apostatized. God used the prophet Hosea to show that He would no longer have mercy toward His people, but would show mercy to another people. To signify this, Hosea was to name his daughter Lo-Ruhamah meaning "no mercy."

> And she conceived again, and bare a daughter. And God said unto him, Call her name Lo-ruhamah: for I will no more have mercy upon the house of Israel; but I will utterly take them away. But I will have mercy upon the house of Judah, and will save them by the LORD their God, and will not save them by bow, nor by sword, nor by battle, by horses, nor by horsemen. (Hosea 1:6–7

God also instructed Hosea to name his next child "Lo-Ammi" which means "not my people." God was making Hosea's son a prophecy that the nation of Israel would rebel against God and that God would no longer call them His people. But much later in time, God gathered together groups of peoples from all nations and they formed a new "people of God."

> She conceived, and bare a son. Then said God, Call his name Lo-ammi: for ye are not My people, and I will not be your God. Yet the number of the children of Israel shall be as the sand of the sea, which cannot be measured nor numbered; and it shall come to pass, that in the place where it was said unto them, Ye are not My people, there it shall be said unto them, Ye are the sons of the living God. (Hosea 1:8b–10)

The Apostle John referenced this "people of God" when writing to the seven churches of Asia. John says we (the Christians) are that prophesied kingdom of priests.

John, to the seven churches which are in Asia: Grace be unto
you, and peace, from Him which is, and which was, and which
is to come; and from the seven Spirits which are before His
throne; And from Jesus Christ, who is the faithful witness, and
the first begotten of the dead, and the prince of the kings of the
earth. Unto Him that loved us, and washed us from our sins in
His own blood, And hath made us kings and priests unto God
and His Father; to Him be glory and dominion for ever and
ever. Amen. (Revelation 1:4–6)

The Apostle Peter agreed with the apostle John by saying that the
Gentile believers that were without Christ in the world have now become
a "royal priesthood" and a "holy nation."

But ye are a chosen generation, a royal priesthood, an holy nation,
a peculiar people; that ye should shew forth the praises of Him who
hath called you out of darkness into His marvellous light: Which
in time past were not a people, but are now the people of God:
which had not obtained mercy, but now have obtained mercy.
Dearly beloved, I beseech you as strangers and pilgrims, abstain
from fleshly lusts, which war against the soul. (1 Peter 2:9–11)

We know that Jesus is our eternal high priest. He will never pass the
priesthood over to another. So, in what sense are we priests and kings
with Him? Christians do not offer animal sacrifices as a priest might do,
we do not give orders to be obeyed as a king would do, and very few of
us give new prophecies by the leading of the Holy Spirit. So, in what
sense are we kings, priests, and prophets?

As Kings

We represent the King by being His ambassadors. This means we do not
judge or give orders, but we teach His judgments and teach His orders.

Paul tells Timothy to:

Preach the Word, be instant in season and out of season, reprove, rebuke, exhort with all long-suffering and doctrine. For a time will be when they will not endure sound doctrine, but they will heap up teachers to themselves according to their own lusts, tickling the ear. And they will turn away their ears from the truth and will be turned to myths. But you watch in all things, endure afflictions, do the work of an evangelist, fully carry out your ministry. (2 Timothy 4:2–5 MKJV)

For the grace of God that bringeth salvation hath appeared to all men, Teaching us that, denying ungodliness and worldly lusts, we should live soberly, righteously, and godly, in this present world; Looking for that blessed hope, and the glorious appearing of the great God and our Saviour Jesus Christ; Who gave Himself for us, that He might redeem us from all iniquity, and purify unto Himself a peculiar people, zealous of good works. These things speak, and exhort, and rebuke with all authority. Let no man despise thee. (Titus 2:11–15)

As Priests

A priest acts as an intercessor to help people come before the Lord. As priests we pray with unbelievers to lead them to the Lord. We pray with believers for peace, safety, and the guidance of the Holy Spirit in their lives. We listen and try to help where God allows us to.

Pray without ceasing. In everything give thanks, for this is the will of God in Christ Jesus toward you. (1 Thessalonians 5:17–18 LITV)

First of all then, I exhort that petitions, prayers, supplications, and thanksgivings be made on behalf of all men, for kings and all the ones being in high position, that we may lead a tranquil and quiet existence in all godliness and dignity. For this is good and acceptable before God our Savior, who desires all men to be saved and to come to a full knowledge of truth. (1 Timothy 2:1–4 LITV)

Let love be without dissimulation. Abhor that which is evil; cleave to that which is good. Be kindly affectioned one to another with brotherly love; in honour preferring one another; Not slothful in business; fervent in spirit; serving the Lord; Rejoicing in hope; patient in tribulation; continuing instant in prayer; Distributing to the necessity of saints; given to hospitality. Bless them which persecute you: bless, and curse not. Rejoice with them that do rejoice, and weep with them that weep. Be of the same mind one toward another. (Romans 12:9–16a)

By Him, then, let us offer the sacrifice of praise to God continually, that is, the fruit of our lips, confessing His name. But do not forget to do good and to share, for with such sacrifices God is well pleased. (Hebrews 13:15–16 MKJV)

As Prophets

The prophet is the opposite of the king. He doesn't tell you what you must do for God, but he tells you what God is doing for mankind. He instructs in history and future history, which is called prophecy. To be a "son of the prophets" means to carefully study all the prophecies.

Study earnestly to present yourself approved to God, a workman that does not need to be ashamed, rightly dividing the Word of Truth. (2 Timothy 2:15 MKJV)

Do not despise prophecies. Test all things, hold fast the good.
(1 Thessalonians 5:20–21 LITV)

As I said before, the Essenes believed they were led directly by the
Holy Spirit. The community in Qumran called themselves "Yahad."
This is a contraction of two Hebrew words. "Yah" is the name of God
and "ehad" means "one" in the sense of one group of brothers. So, the
name "Yahad" means a group of believers united together as one by the
leading of the Holy Spirit.

Some even teach that Yahovah is a name for the Father, Yeshua is a
name for the Son, and Yah is a name for the Holy Spirit.

Zadok Priests in the Millennium

If the order of Levi has been abolished, then why does the prophet Ezekiel say that there will be Zadok priests (of the order of Levi) serving in a
rebuilt temple in Jerusalem during the one-thousand-year reign of Jesus
Christ?

It shall be for the priests that are sanctified of the sons of Zadok;
which have kept My charge, which went not astray when the
children of Israel went astray, as the Levites went astray. (Ezekiel
48:11)

I think the answer to this is found in the Dead Sea Scrolls known as
the Damascus Document and the Community Rule.

They describe that the Pentecost dates remain the same, but the
rituals and dispensations change. On a Pentecost, believers received
the Noahide Covenant (Genesis 9), the Law of Moses on Mount Sinai
(Exodus 19), and the giving of the New Covenant of Grace (Acts 2).

In addition to this, the scrolls teach the date of Passover remains
the same, but the rituals and dispensations change. The texts describe
that there was a ritual of bread and wine performed by Melchizedekian

priests during the Age of Chaos (1–2000 AM). When the covenant of Moses came, the Melchizedekian ritual was replaced with what we know as the Passover Seder ritual. They predicted that during the next age, the Age of Grace, the ritual would change again. Bread and wine would still be used, but the Messiah Himself, would change the ritual. This happened. Today this modified ritual is called Christian communion. They went on to say that after the Second Coming, the Messiah would again change the ritual to point to the New Covenant of the Kingdom Age. One reason given is that there would be not only Jews and Gentiles observing the ritual, but also the Messiah Himself, along with His angels and His immortal ones. The immortal ones would be the Church Age Christians who were resurrected or raptured and at that time rule with the Messiah in His kingdom. Amazing, isn't it?

So, back to the original question: Why Zadok priests? There is something in that new ritual that points to the Messiah and His kingdom. All we really know is that at that point in time the rituals will not be the same as they were back in the days of Moses. We shall see.

Conclusion

Pulling together the teachings from the apostles and the Dead Sea Scrolls, we can see that the Messiah is the one and only Melchizedekian high priest and He will be that for all of eternity. We are His representatives on earth. We are king-priest-prophets only in the sense of representing Him. We represent Him as kings by teaching His commands. We represent Him as priests by counseling nonbelievers to accept Him as their Savior and to counsel believers in the whole council of God. We represent Him as prophets when we teach the prophecies. Sometimes the Holy Spirit may give us a word of wisdom or knowledge for our brothers.

God equips Christians with spiritual gifts that help them do the things He commands. None of us have all gifts and none of us can do everything effectively. Some have ministries of teaching. Others have ministries of consolation, counseling, and evangelism. Still others have prophetical gifts. If you are not a believer, you should become one. If you are a believer, you need to find out what your spiritual gift is and begin exercising it.

12

MELCHIZEDEKIAN PROPHECY

The Patriarchs

The Essenes taught that the ancient patriarchs, Adam through Aaron, wrote testaments for their children. These testaments contain moral wisdom and Messianic prophecy. The Pharisees agreed that these patriarchal texts did exist, but said they were lost long ago. Nothing is ever lost except that which you choose to throw away because it does not fit your doctrine. The Essenes rejected the Pharisee's Oral Torah because of what is taught in the Testaments of the Patriarchs. The Pharisees reject the Essene testaments because of what their Oral Torah says. Jesus said the Pharisees' "Traditions of the Elders," their Oral Torah, makes void the Word of God.

First Chronicles states there were those of the tribe of Issachar who understood the division of the four "ages," which means they were serious students of the biblical and patriarchal prophecies. They were called the "sons of the prophets."

> And of the children of Issachar, which were men that had understanding of the times, to know what Israel ought to do; the heads of them were two hundred; and all their brethren were at their commandment. (1 Chronicles 12:32)

This is also referred to as the "tabernacle of David." This tabernacle, or school, of David followed the Law and prophets correctly. With the rise of the Sadducees and Pharisees, an apostate form of Judaism was established. But with the advent of the Messiah, all was restored.

After this I will return, and will build again the tabernacle of David, which is fallen down; and I will build again the ruins thereof, and I will set it up: That the residue of men might seek after the Lord, and all the Gentiles, upon whom My name is called, saith the Lord, who doeth all these things. Known unto God are all His works from the beginning of the world [Age]. (Acts 15:16–18)

The following is a list of the major prophecies given by the biblical patriarchs. For a complete study in the fragments of the Testaments of the Patriarchs found in the Dead Sea Scrolls, see the book Ancient Testaments of the Patriarchs by this author:

Messiah is the Son of God, Levi 4

Messiah is God incarnate, Simeon 6, 7; Zebulun 9; Naphtali 8; Asher 7; Benjamin 10

Levi's priesthood is only until Messiah, Reuben 6; Levi 4, 5; Benjamin 9

Levi's ordinances and sacrifices are only until Messiah Reuben 6

Tribes rebel against Judah and Levi, Reuben 6 and Dan 5

Messiah is the seed of Judah, Reuben 6; Judah 24; Gad 8

Messiah is virgin-born, Joseph 19

We worship the Messiah, Reuben 6

Messiah is an everlasting King, Reuben 6; Joseph 19

Messiah dies for us, Reuben 6

Physical resurrection, Simeon 6; Judah 25; Zebulun 10; Benjamin 10

Messiah brings salvation, Simeon 6; Levi 4; Asher 7; Joseph 19; Benjamin 3

Levites crucify the Messiah, Levi 4, 16; Aaron 4, 6; Benjamin 9

There will be two expulsions, Levi 15; Zebulun 9; Naphtali 4; Asher 7

Messiah resurrects, Levi 16

Messiah ascends, Levi 18

Messiah creates a new priesthood, Levi 18; Aaron 4

Book of Enoch mentioned, Levi 16; Judah 18; Zebulun 3; Naphtali 4; Benjamin 9

The Writings of the Fathers existed, Zebulun 9; Kohath 2

Messiah appears in Zebulun, Zebulun 9

New Jerusalem mentioned, Dan 5

Old Jerusalem mentioned, Jacob 2

The Watchers mentioned, Naphtali 3

Messiah's priesthood is eternal, Amram-4Q547; Aaron 4

Veil of the Temple Rent, Benjamin 9

For the purpose of our study, we want to show what the patriarchs teach about (1) the Messiah, (2) the apostasy at the time of the first coming of the Messiah, and (3) the new covenant that the Messiah would bring at the beginning of the Age of Grace.

The Messiah

In this section we will see the prophecies that the scrolls reveal about the Messiah Himself.

The Messiah will be God incarnate.

Believers will worship the Messiah as God.

He will be born of a virgin.

He will die for our sins to reconcile us to God.

Messiah Is God Incarnate

Then the world will rest from war and Shem will be glorified, because the Lord God, the Mighty One of Israel, will appear upon earth as man, and save the seed of Adam. (Testament of Simeon, 6)

After these things the Lord Himself will arise to you. The light of righteousness, healing, and compassion will be in His wings. He will redeem all captivity of the sons of men from Belial, and every spirit of error will be trodden down. He will bring back all the nations to zeal for Him, and you will see God in the fashion of a man whom the Lord will choose. (Testament of Zebulun, 9)

For through Judah will salvation arise to Israel, and Jacob will be blessed through him. For through his tribe God will be seen dwelling among men on the earth, to save the race of Israel. He will gather together the righteous from the Gentiles. (Testament of Naphtali, 8)

Until the Most High will visit the earth. He will come as man, eating and drinking with men, and in peace He will break the head of the dragon through water. He will save Israel and all nations, God speaking in the person of man. Therefore, teach these things to your children, so they will not disobey Him. (Testament of Naphtali, 8)

The Lord will judge Israel first, even for the wrong they did unto Him; for when He appeared as a deliverer, God in the flesh, they did not believe Him. Then He will judge all the Gentiles, as many as did not believe Him when He appeared on earth. He will reprove Israel among the chosen ones of the Gentiles, even as He reproved Esau among the Midianites. (Testament of Benjamin, 10)

Believers Will Worship the Messiah as God

For He will bless Israel; and specially Judah, because the Lord
chose him to rule over all the people. We will worship his Seed,
because He will die for us in wars visible and invisible, and will
be among you an everlasting king. (Testament of Reuben, 6)

Messiah Will Be Virgin Born

The book of Enoch hints at the virgin birth of the Messiah.

They will be downcast of countenance and pain will seize them
when they see that Son of Man sitting on the throne of His
glory. (Ancient Book of Enoch 62:5)

Some manuscripts of Enoch replace "Son of Man," the common
messianic title, with the more uncommon messianic title of "Son of
Woman." The son of woman carries the same meaning as the "seed of
the woman" as seen in Genesis.

And I will put enmity between thee and the woman, and
between thy seed and her seed; it shall bruise thy head, and thou
shalt bruise His heel. (Genesis 3:15)

The idioms "son of woman" and "seed of woman" both mean virgin
born. The prophet Isaiah makes this clearer.

Therefore the Lord Himself shall give you a sign; Behold, a
virgin shall conceive, and bear a son, and shall call His name
Immanuel. (Isaiah 7:14)

Another clear reference is in the Testament of Joseph 19.

Hear also, my children, the visions which I saw. There were twelve deer feeding, and the nine were divided and scattered in the land, likewise also the three. I saw that from Judah was born a virgin wearing a linen garment, and from her went forth a Lamb, without spot, and on His left hand there was a lion. All the beasts rushed against Him, and the Lamb overcame them, destroyed them, and trampled them under foot. Because of Him, the angels, men, and all the earth rejoiced. These things will take place in their season, in the last days. Therefore, my children, observe the commandments of the Lord, and honor Judah and Levi. From them will rise unto you the Lamb of God, by grace saving all the Gentiles and Israel. For His kingdom is an everlasting kingdom, which will not be shaken; but my kingdom among you will come to an end as a watcher's hammock, which after the summer will not appear. (Testament of Joseph 19)

According to Hippolytus' record of the School of the Prophets, Nathan was a leader of the school and therefore his writings would have been in the Dead Sea Scrolls. No copy has yet been found in the Judean hills, but I am sure there will be in the future. In the meantime, we will look at fragments of the Book of Nathan that clearly prove the virgin birth of the Messiah. This first fragment records part of a vision that King David saw about the Messiah and His mother. Notice that here, David calls the incarnation the "mystery of Yahweh," while the Apostle Paul in 1 Timothy 3:16 calls this the "mystery of godliness."

I admonish you, O my son, Solomon. Carry out my will and remember the Mystery of Yahweh that I saw in a vision (wonders) from the Lord about His virgin mother, who is to emerge from our tribe. (Fragment of the Testament of Nathan)

This second portion is Nathan's own vision about the virgin birth. Notice Nathan does not use any word for virgin so it cannot be debated whether the word could mean virgin or just young woman. The description is clear. A young woman who has never been with a man is a virgin! Her child is the Lord of the earth. Adam and Noah were the only kings of the whole earth and they both lost control of it. This future king of the world will not lose control of it.

> I saw one, a maiden and without touch of man, and a man child in her arms, and that was the Lord of the earth unto the ends of the earth. (Fragment of the Testament of Nathan)

Messiah Will Die for Our Sins to Reconcile Us to God

The Messiah dies for us and this makes salvation possible to all mankind

> We will worship his Seed, because He will die for us in wars visible and invisible, and will be among you an everlasting king. (Testament of Reuben 6)

> Therefore, my children, observe the commandments of the Lord, and honor Judah and Levi. From them will rise unto you the Lamb of God, by grace saving all the Gentiles and Israel. For His kingdom is an everlasting kingdom. (Testament of Joseph 19)

> In you will be fulfilled the prophecy of heaven concerning the Lamb of God, even the Savior of the world. He will be delivered up spotless for transgressors. He will be sinless, yet put to death for ungodly men in the blood of the covenant, for the salvation of the Gentiles and of Israel. He will destroy Belial, and them that serve him. (Testament of Benjamin 3)

> The Lord will cast their lot amid the portions of Melchizedek, who will make them repent and will proclaim freedom to them, to free them from the debt of all their iniquities. (11QMelchizedek)

The Apostasy

The apostasy that the scrolls describe can be broken down into several points.

The Levites will reject the Messiah.

Messiah will be crucified.

God will end the Levitical priesthood.

The apostasy will bring total madness.

The veil in the temple will be torn in two.

The Levites Reject the Messiah and Crucify Him

You and all your seed will be blessed until the Lord visits all the heathen in the tender mercies of His Son, even forever. Nevertheless, your sons will lay hands upon Him to crucify Him. Therefore, you have been given counsel and understanding to instruct your sons about Him, because he who blesses Him will be blessed, but they that curse Him will perish. (Testament of Levi, 4)

I have also learned in the book of Enoch that for seventy weeks you will go astray, will profane the priesthood, pollute the sacrifices, corrupt the law, and ignore the words of the prophets. In perverseness, you will persecute righteous men, hate the godly, and abhor the words of the faithful. The man who renews the law in the power of the Most High you will call a deceiver. At last, as you suppose, you will slay Him, not understanding His resurrection, wickedly taking upon your own heads the innocent blood. Because of Him will your holy places be desolate, polluted even to the ground, and you will have no place that is clean; but you will be among the Gentiles a curse and a dispersion, until He will again look on you, and in pity will take you to Himself through faith and water. (Testament of Levi, 16)

Let not the nail touch him. Then you will raise up for your father a name of rejoicing and for all your brothers a firm foundation. You will understand and rejoice in the eternal light and you will not be one whom God hates. (Testament of Aaron, Col. 6)

God Ends the Levitical Priesthood

Obey Levi, because he will know the law of the Lord, and will create ordinances for judgment and sacrifice for all Israel until the time of Messiah, the High Priest whom the Lord has declared. (Testament of Reuben, 6)

You and all your seed will be blessed until the Lord visits all the heathen in the tender mercies of His Son, even forever. Nevertheless, your sons will lay hands upon Him to crucify Him. (Testament of Levi 4)

He said to me "Levi, I have given you the blessings of the priesthood until I will come and sojourn in the midst of Israel." (Testament of Levi 5)

The words of the righteous Enoch teach that even your descendants will practice evil. They will commit fornication like the fornication of Sodom, and all but a few will perish, and will multiply inordinate lusts with women; and the kingdom of the Lord will not be among you, for immediately He will take it away. (Testament of Benjamin 9)

The Apostasy Brings Total Madness

In their days, pride will cause many to act wickedly against the covenant and become the slaves of foreign things. Israel will be rent asunder in that generation, each man fighting against his neighbor over the Torah and the Covenant. I will send hunger upon the land, but not for bread or water, but to hear the Word of the Lord. (4Q385a Fragment 5)

At the completion of ten jubilees, Israel will be walking in madness. (4Q387)

The Sign of the Veil of the Temple

The scrolls speak of a beautiful Jewish temple being the glory for both Jews and Gentiles. But one prediction says that when the Levites reject the Messiah, God would reject and end the Levitical priesthood. The public sign of this would be the veil in the temple would be torn in two.

The New Testament does not tell us this was predicted, but it does speak of its fulfillment.

Nevertheless, the temple of God will be built in your portion, and will be glorious among you. For He will take it, and the twelve tribes will be gathered together there, and all the Gentiles, until the Most High will send forth His salvation in the visitation of His only-begotten One. He will enter into the front of the temple, and there will the Lord be treated with outrage, and He will be lifted up on a tree. The veil of the temple will be rent, and the Spirit of God will descend upon the Gentiles as fire poured forth. (Testament of Benjamin 9)

Jesus, when he had cried again with a loud voice, yielded up the ghost. And, behold, the veil of the temple was rent in twain from the top to the bottom; and the earth did quake, and the rocks rent. (Matthew 27:50–51)

Messiah's Covenant / Priesthood

The scrolls also reveal several points about the covenant and priesthood that the Messiah brings at His first coming.

Messiah's Covenant replaces Levi's.

Messiah's Covenant would be a Gentile one.

Messiah's Priesthood / Covenant is eternal.

There would be a New Testament.

Messiah's Covenant / Priesthood Replaces Levi's

When Levi was given the priesthood, he understood that his priesthood was different from the previous Melchizedekian priesthood and when the Messiah came the priesthood would change again. It would become a Gentile priesthood headed by the Messiah who would be from the tribe of Judah, not the tribe of Levi. Levi was told in a dream the following:

> They said to me, "Levi, your seed [the priesthood] will be divided into three branches, for a sign of the glory of the Lord who is to come. The first will be he who has been faithful; no portion will be greater than his. The second will be in the priesthood. The third—a new name will be called over Him, because He will arise as King from Judah, and will establish a new priesthood, after the fashion of the Gentiles, to all the Gentiles. His appearing will be unutterable, as of an exalted prophet of the seed of Abraham our father." (Testament of Levi 8)

The Mosaic Covenant Replaced

Levi's priesthood would only exist until Messiah came.

> For the Lord made Levi, Judah, Dan, Joseph, and me rulers over you. Therefore, I command you to obey Levi, because he will

know the law of the Lord, and will create ordinances for judgment and sacrifice for all Israel until the time of Messiah, the High Priest whom the Lord has declared. (Testament of Reuben, 6)

Age of Grace

The School of Elijah taught a dispensational view of history, according to an ancient commentary on Elijah's school called the Tanna Eliyahu. They divided history into four "Ages." First was the "Age of Chaos." Its name was taken from Genesis 1:2 (the earth was "without form" or in chaos). This was the age spanning from Creation to when God called Abraham. The second was called the "Age of Torah." This was the age of temples and sacrifices. It was supposed to last until the first coming of the Messiah. The Messiah would usher in the third age called the "Age of Grace." The Dead Sea Scrolls talk about the Messiah's New Covenant coming in the Age of Grace. One such document is called the Community Rule. It looks forward to the next age when Jews and Gentiles can enter the New Covenant together. The Community Rule actually says they will welcome the Gentiles into the Kingdom when the Age of Grace starts.

> Welcome all those who freely choose to obey God's decrees and enter the Covenant of Grace. (Community Rule, section 1)

The Essenes believed the Messiah's first coming would start this new Age of Grace.

The Messiah's New Eternal Priesthood

When the Messiah comes, the New Covenant He would create will last forever.

And will be chosen as a priest forever. (Testament of Amram, 4Q547)

His wisdom will be great. He will make atonement for all the children of His generation. He will be sent to all the sons of His [generation]. His word will be as the word of heaven, and His teaching will be in accordance with the will of God. His eternal sun will burn bright. The fire will be kindled in all the corners of the earth. It will shine into the darkness. Then the darkness will vanish from the earth and the deep darkness from the dry land. They will speak many words against Him. There will be numerous lies. They will invent stories about Him. They will say shameful things about Him. He will overthrow His evil generation and there will be great wrath. When He arises, there will be falsehood and violence, and the people will wander astray in His days and be confounded. (Testament of Amram, Col. 4)

Messiah Is an Everlasting King

Therefore, my children, observe the commandments of the Lord, and honor Judah and Levi. From them will rise unto you the Lamb of God, by grace saving all the Gentiles and Israel. For His kingdom is an everlasting kingdom, which will not be shaken; but my kingdom among you will come to an end as a watcher's hammock, which after the summer will not appear. (Testament of Joseph 19)

Messiah Creates a New Priesthood

His wisdom will be great. He will make atonement for all the children of His generation. He will be sent to all the sons of His [generation]. His word will be as the word of heaven, and

His teaching will be in accordance with the will of God. His eternal sun will burn bright. The fire will be kindled in all the corners of the earth. It will shine into the darkness. Then the darkness will vanish from the earth and the deep darkness from the dry land. They will speak many words against Him. There will be numerous lies. They will invent stories about Him. They will say shameful things about Him. He will overthrow His evil generation and there will be great wrath. When He arises, there will be falsehood and violence, and the people will wander astray in His days and be confounded. (Testament of Aaron, Col. 4)

After the Lord punishes them, He will raise up to the priesthood a new Priest, to whom all the words of the Lord will be revealed…. He will give the majesty of the Lord to His sons in truth for evermore; and there will none succeed Him for all generations, even forever. In His priesthood the Gentiles will be multiplied in knowledge on the earth and enlightened through the grace of the Lord. In His priesthood all sin will come to an end, the lawless will rest from evil, and the just will rest in Him. (Testament of Levi 18)

The New Testament Scriptures

It is very fascinating that not only do we have the prediction of a New Covenant and new priesthood, but there would also be a New Testament. Think about that for a moment. They hallowed the writings of the patriarchs as a revelation from God; a kind of pre-Old-Testament covenant. Then there would be a covenant written for the second age, the Age of Torah. This was written by Moses. At the beginning of the Age of Grace there would be another set of books that believers would live their lives by. We call this the New Testament.

I will no longer be called a ravening wolf on account of your ravages, but a worker of the Lord, distributing food to them that work what is good. One will rise up from my seed in the latter times, beloved of the Lord, hearing His voice on the earth, enlightening with new knowledge all the Gentiles, bursting in on Israel for salvation with the light of knowledge, and tearing it away from them like a wolf, and giving it to the synagogue of the Gentiles. Until the consummation of the ages he will be in the synagogues of the Gentiles, and among their rulers, as a strain of music in the mouth of all; and he will be inscribed in the holy books, both his work and his word, and he will be a chosen one of God forever; and because of him my father Jacob instructed me, saying,"He will fill up that which lacks from your tribe." (Testament of Benjamin 11)

The Apostle Paul became aware of the prophecy that he (the predicted Benjamite) would become the apostle to the Gentiles. His life (the Book of Acts) and his teachings (the epistles of Paul) would be written down and placed in a New Testament which would be located in the synagogue of the Gentiles (the Christian church) for all time.

Let me make this clear. According to the Dead Sea Scrolls, if we are not sure about doctrine, all the answers will be written in the epistles of Paul!

Until the Messiah of righteousness comes, the branch of David, for to Him and His children have been given the covenant of the kingship of His people for everlasting generations. (Q252 Col. 5)

The Date of the First Coming

There is another Dead Sea Scroll referenced as 11QMelchizedek. It starts out explaining that the Old Testament law of the Jubilee period of debt forgiveness is actually a concealed prophecy about the coming of the Messiah. He would forgive the debts of our sin. This would reconcile us to God the Father. The Messiah is called Melchizedek because He is the tenth and final Melchizedekian priest and He begins the new order of the Age of Grace.

> Moses said, "In the year of the jubilee, each of you will be freed to return home [Lev. 25:13]" and he described how, saying, 'Now this is the manner of the release: Let every creditor remit what he has lent his neighbor. He shall not press his neighbor or his brother for repayment, for the LORD's release has been proclaimed [Deut. 15:2].' Its interpretation pertains to the end of days. The captives Moses speaks of are those whom Isaiah says, 'To proclaim freedom to the captives [Isa. 61:1].' Its interpretation is that the LORD will assign those freed to the sons of heaven and the lot of Melchizedek. Even those, whose teachers had deliberately hidden and kept secret from them the truth about their inheritance through Melchizedek. The LORD will cast their lot amid the portions of Melchizedek, who will make them return [or repent] and will proclaim freedom to them, to free them from the debt of all their iniquities. (11QMelchizedek)

Now notice what it says about the timing of the arrival of the Messiah, Melchizedek, will die for our sins.

> This event will take place in the first week of the jubilee that occurs after the ninth jubilee. (11QMelchizedek)

Let's break this down. There are several ways to figure the timeline and we have written about this in many books, the Ancient Seder Olam, the Ancient Dead Sea Scroll Calendar, Ancient Post-flood History, etc. Basically, Abraham was called when he was fifty-two years old. That was the turn of the age, the year 2000 AM (two thousand years exactly from Creation to Abraham's call). The second two thousand years lasted from Abraham's call to just past the destruction of the Jewish temples. The Jerusalem temple was destroyed in AD 70 and the Alexandrian temple was shut down in AD 73. The end of the age was AD 75 on their calendar. An age lasts two thousand years. An age is made up of four five-hundred-year periods called "onahs." Each five-hundred-year period is made up of ten fifty-year periods called "jubilees." Each jubilee is made up of seven seven-year periods called "shemitahs." There are seven shemitahs and then a jubilee year, making fifty total.

So, if the end of the age is AD 75, that would be the end of the tenth jubilee. One jubilee back would be the end of the ninth jubilee or AD 25. The text says one shemitah after the end of the ninth jubilee, so, AD 25 plus seven years would bring us to AD 32. This is the year the Melchizedekian Messiah, Jesus Christ, died for our sins.

Next, we see the Messiah creates a "Day of Grace" also known as the "Age of Grace."

> Now the Day of Atonement is the end of the tenth jubilee, when atonement (is made) for all the sons of heaven, for the men of the lot of Melchizedek... It is the time of Melchizedek's 'Day of Grace.' He will, by His strength, raise up the holy ones of God to execute judgment as it has been written concerning Him in the songs of David, as it says, 'Elohim stands in the divine assembly, in the midst of Elohim He judges [Ps 82:1].' He said, 'Above it, to the heights, return. El will judge the nations [Ps 7:8-9].' When he said, 'How long will you judge unjustly and show impartiality to the wicked? Selah [Ps 82:2].' Its interpretation concerns Belial and the spirits of his lot who turn away from the commandments of El in wickedness. Melchizedek will exact the vengeances of the judgments of El. (11QMelchizedek)

By the end of the age (the end of the tenth jubilee) vengeance will come to the nation of Israel. Both temples will be destroyed, and the time of animal sacrifices will come to an end.

This is interesting to me as a Christian trying to figure out the exact dates of prophecy. You could say the new age started with the birth of the Messiah at 2 BC, His death and the birth of the church in AD 32, the destruction of one of the temples in AD 70–73, the end of the age proper in AD 75, or the expulsion of the nation of Israel in AD 135. This needs further study. The Essenes went on to say that this Age of Grace is a fulfillment of several Old Testament prophecies. These same passages were quoted in the New Testament by Paul and Jesus Christ.

> This is the "Day of Peace" about which God spoke through Isaiah the prophet [52:7] who said, "How beautiful on the mountains are the feet of the Messenger who proclaims peace, the Messenger of good who proclaims salvation, saying to Zion, 'Your God reigns!' Its interpretation is that the mountains are prophets' predictions about the Messenger and the Messenger is the one anointed of the Spirit about whom Daniel said, "Until Messiah, the Prince, (there will be) seven weeks [Dan. 9:25]. 'He is the Messenger of good who proclaims salvation. He is the one about whom it is written, when it says, 'to comfort those who mourn... [Isa. 61:2-3],' to instruct them in all the ages of the world in truth.'" (11QMelchizedek)

His salvation is true for "all the ages of the world." It is for all time. Salvation has always been by faith in the Messiah and not works. A very important point is that they accepted the Messiah not only as their Melchizedekian priest but as God incarnate. The text says, "your God is Melchizedek."

Zion is those who uphold the covenant, those who turn aside from walking in the ways of the people. But "Your God" is Melchizedek, who will save them from the hand of Belial. (11QMelchizedek)

The very last part begins to speak of the time of the end of our age when the trumpet is blown, and the Rapture / Resurrection occurs. Unfortunately, it is too fragmented to give us a date or record the sequence of the events.

> As for that which he has said, "You will blow the signal-horn in the seventh month [Lev 23:24; 25:9]." ...the divisions of the times.... (11QMelchizedek)

Conclusion

In Daniel 9 the Scriptures clearly reveal the Messiah's death in AD 32. Separate from that we have the Dead Sea Scroll 11QMelchizedek that gives us the exact year of the Messiah's death. It also reveals that His death is a work of the Father to pay for our sin nature and reconcile us to God. It is truly amazing that the Zadok priests would have the exact same theology as the Christian church.

APPENDIX A

∽

ANCIENT CHRONOLOGY

The year count is taken from the Bible, Jasher, Seder Olam, Enoch, and other Dead Sea Scrolls.

1   Adam created   (1-930)
130   Seth born (130-1042)
235   Enos born (235-1140)
325   Cainan born (325-1235)
395   Mahalaleel born (395-1290)
460   Jared born (460-1422)
622   Enoch born (Raptured in 987)
687   Methuselah born (687-1656)
874   Lamech born (874-1651)
1056 Noah born (1056-2006)
1558 Shem born (1558-2158)
1656 Flood occurred (Nisan 17)
1658 Arphaxad born (1658-2096)
1693 Selah born (1693-2126)
1723 Eber born (1723-2187)
1757 Peleg born (1757-1996)
1787 Reu born (1787-2026)

1819 Serug born (1819-2048)

1849 Nahor born (1849-1997)

1878 Terah born (1878-2083)

1948 Abraham born (1948-2123)

2018 Abraham's covenant

2048 Isaac born (2048-2228)

2108 Jacob born (2108-2255)

2194 Levi born (2194-2331)

2199 Joseph born (2199-2309)

2216 Kohath born (2216-2349)

2216 Joseph enslaved

2228 Joseph becomes vice-pharaoh

2237 7-yr Famine began

2238 Jacob migrated to Egypt

2255 Jacob died

2309 Joseph died

2368 Moses born (2368-2488)

2448 Exodus from Egypt (Nisan 15)

2516 Joshua died (2406-2516)

2935 Solomon's Temple dedicated (Cheshvan 1)

3338 Solomon's Temple destroyed

3388 Cyrus' decree

3407 Darius' decree

3408 Second Temple constructed

3481 Artaxerxes' decree

3957 Crucifixion (Nisan 15)

3995 Second temple destroyed (AD 70)

5873 Israel reborn (AD 1948)

5892 Israel takes Temple Mount (AD 1967)

5898 Yom Kippur war (AD 1973)

5907 First Lebanese war (AD 1982)

5929 Sanhedrin reestablished (AD 2004)

5931 Second Lebanese war (AD 2006)

6000 Year 6000 AM (AD 2075)

APPENDIX B

SIX-YEAR CALENDAR

This section is a recreation of the priestly courses of 4Q320-321. These Dead Sea Scrolls contain the basic solar calendar with each week's priestly course and the lunar phases.

The recreation has the name of the priestly course for the week, Sunday through Saturday, then lists which week of the year and month of the year that week falls in. The symbol of the full moon on the calendar is O while the new moon symbol is ●. Whenever a second full moon occurs in one calendar month it is called a blue moon and is symbolized with ②.

	Sun	Mon	Tue	Wed	Thu	Fri	Sat	W	M
1 Gamul				1O	2	3	4	1	1
2 Delaiah	5	6	7	8	9	10	11	2	
3 Maaziah	12	13	14	15	16	17☽	18	3	
4 Jehoiarib	19	20	21	22	23	24	25	4	
5 Jedaiah	26	27	28	29	30②	1	2	5	2

#	Division								Week	Month
6	Harim	3	4	5	6	7	8	9	6	
7	Seorim	10	11	12	13	14	15	16	7	
8	Malchijah	17☽	18	19	20	21	22	23	8	
9	Mijamin	24	25	26	27	28	29	30○	9	
10	Hakkoz	1	2	3	4	5	6	7	10	3
11	Abijah	8	9	10	11	12	13	14	11	
12	Jeshua	15	16☽	17	18	19	20	21	12	
13	Shecaniah	22	23	24	25	26	27	28	13	
14	Elishib	29○	30		1	2	3	4	14	4
15	Jakim	5	6	7	8	9	10	11	15	
16	Huppah	12	13	14	15☽	16	17	18	16	
17	Jeshebeab	19	20	21	22	23	24	25	17	
18	Bilgah	26	27	28○	29	30	1	2	18	5
19	Immer	3	4	5	6	7	8	9	19	
20	Hezir	10	11	12	13	14☽	15	16	20	
21	Happizzez	17	18	19	20	21	22	23	21	
22	Pethahiah	24	25	26	27○	28	29	30	22	
23	Jehezkel	1	2	3	4	5	6	7	23	6
24	Jachin	8	9	10	11	12	13	14☽	24	
1	Gamul	15	16	17	18	19	20	21	25	
2	Delaiah	22	23	24	25	26	27○	28	26	
3	Maaziah	29	30		1	2	3	4	27	7

		Sun	Mon	Tue	Wed	Thu	Fri	Sat	W	M
4	Jehoiarib	5	6	7	8	9	10	11	28	
5	Jedaiah	12☽	13	14	15	16	17	18	29	
6	Harim	19	20	21	22	23	24	25○	30	
7	Seorim	26	27	28	29	30	1	2	31	8
8	Malchijah	3	4	5	6	7	8	9	32	
9	Mijamin	10	11	12☽	13	14	15	16	33	
10	Hakkoz	17	18	19	20	21	22	23	34	
11	Abijah	24	25○	26	27	28	29	30	35	
12	Jeshua	1	2	3	4	5	6	7	36	9
13	Shecaniah	8	9	10	11☽	12	13	14	37	
14	Elishib	15	16	17	18	19	20	21	38	
15	Jakim	22	23	24○	25	26	27	28	39	
16	Huppah	29	30		1	2	3	4	40	10
17	Jeshebeab	5	6	7	8	9	10☽	11	41	
18	Bilgah	12	13	14	15	16	17	18	42	
19	Immer	19	20	21	22	23○	24	25	43	
20	Hezir	26	27	28	29	30	1	2	44	11
21	Happizzez	3	4	5	6	7	8	9☽	45	
22	Pethahiah	10	11	12	13	14	15	16	46	
23	Jehezkel	17	18	19	20	21	22○	23	47	
24	Jachin	24	25	26	27	28	29	30	48	

	1	2	3	4	5	6	7		
1 Gamul	1	2	3	4	5	6	7	49	12
2 Delaiah	8	9☽	10	11	12	13	14	50	
3 Maaziah	15	16	17	18	19	20	21	51	
4 Jehoiarib	22○	23	24	25	26	27	28	52	
	29	30							

Second Year

5 Jedaiah				1	2	3	4	1	1
6 Harim	5	6	7☽	8	9	10	11	2	
7 Seorim	12	13	14	15	16	17	18	3	
8 Malchijah	19	20○	21	22	23	24	25	4	
9 Mijamin	26	27	28	29	30	1	2	5	2
10 Hakkoz	3	4	5	6	7☽	8	9	6	
11 Abijah	10	11	12	13	14	15	16	7	
12 Jeshua	17	18	19	20○	21	22	23	8	
13 Shecaniah	24	25	26	27	28	29	30	9	
14 Elishib	1	2	3	4	5	6☽	7	10	3
15 Jakim	8	9	10	11	12	13	14	11	
16 Huppah	15	16	17	18	19○	20	21	12	
17 Jeshebeab	22	23	24	25	26	27	28	13	
18 Bilgah	29	30		1	2	3	4	14	4
19 Immer	5☽	6	7	8	9	10	11	15	
20 Hezir	12	13	14	15	16	17	18○	16	

#	Name	Sun	Mon	Tue	Wed	Thu	Fri	Sat	W	M
21	Happizzez	19	20	21	22	23	24	25	17	
22	Pethahiah	26	27	28	29	30	1	2	18	5
23	Jehezkel	3	4☽	5	6	7	8	9	19	
24	Jachin	10	11	12	13	14	15	16	20	
1	Gamul	17○	18	19	20	21	22	23	21	
2	Delaiah	24	25	26	27	28	29	30	22	
3	Maaziah	1	2	3	4☽	5	6	7	23	6
4	Jehoiarib	8	9	10	11	12	13	14	24	
5	Jedaiah	15	16	17○	18	19	20	21	25	
6	Harim	22	23	24	25	26	27	28	26	
7	Seorim	29	30		1	2☽	3	4	27	7
8	Malchijah	5	6	7	8	9	10	11	28	
9	Mijamin	12	13	14	15○	16	17	18	29	
10	Hakkoz	19	20	21	22	23	24	25	30	
11	Abijah	26	27	28	29	30	1	2☽	31	8
12	Jeshua	3	4	5	6	7	8	9	32	
13	Shecaniah	10	11	12	13	14	15○	16	33	
14	Elishib	17	18	19	20	21	22	23	34	
15	Jakim	24	25	26	27	28	29	30	35	
16	Huppah	1☽	2	3	4	5	6	7	36	9
17	Jeshebeab	8	9	10	11	12	13	14○	37	

18 Bilgah	15	16	17	18	19	20	21	38	
19 Immer	22	23	24	25	26	27	28	39	
20 Hezir	29	30	☽	1	2	3	4	40	10
21 Happizzez	5	6	7	8	9	10	11	41	
22 Pethahiah	12	13○	14	15	16	17	18	42	
23 Jehezkel	19	20	21	22	23	24	25	43	
24 Jachin	26	27	28	29☽	30	1	2	44	11
1 Gamul	3	4	5	6	7	8	9	45	
2 Delaiah	10	11	12○	13	14	15	16	46	
3 Maaziah	17	18	19	20	21	22	23	47	
4 Jehoiarib	24	25	26	27	28	29☽	30	48	
5 Jedaiah	1	2	3	4	5	6	7	49	12
6 Harim	8	9	10	11	12○	13	14	50	
7 Seorim	15	16	17	18	19	20	21	51	
8 Malchijah	22	23	24	25	26	27	28☽	52	
	29	30		1	2	3	4		

Third Year

9 Mijamin				1	2	3	4	1	1
10 Hakkoz	5	6	7	8	9	10○	11	2	
11 Abijah	12	13	14	15	16	17	18	3	
12 Jeshua	19	20	21	22	23	24	25	4	
13 Shecaniah	26	27☽	28	29	30	1	2	5	2

		Sun	Mon	Tue	Wed	Thu	Fri	Sat		
14	Elishib	3	4	5	6	7	8	9	6	
15	Jakim	10○	11	12	13	14	15	16	7	
16	Huppah	17	18	19	20	21	22	23	8	
17	Jeshebeab	24	25	26☽	27	28	29	30	9	
18	Bilgah	1	2	3	4	5	6	7	10	3
19	Immer	8	9○	10	11	12	13	14	11	
20	Hezir	15	16	17	18	19	20	21	12	
21	Happizzez	22	23	24	25	26☽	27	28	13	
22	Pethahiah	29	30		1	2	3	4	14	4
23	Jehezkel	5	6	7	8○	9	10	11	15	
24	Jachin	12	13	14	15	16	17	18	16	
1	Gamul	19	20	21	22	23	24☽	25	17	
2	Delaiah	26	27	28	29	30	1	2	18	5
3	Maaziah	3	4	5	6	7○	8	9	19	
4	Jehoiarib	10	11	12	13	14	15	16	20	
5	Jedaiah	17	18	19	20	21	22	23	21	
6	Harim	24☽	25	26	27	28	29	30	22	
7	Seorim	1	2	3	4	5	6	7○	23	6
8	Malchijah	8	9	10	11	12	13	14	24	
9	Mijamin	15	16	17	18	19	20	21	25	
10	Hakkoz	22	23☽	24	25	26	27	28	26	

		Sun	Mon	Tue	Wed	Thu	Fri	Sat	W	M
11	Abijah	29	30		1	2	3	4	27	7
12	Jeshua	5○	6	7	8	9	10	11	28	
13	Shecaniah	12	13	14	15	16	17	18	29	
14	Elishib	19	20	21	22☽	23	24	25	30	
15	Jakim	26	27	28	29	30	1	2	31	8
16	Huppah	3	4	5○	6	7	8	9	32	
17	Jeshebeab	10	11	12	13	14	15	16	33	
18	Bilgah	17	18	19	20	21☽	22	23	34	
19	Immer	24	25	26	27	28	29	30	35	
20	Hezir	1	2	3	4○	5	6	7	36	9
21	Happizzez	8	9	10	11	12	13	14	37	
22	Pethahiah	15	16	17	18	19	20	21☽	38	
23	Jehezkel	22	23	24	25	26	27	28	39	
24	Jachin	29	30		1	2	3○	4	40	10
1	Gamul	5	6	7	8	9	10	11	41	
2	Delaiah	12	13	14	15	16	17	18	42	
3	Maaziah	19☽	20	21	22	23	24	25	43	
4	Jehoiarib	26	27	28	29	30	1	2○	44	11
5	Jedaiah	3	4	5	6	7	8	9	45	
		Sun	Mon	Tue	Wed	Thu	Fri	Sat	W	M
6	Harim	10	11	12	13	14	15	16	46	
7	Seorim	17	18	19☽	20	21	22	23	47	

8 Malchijah	24	25	26	27	28	29	30	48	
9 Mijamin	1	2O	3	4	5	6	7	49	12
10 Hakkoz	8	9	10	11	12	13	14	50	
11 Abijah	15	16	17	18☽	19	20	21	51	
12 Jeshua	22	23	24	25	26	27	28	52	
	29	30							

This re-creation of the priestly courses shows us that the Essenes recorded the moon phases to show there is no leap day each year and to prove the moon phases are not a necessary part of the original calendar.

OTHER BOOKS BY
KEN JOHNSON, THD

Ancient Post-Flood History — Historical documents that point to a
biblical Creation.

Ancient Seder Olam — A Christian translation of the 2000-year-old
scroll.

Ancient Prophecies Revealed — 500 prophecies listed in order of
when they were fulfilled.

Ancient Book of Jasher — Referenced in Joshua 10:13; 2 Samuel
1:18; 2 Timothy 3:8.

Third Corinthians — Ancient Gnostics and the end of the world

Ancient Paganism —The sorcery of the fallen angels

The Rapture — The pretribulational Rapture of the church viewed
from the Bible and the ancient church

Ancient Epistle of Barnabas — His life and teaching

The Ancient Church Fathers — What the disciples of the apostles
taught

Ancient Book of Daniel — Ancient Epistles of John and Jude

Ancient Messianic Festivals — And the prophecies they reveal

Ancient Word of God — Cults and the Trinity

Ancient Book of Enoch

Ancient Epistles of Timothy and Titus
Fallen Angels
Ancient Book of Jubilees
The Gnostic Origins of Calvinism
The Gnostic Origins of Roman Catholicism
Demonic Gospels
The Pre-Flood Origins of Astrology
The End-Times by the Church Fathers
Ancient Book of Gad the Seer
Ancient Apocalypse of Ezra — Called 2 Esdras in the KJV
Ancient Testaments of the Patriarchs — Autobiographies from the
    Dead Sea Scrolls
Ancient Law of Kings — Noahide law
Ancient Origins of the Hebrew Roots Movement — The Noahide and
    Mosaic Laws as seen in the Dead Sea Scrolls
Ancient Origins of Modern Holidays
Ancient Dead Sea Scroll Calendar
DVD 1 – *The Prophetic Timeline*
DVD 2 – *The Church Age*

For more information, visit us at: Biblefacts.org

BIBLIOGRAPHY

Part 1:

Ken Johnson, *Ancient Book of Jasher*, Createspace, 2013
Ken Johnson, *Ancient Seder Olam*, Createspace, 2006
Whiston, William, *The Works of Flavius Josephus*, London, Miller & Sowerby, 1987. Includes *Antiquities of the Jews*.
Ken Johnson, *Ancient book of Enoch*, Createspace, 2012
Mattis Kantor, *Jewish Time Line Encyclopedia*, Jason Aronson, 1993
Ken Johnson, *Ancient Testaments of the Patriarchs*, Createspace, 2017

Part 2:

Schaff, Philip, *Ante-Nicene Fathers*, Eerdmans Publishing, 1893
Ken Johnson, *Ancient Book of Enoch*, Createspace, 2012
Ken Johnson, *Ancient Book of Jubilees*, Createspace, 2013
Ken Johnson, *Ancient Book of Gad the Seer*, Createspace, 2016
Ken Johnson, *Ancient Post-Flood History*, Createspace, 2010

Part 3:

Whiston, William, *The Works of Flavius Josephus*, London, Miller & Sowerby, 1987. *Includes Antiquities of the Jews.*

Ken Johnson, *Ancient Book of Jasher*, CreateSpace, 2008

Ken Johnson, *Ancient Book of Enoch*, CreateSpace, 2012

Eerdmans Publishing, *Ante-Nicene Fathers*, Eerdmans Publishing, 1886

Ken Johnson, *Ancient Dead Sea Scroll Calendar*, independent publisher, 2019

Ken Johnson, *Ancient Testaments of the Patriarchs*, independent publisher, 2017

NOTES

1. 2 Thessalonians 2:7
2. Bath-Enos or daughter of Enos. This is the same name given to her in the Book of Jubilees.
3. Genesis 7:11 and 8:14
4. Noah means "rest" or "comfort" in Hebrew.
5. Emzera can be translated as "seed of my people." In other words, he married a godly relative. According to the *Ancient Book of Jasher*, Noah married Namaah, daughter of Enoch
6. Compare to Jubilees 21.
7. Jewish tradition says this was Rosh Hashanah, the Jewish New Year.
8. Compare to Genesis 21:12 and Hebrews 11:18.
9. "Moreh" means teacher. This says he went around a place called Moreh. This may have been the yeshiva of Shem. It is a show of respect, if you are not going to a holy place to study or sacrifice, to travel around it.
10. The Lord used problems and illnesses to cause people to repent of their sins. We should only pray for non-believers to repent. We pray for healing and blessing for believers.

11. Courtship, not dating.
12. Genesis 29:33
13. Genesis 37:22, 29; 42:22
14. Lit. Cappadocians. Compare Deuteronomy 2:23 LXX and Amos 9:7 LXX
15. John the Baptist
16. Luke 24:21
17. For the Jewish idea of seven heavens, cf. Clement of Alexandra, Strom., iv. 7; and Paul in the third heaven in 2 Corinthians 12:2.
18. Matthew 27:51
19. Genesis 12:3
20. 4Q213b
21. Moses (Law), Aaron (Priesthood) and Jesus (Melchizedek)
22. Noahide Law with a Noahide / Melchizedekian Priesthood
23. 4Q213b
24. Idolatry
25. 4Q214, 4Q214b
26. 4Q214a, Fragments. 2-3
27. 4Q214a, Fragments. 4-6
28. Matthew 27:63
29. Matthew 27:25
30. A return of the Levitical Priesthood?
31. Priesthood becomes more and more corrupt till virtually no real priesthood exists in the 8-10 jubilees, when the Messiah comes.
32. Jubilees 38 has the same story but the Talmud and Jasher tell a different story of Esau's death. One of the texts is corrupted. Most likely one deals with Esau's death and the other deals with the death of one of Esau's sons.
33. Genesis 30:14-18
34. This was most likely Isaac. Shem, Eber, and Abraham were already dead.

35. The Melchizedekian priesthood (Shem and Eber) and the priesthood of Levi existed at this time. The Aaronic priesthood was not yet established.
36. Either thinking he has plenty of time to repent or seeking ungodly ways to extend his life.
37. Mathew 4:14-16. Zebulon and Naphtali, the Galilee of the Gentiles.
38. 1 Timothy 2:5
39. Yeshua
40. 4Q215 Fragment 1
41. Genesis 49:21
42. Ephesians 5:6
43. Aramaic adds "we each caught a star except for Joseph."
44. "Elamites and Gelachaeans" are not in some manuscripts.
45. "Full of dried flesh" is not in some manuscripts.
46. Daniel 11:35
47. Philippians 2:10-11; Isaiah 45:23-24; Every knee will bow and every tongue confess that Jesus is LORD.
48. Luke 7:35; Wisdom is vindicated by her children.
49. See *Ancient Book of Gad the Seer 1-2*.
50. Twenty pieces of silver; Genesis 37:28.
51. 2 Timothy 3:5
52. Leviticus 11:6-8
53. Genesis 39:1 LXX and Josephus Ant. 2.4.1
54. This sentence is confusing.
55. The apostle Paul's writings will be included in the Scriptures forever.
56. King of Rosh, see Ezekiel 38.